To Luke
David Shall

Papercopia

Origami Designs
by David Shall

Edited by
deg farrelly

Harrisburg, Pennsylvania

Papercopia Publishing
Harrisburg, Pennsylvania 17110

www.papercopia.com

ISBN: 978-0-9796487-0-0

Printed in the United States of America

This book is dedicated to my father Herman,
who introduced me to origami,
and
to my brother Michael,
whose passion for origami inspired and encouraged me.

Acknowledgements

Much appreciation is felt for my family, especially my wife Mara, and my daughters Zoe and Lisa, who encouraged me, folded with me, and tolerated the greater attention I gave at times to my immersions in various origami projects. My mother Tillie Shall, although rarely a folder herself, was a big supporter of my love of origami, and always maintained in her home a glass display case filled with origami, as well as a collection of origami books, articles and photos. My brother Don has encouraged me over the years and helped promote my work through teaching my models to others. Thanks especially to my sister Maxine Burkholder for the photo of a section of her family quilt used for the back cover of this book. Thanks also to Mara who proofread the entire text.

My late brother Michael Shall significantly influenced my origami career. I speak of him in greater detail in the Introduction to this book.

I have been nurtured throughout several decades by my relationships with many folders, too numerous to name. At the risk of neglecting to mention someone, I nonetheless acknowledge those who have been particularly supportive. In no particular order, Jackie Humphries-Bickley, Nate Segal, Jim Troutman (who provided use of his scanner to digitize the diagrams), Rae Urban, and Rob Hudson, all members of my on-again, off-again local folding group. In addition, I want to thank my origami friends Kathleen O'Regan, Michael Wrenn, Martha Landy, Gay Merrill Gross, Mark Kennedy, Andrew Hans, and lastly, Ravi Apte, who was the first to move me to actually begin planning and designing this book.

Alan Godwin at Arizona State University provided exceptional guidance on the digital processes used in this book's production, and Aaron Rostad, also at Arizona State University, worked wonders turning my digital photos into the front and back covers.

The long, hard work, which ultimately resulted in the publication of this book, would never have happened without the endless support and thankfully stubborn persistence of deg farrelly, my editor and closest origami friend for nearly 25 years. He has helped turn my unfulfilled wish, to someday have my own book, into a reality. For this I will be always grateful.

Lastly, like so many other folders, I feel a special sense of gratitude for Lillian Oppenheimer and Alice Gray for their many years of encouragement and support.

David Shall

Foreword

Long before I knew the man, I knew David Shall's work. Not that I knew *how* to fold his models, as they were heretofore unpublished. But from the moment I spotted a miniature version of his Candlestick displayed in Lillian Oppenheimer's Union Square loft sometime in the late 1970's I was instantly captivated and longed to fold the model. Sadly, Lillian could recall neither the designer's name, nor if the model was diagrammed. It wasn't. Some years later I spotted a Claw Hammer model on Japan Air Lines' "Exhibition in the Window" on 5th Avenue in New York City. Once again, without knowing the designer or the availability of diagrams, I was instantly charmed by a model that I longed to fold.

It wasn't until I attended my first Friends of the Origami Center of America Annual Convention in 1983 that, in response to my query regarding diagrams for this Claw Hammer, Michael Shall informed me it was David's design. "I don't know if it's diagrammed, but it's my brother's design. He doesn't live far from you, I'm sure he'd be happy to teach you," Michael enthused. Thus I was led to David's door, and to what has become a lifelong friendship.

Over the ensuing years David has become far more than my friend. He has been my teacher, my mentor, my brother. We have collaborated with, challenged, and complemented each other. David's design aesthetic, his diagramming style, and his use of foil papers have profoundly influenced my own origami work. His admonition led to my design of High Heel, and both my Howling Coyote and Flapping Butterfly models were invented while sitting in his kitchen.

Diagrams for some of David's models have been distributed piecemeal: in *The Origamian*, in convention programs, or given privately to friends or students. In the years that David could not attend OUSA annual conventions he permitted me both to teach his models and distribute diagrams for them, including the first of his models to charm me: Candlestick and Claw Hammer (1997 and 1999 respectively). For the most part, however, diagrams of David's models have not been widely disseminated. Thus, sadly, they remain largely unknown to the origami community.

It has been a pleasure to be able to share David's unique vision by teaching his models. It is with even greater joy and considerable honor that I have played a part in the production of this book, to finally bring his origami designs to the larger audience they so richly deserve.

I am certain the designs in this book will captivate you, as I was, all those many years ago.

deg farrelly, Editor

Contents

Introduction

"I will do it some day" was the answer I gave so many times over many years to all the folders, family and friends who asked me, "When are you going to do a book of your models?" Finally it is here, and I sincerely hope your support and patience will be rewarded.

Memories

I began folding in 1955 when I was 10 years old. According to my sister, Maxine, she interested our father in origami and he in turn introduced origami to my brothers Don and Michael, and me. There were few origami books published and available in the 1950s but Dad began searching out and collecting them. These he obtained from Lillian Oppenheimer at the Origami Center in New York City. Among them were several early, very basic books, but also larger works such as Solórzano's *Papiroflexia Zoomorfica* and Montero's *El Mundo de Papel.* None of these interested me much; the models were often too abstract or primitive, or employed cuts.

Fortunately there were others Dad collected that I liked much better. Of my first books my favorite was Isao Honda's *How To Make Origami*, one in a series of small books with models glued to the pages. I also liked *Paper Magic* by Robert Harbin. By the early 1960's it was a great influence to have a father who had regular contact with Lillian Oppenheimer, Fred Rohm, and also James Sakoda, who sent him the pre-publication manuscript of *Modern Origami* for comment. After the Randletts' books *Art of Origami* and *Best of Origami* arrived in our house, I was completely hooked.

Dad co-owned a company manufacturing quartz crystal frequency control devices, and traveled a lot to sell his products. He often folded paper while in business meetings, and liked to give models to his customers. His favorite was Cerceda's peacock folded from a dollar bill. He recruited all three sons to fold these in quantity and pack them, perfectly fitted, into plastic boxes. We must have folded hundreds of peacocks, earning some pocket money for our effort.

We were mostly lone folders until 1966 when I went with Mom, Dad, and my fiancé Mara, to New York City. While Mara and Mom went off to see some musicals I accompanied Dad to an "origami convention" at Lillian's home on West 11th Street. Regrettably, my memory of this event is poor, but I recall there were 20 or 25 folders sitting around a large table with a few people taking turns throughout the day teaching models to the group. Lillian and her friends provided refreshments, and guests could examine her collections of origami models and publications, or purchase books and paper she had for sale. Origami became and remained my favorite hobby.

My first original design was the Puzzle Cube in 1961. Sometime thereafter I figured out a folded lock for the pleated tail on the Cerceda peacock, which up to then required glue. Although I did not design another model until 1978 an explosion of creativity began at that time. In 1978 and 1979 I developed nearly 45 original designs, while simultaneously helping to raise our two elementary school age daughters, Zoe and Lisa. Among these designs was my first published model: a modular Tree, diagrammed by Mick Guy and published in the *British Origami Magazine* #76 in 1979.

Some of my very early designs are included in this book: the Collapsing Box, the Basket, the Triangular Solid, the Paper Chain, a Letterfold, the Candlestick, the Expanding Ball, the Claw Hammer, the Soccer Ball, and the Daffodil.

In 1980, I diagrammed the Paper Chain and was quite pleased with the result. After 1980 I managed to complete an occasional diagram but my pace of designing models far outstripped my rate of drawing them. In addition, it took a few years to arrive at anything close to a consistent style. Around 1990 or 1991 I experimented with diagramming a model using the draw program on Lisa's Mac-Plus. I was too frustrated and lacking in patience, and then the computer went back to school with her.

My brother Michael conducted origami programs while working as a teacher in New Jersey. When he relocated to New York City in the mid-1970s he became actively involved with Lillian Oppenheimer, Alice Gray, and others in the New York area origami community. Eventually this involvement led to his decision to pursue origami as a career. His intense activity, volunteering with the Origami Center, conducting workshops, commissioned folding for advertising, and mounting commercial exhibits, coincided with my sudden surge in origami design.

A symbiotic origami relationship emerged in which Michael responded enthusiastically to every new design I showed or taught him. This in turn encouraged me to design new models and experience this enthusiasm again and again. Although Michael obtained the use of many designers' models, he also loved to use my models in his workshops, publicity pictures, and especially his annual Christmas tree displays in the Fifth Avenue window of Japan Airlines. These were produced with the support of the Origami Center and it's members, beginning in the late 1970's and continuing into the 1980's.

Similarly, during this same time and under Michael's influence, I also became more active in organized origami activities. These included facilitating a local folding group; teaching origami workshops at camps, the State Museum, the community college, and many public libraries, volunteering and teaching at New York origami conventions, and producing folds or new designs on commission for advertising contracts.

From 1992 through 1999 my origami activities greatly diminished. I folded and designed models far less often and attended no origami conventions. I believe several factors greatly influenced my diminished activity: new career demands, the progressive and lengthy illness of my brother Michael followed by loss and grief, and perhaps also, the discontinuation of our local folding group (York PAperfolders) when deg farrelly relocated to Phoenix. Happily, by 2000 the passage of time and my love of origami restored my motivation. I have again become as busy as ever with origami, especially with diagramming my models and attending the New York conventions again.

Thoughts On Designing and Folding

On rare occasions a design idea emerges from some random doodling folds, but most often I have the model in mind before I start. I try to think of subject ideas that, to my knowledge, have not been created previously. Or, I choose a subject that has been done already, but I feel a desire to make a different version more to my liking. I maintain a list of model ideas and occasionally pick one to try. There are subject ideas I have never succeeded in folding. Other times I have folded something I thought may be too difficult only to have folded it rather quickly, and wondered to myself "how did I ever do that?"

I have a few designs of animal and human subjects but most of my models are a mix of common objects, geometric modulars, flowers, and decorative pieces. My designs also include a large assortment of practical-use models, including boxes and containers, coin purses, letterfolds and greeting cards, a photo cube, and a checkbook cover. The crane is a favorite motif and appears in several of my models.

My designs do not depend on traditional bases. After I visualize a model I think about the paper shape that would likely work and mentally divide the paper into broad areas of size and location. These will be used to create features: appendages, handles, tabs or flaps for locking modules together, etc. The rest is pretty much trial and error. I have never felt the need to fold only from squares. When a square hasn't provided satisfactory results I switch to using a rectangle. None of my designs use glue, nor do they involve cutting, except to prepare the size and shape of the paper before the folding begins.

It is very useful for paper folders to have a reliable method of rating model difficulty. I once contributed an article proposing a numerical rating system on a scale from 1-to-10 (see "It's Definitely A Ten!," *The Origamian*, Vol. 16, No. 1, p. 3), but I have since concluded that functional descriptions are more meaningful and I support OrigamiUSA's effort to define the skills needed at each level of difficulty.

Most of my designs fall in the intermediate range. A few would be regarded as complex; in this volume specifically, these would include the Claw Hammer and the Daffodil. Possibly, the Expanding Ball and the Soccer Ball might be considered complex as well, due to the total number of folds and the somewhat tricky assembly required.

I have designed very few simple models. The easiest models in this book include the Letterfold, Michael Shall's Coin Purse, and especially the Paper Chain. While paperfolders and non-paperfolders alike marvel at the beauty and sophistication of many complex and super-complex designs, I often think that it is just as difficult, or nearly so, to design a great simple model that comes to have broad, popular appeal.

More of my ideas about origami design appear in the transcription of "Creativity in Origami," a panel discussion at the 1984 Convention of the Friends of the Origami Center of America, published in *The Origamian*, Volume 16, Issue 1, pages 9-14.

Paper Selection and Preparation

Models folded from traditional origami paper often tend to lose shape and unfold. I have always preferred folding paper with a foil layer to maintain shape and increase durability. I use Alufoil ("American foil") for most of my practice and design folding. Because the foil surface often makes an unattractive appearance, over the years I have resorted to modifications such as pre-coloring the paper or bonding layers of paper together. For example, in the early-to-mid 1980s I began using liquid watercolor or ink washes on the white side of foil papers.

I also like to use tissue foils, which I make myself. The materials chosen depend on what I feel a particular model needs, the desired thickness of the paper, and whether the reverse side of the paper shows on the finished model. Thus, I may bond tissue to one or both sides of a backing sheet, using Alufoil for thicker, or Japanese foil for thinner results. Sometimes I will bond tissue to heavy kitchen foil, although such paper is tricky to work with. "Foil never forgives; foil never forgets," Michael used to say. I also like to bond wallpaper and decorative gift-wrap to kitchen foil. For bonding I have always used 3M Super 77, a spray adhesive. This is a particularly noxious material to work with, so I always take precautions to protect my eyes and my breathing from the mist.

Many of the models photographed for this book were folded from papers modified using these techniques. For example, the Candlestick, Dodecahedron and Lily were folded from papers with color washes (Mark Kennedy made the paper for the Lily) and the Mouse, Rabbit, and Daffodil use papers bonded to foil layers.

How I Diagram

Learning to diagram was a slow process for me. My greatest diagramming influence was the British author Dave Venables, perhaps best known for the 1978 booklet *Focus On Neal Elias*, published by the British Origami Society. While I had already been folding from diagrams by a range of international authors for 20 years, there was something special about Venable's drawings that affected me strongly. I especially liked the way they looked and how effectively they communicated directions for what were, at the time, above average to complex models. Their effect on me was to inspire hope that I could learn to make attractive drawings that communicated as well. The readers of this book will be able to notice differences among the diagrams as over time I explored a variety of layouts and styles.

As I gained confidence in my knowledge and diagramming ability I contributed a series of articles to the *Newsletter of the Friends of the Origami Center of America*, published as "Diagramming Technique and Symbol Language" in issues 27-29. Although I was neither an expert nor a book author, these articles shared methods I was learning and that others were using, and promoted some thoughts about minimal standards for successful folding communication using diagrams. Now, nearly 20 years later, I can see this effort helped refine my own methods and style. These articles coincided with the emerging availability and use of computer drawing software to generate origami diagrams, although I did not choose that path.

All my diagrams are drawn and lettered by hand, and are made in four stages. The first, and most challenging and interesting for me, is an informal pencil sketch of the complete folding sequence. These are usually done on plain office paper with just a pencil and without the use of drawing tools. Here, I work out what I perceive to be the best folding sequence that can be communicated by a drawing and accompanying text explanation. The need to communicate effectively on paper often causes me to draw a folding sequence that is different from how I fold or teach the model. I also develop the layout and scale of the drawings from start to finish. During this process I determine where to employ "picture gets larger," to enlarge the diagram for detail, and where to leave open space for an illustration to be inserted later. The first stage is complete when I have a sketched version of the complete diagram from start to finish: the folding sequence and diagram symbols, the scale, the layout, and space for inserts and text explanations.

The second stage is a finished pencil drawing on artists' drawing paper. I currently use Strathmore Bristol, heavy weight, smooth finish, cut to 8 ½ X 11 inch. I use a size .03 mechanical pencil and a good assortment of tools including T-square, protractor, rulers, curves and templates for circles and ovals. I make only light pencil marks and lines because they all will be erased later. Margin lines on all four sides and a vertical centerline help guide the layout. Then I replicate the entire first stage sketch in a high quality, finished drawing.

In the third stage, I ink over each of the finished pencil drawings with Rapidograph pens, using .35 for edges and symbols, and .25 for existing creases. First, I ink the drawings; then I go back and ink the text explanations, which I also penciled in earlier. Lastly, I number all the steps.

In the fourth and final stage I erase all the pencil marks, attach any illustrations made by the acetate drawing method described below, and correct any errors in the ink work with a correcting fluid pen, followed by using the ink pens to fill in whatever is missing.

At this point, in my early diagrams, I cut and placed commercial shading film on the drawings to indicate the color side of the paper. Later I discovered that this film degrades over time, ruining the original drawings. My subsequent diagrams use text to describe and direct the positioning of the paper's color side.

Normally I inscribe my diagrams with two dates. The first shows the year I diagrammed the model and the second indicates the year I designed the model. With this addition the master copy of the model's diagram is complete. For this book these dates have been removed from the diagrams but are noted in the Additional Model Information section.

Tracing and Acetate Drawing Techniques

All the diagrams in this book use some form of tracing technique. For illustrations of flat steps I lay a small step fold on the drawing paper marking corners, lines, and intersections as needed, with pencil. After I move the step fold away I use the marks to fill in missing details.

To illustrate any step that has become 3-D, if the details are simple, I place the model on the page where I will insert the drawing. I then stare at it, one-eyed, until I find a 3-D view I like. After pencil-marking the corners and edges that touch the paper's surface, using the one-eye view, and without changing my line-of-sight, I mark the position of any corners or edges that are above the paper. If I marked the paper reasonably accurately, and filled in the detail, this method can produce a satisfactory 3-D drawing. This approach takes some practice; sometimes I need to repeat the process from a different view to produce a drawing I like.

For more complex 3-D images I take a close-up digital photograph of the step. While I prefer to use a photograph made from the digital image, sometimes a computer print is sufficient. With a good image in hand I tape the photo to my drawing board. I cover the photo with a piece of taped-down prepared acetate, an artist medium made to accept ink drawing. To remove any dust or other substance that may be present I gently wipe the surface of the acetate with a soft, clean, non-abrasive cloth. Then, using my pen and drawing tools, I trace the edges and creases in the photograph onto the acetate. I photocopy the finished drawing, covered with a clean blank sheet. By using a copier that allows image size adjustments I am able to match the scale of the other diagrams on the page where the copy will be trimmed and pasted. Any errors on the acetate drawing now can be repaired on the photocopy with correction fluid and pen. With these additions the master copy of the model's diagram is complete.

The 24 projects in this book cover the range of my designs and diagrams from the earliest to some of my most recent work. I hope that everyone who enjoys origami will find something of interest here.

Diagram Symbols and Folding Techniques

Origami diagrams typically use symbols (lines, arrows, and other graphics) to explain the steps necessary to fold a model. Variations in dotted lines and arrows distinguish valley and mountain folds; other arrows and symbols indicate whether to push, pull, hold, turn, or look at the paper another way. Since emerging in the mid-20th century this symbolic language has become relatively standard around the world. While origami designers and diagrammers may use slightly different variations of these symbols, the overall result is that paper folders generally understand and can follow an origami diagram regardless of the designer's nationality or language.

This section illustrates and discusses symbols used in the diagrams and folding techniques for the models in this book.

Picture Sequence

The first drawing in any pair of diagram steps shows the paper's starting appearance, along with symbols and explanatory text to complete the step. The next drawing illustrates the resulting appearance and so on, step-by-step, until the model is completed.

Steps are numbered and the model should be folded in sequential order. Some numbered steps contain multiple sub-steps, which are labeled and explained.

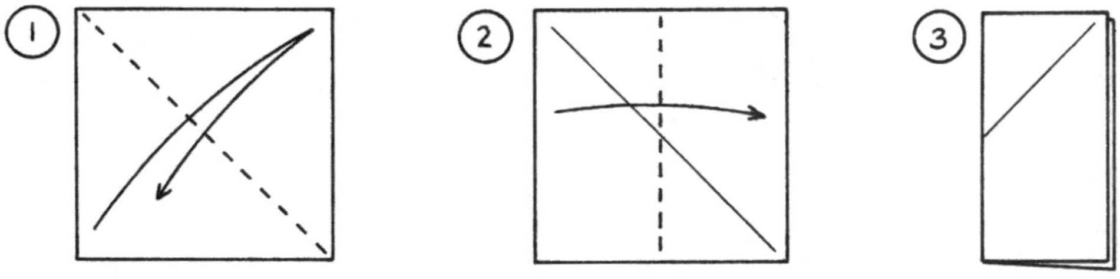

Lines, Creases, and Directions of Folds

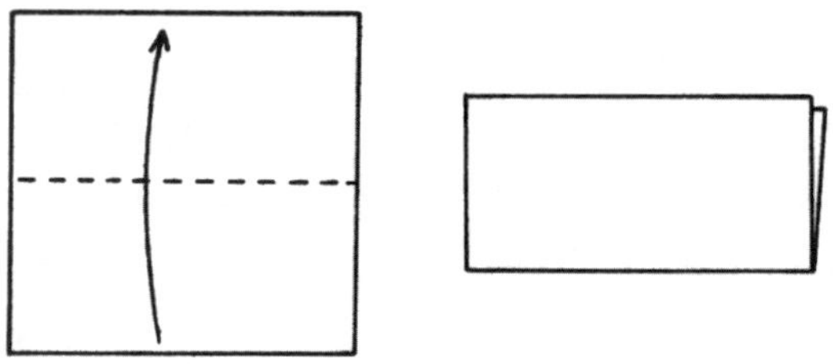

Fold in this direction on the front
(Valley fold)

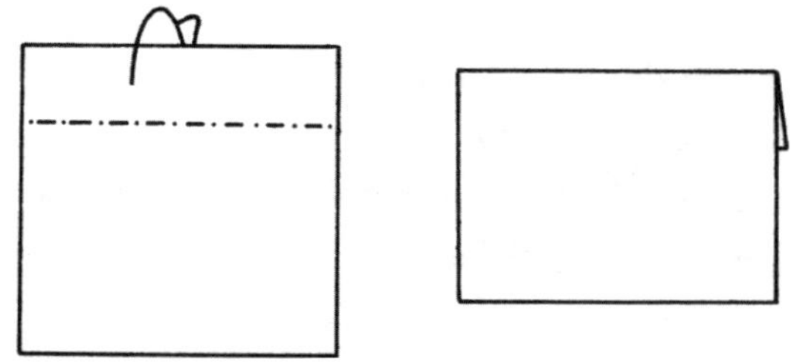

Fold behind to the rear
(Mountain fold)

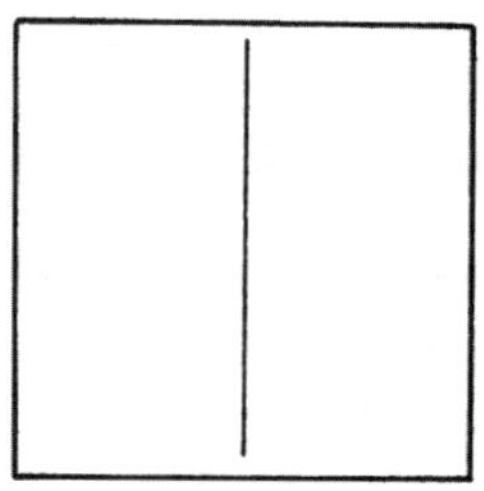

Existing crease(s)

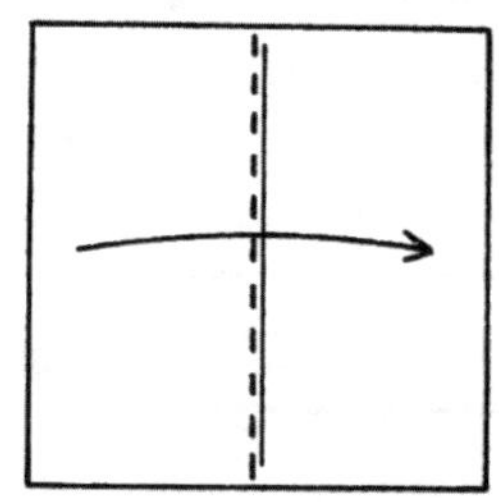

Fold along an existing crease

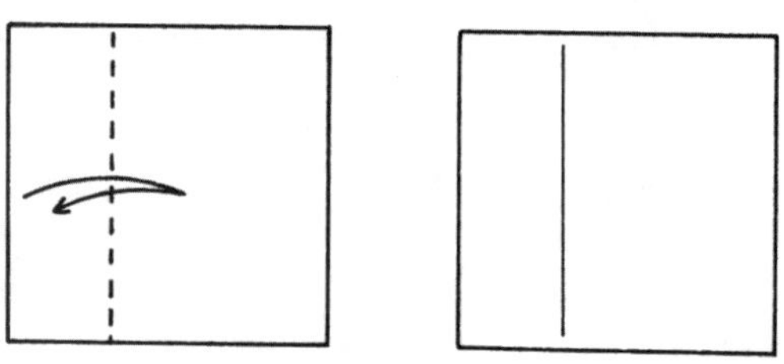

Fold and unfold (Valley fold)

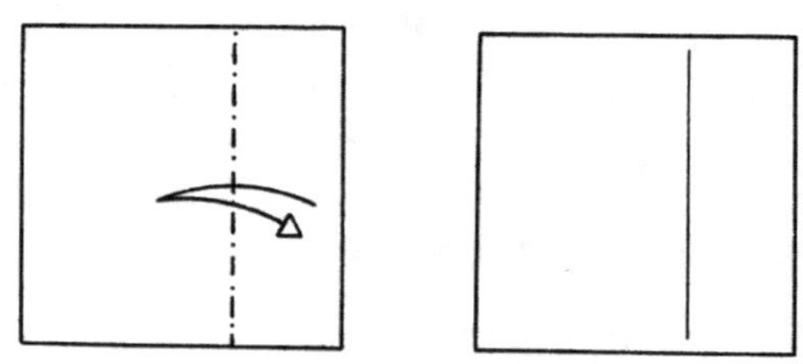

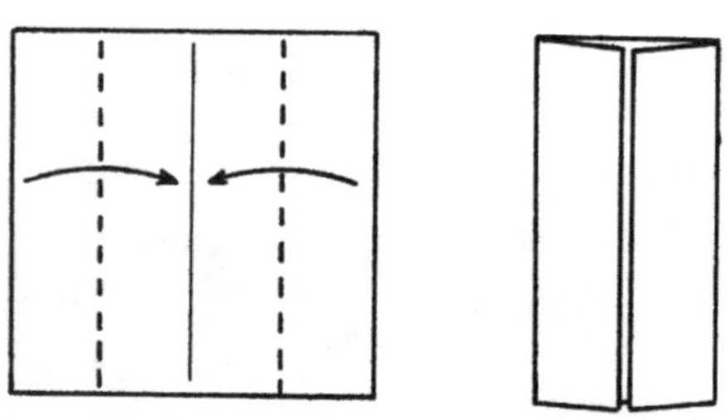

Cupboard fold

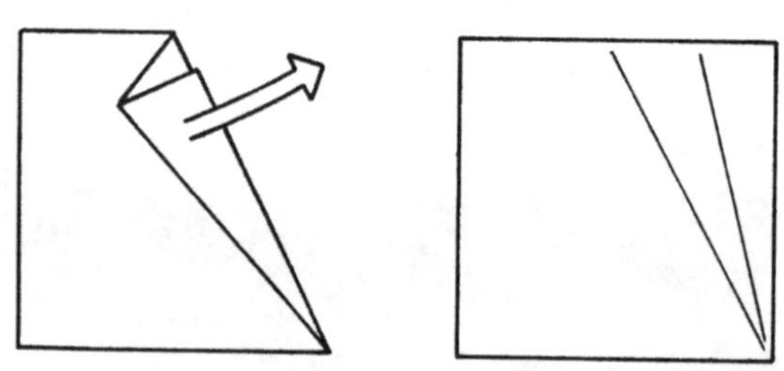

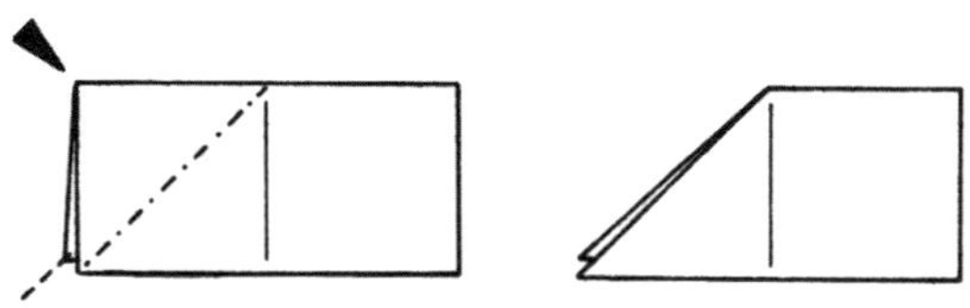

Inside reverse fold
with Push symbol

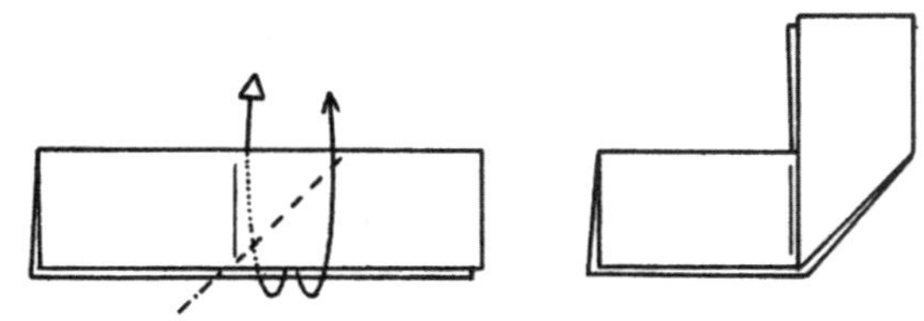

Outside reverse fold

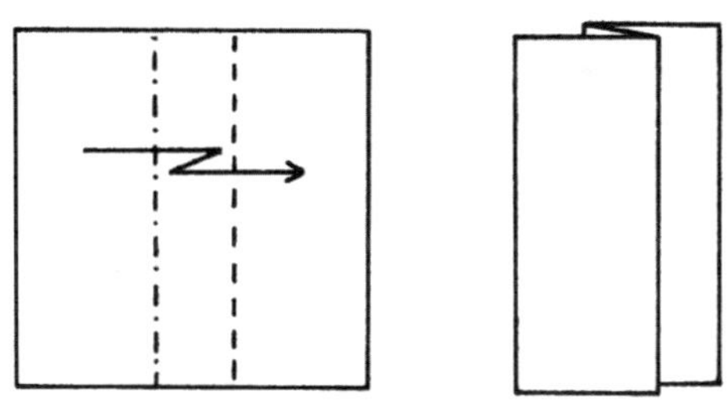

Pleat fold

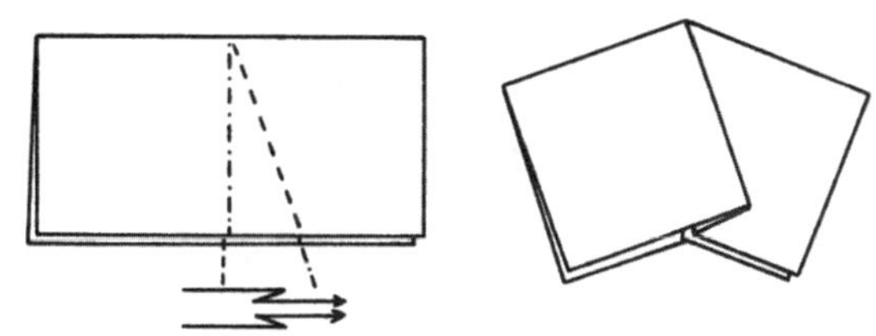

Crimp fold

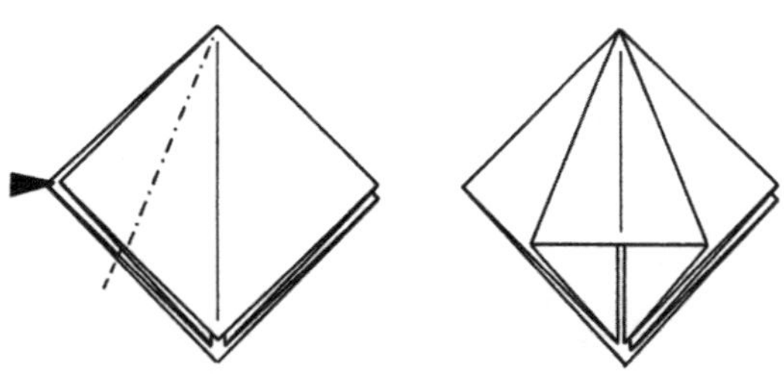

Squash fold

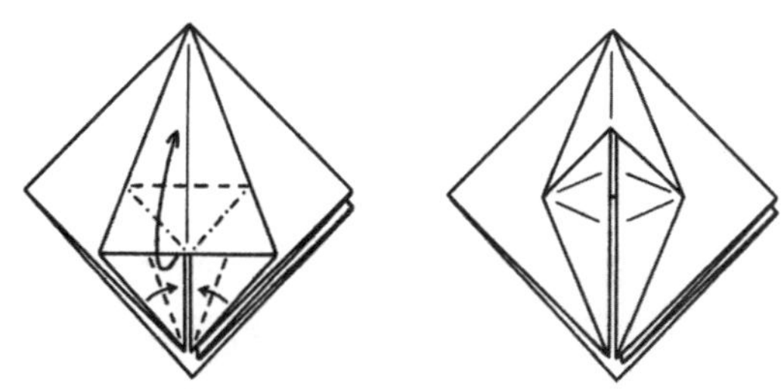

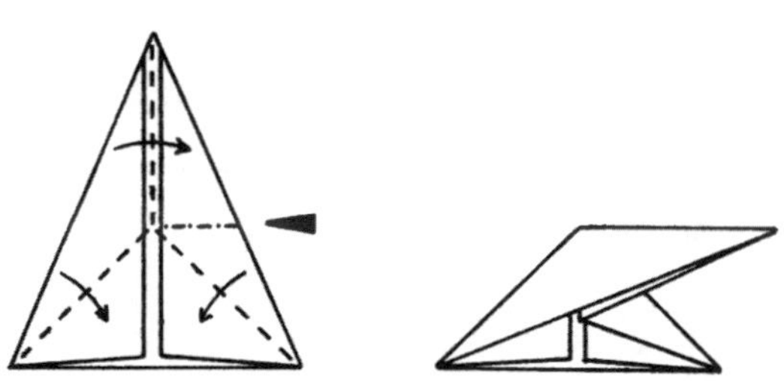

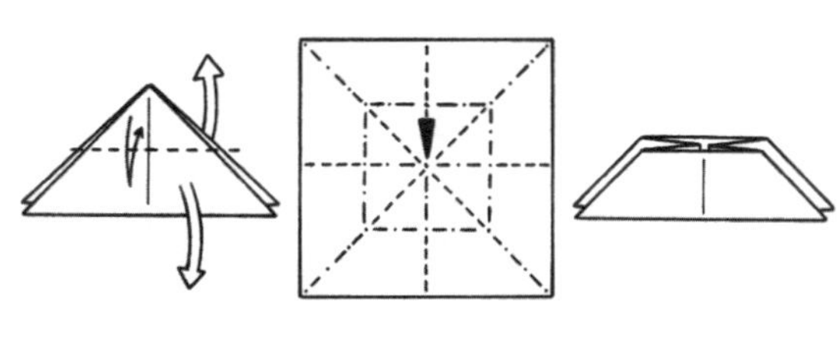

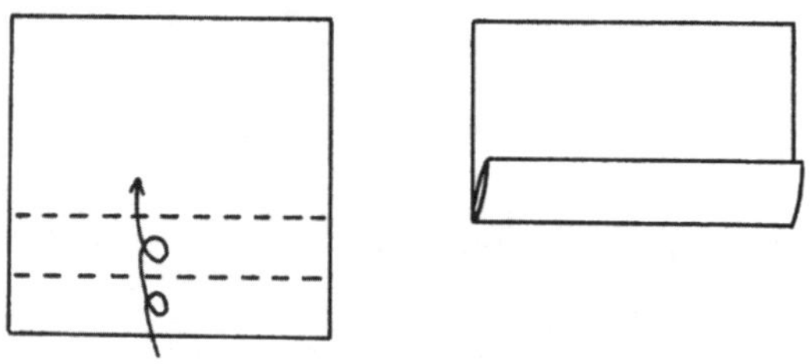

Fold or roll over twice

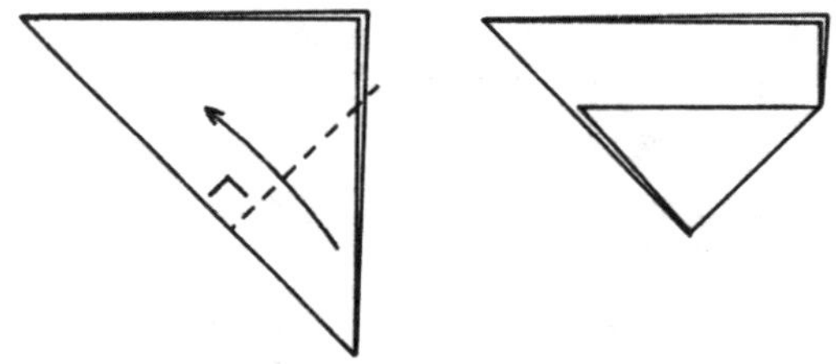

Fold at right angle to a line or edge

Positioning Symbols and Instructions

The diagrams use several different repositioning symbols to direct turning the model prior to making a fold.

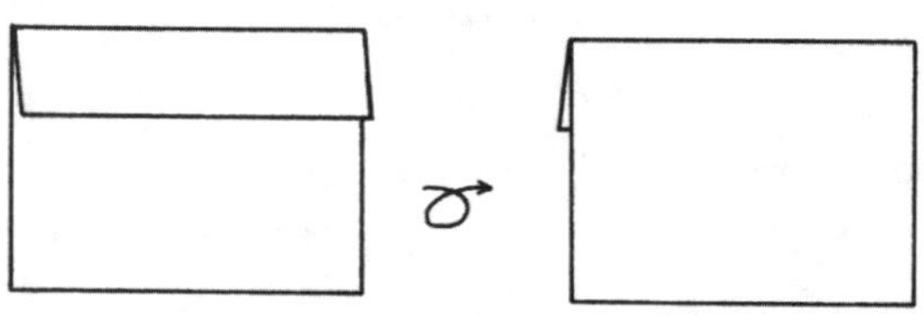

Turn model over, side-to-side

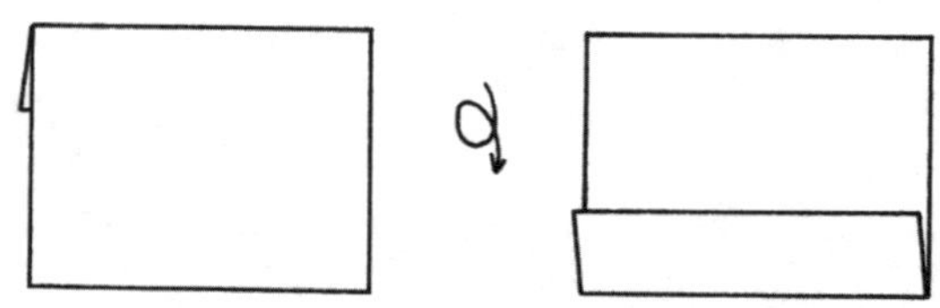

Turn model over, top

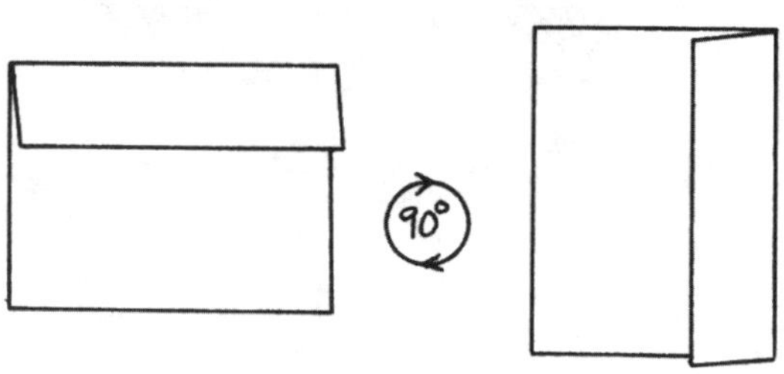

Rotate model
In direction and amount shown

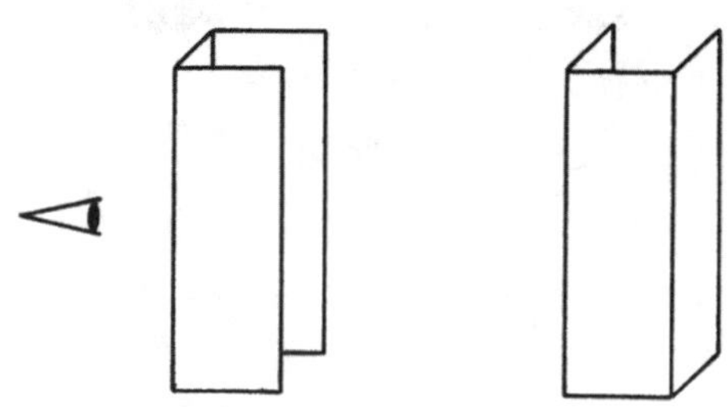

Reference Points

Reference points are graphic indications for precisely locating placement of the paper before forming a crease. Most folding steps in this book use reference points. Common reference points are an edge, an existing crease, a corner, a tip at the end of a flap, or an intersection of creases. Some reference points are labeled with a *capital letter* or a *heavy dot* (●). A line segment may be identified by *two letters* appearing at either end of the segment, such as "AB."

Any time a reference point is either unclear or not given, look at the next diagram in the folding sequence and approximate the position shown. This is often referred to as a *judgment* fold. Landmarks are specific reference points. Usually, folding directions will indicate how to locate a landmark.

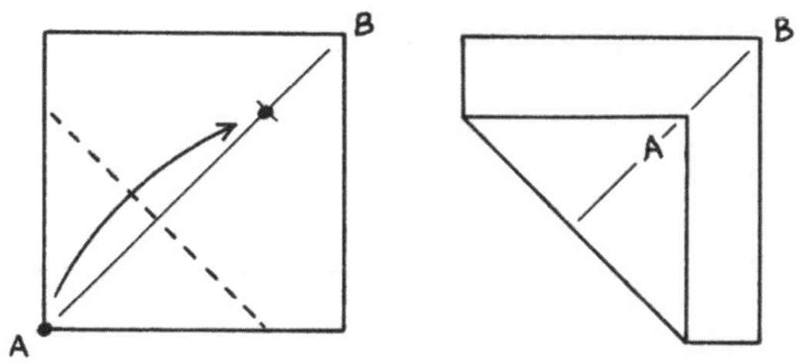

Letter and Dot Reference Points

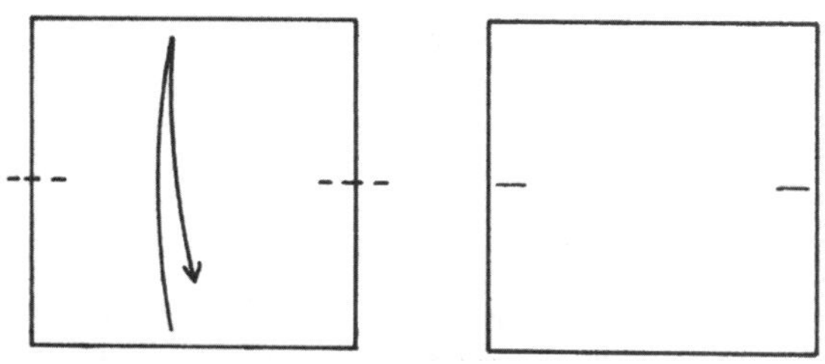

Landmarks

Some directions specify a "pre-crease." Pre-creases may provide landmarks for subsequent folds, or may serve as an efficient, early step for a group of folds, often in a grid or pattern, needed later.

Occasionally it is necessary to subdivide a portion of the paper into equal parts. The diagram symbols for subdividing look like this:

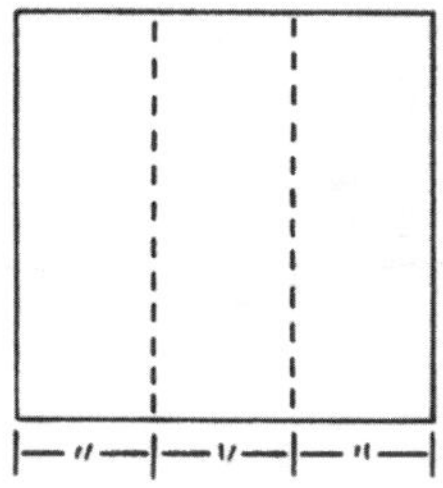

Equal subdivision of an edge

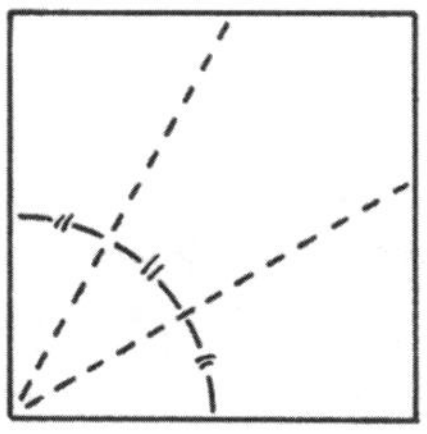

Equal subdivision of an angle

Scale of Drawings

Obviously, when folding a model, a larger sheet of paper becomes progressively smaller. The problem this creates for fitting diagrams to standard pages is overcome by beginning with small drawings and, when needed, changing the scale to a larger view. Symbols illustrate this change in scale.

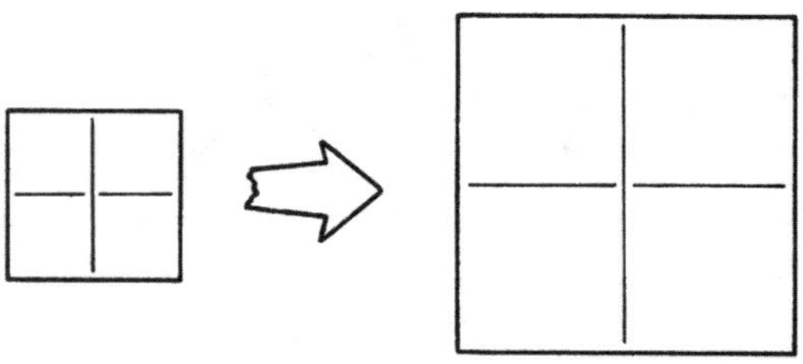

Picture gets larger

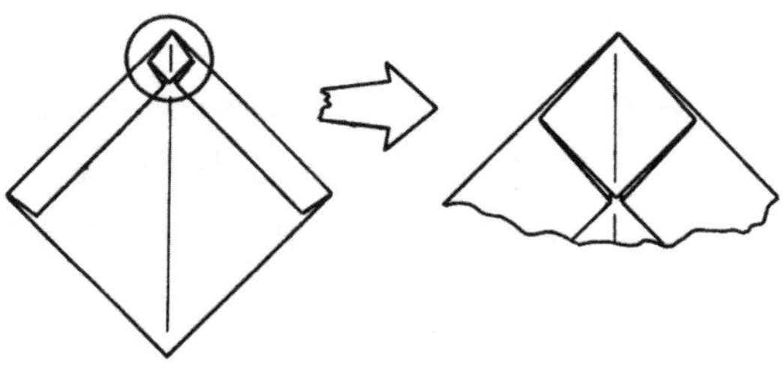

Enlarged detail view

Seeing the Invisible or Hiding the Visible

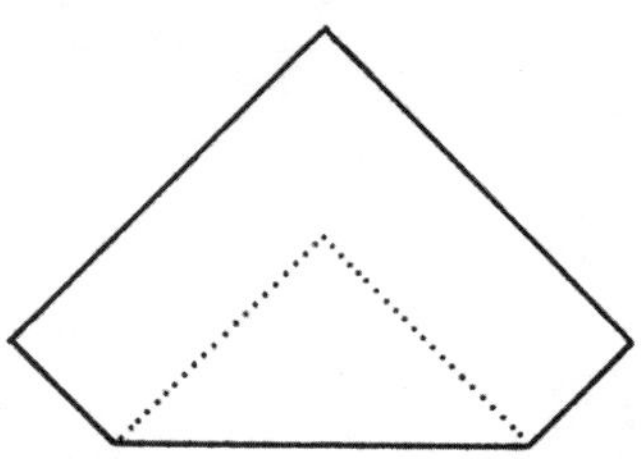

Location of a hidden edge, line, or crease

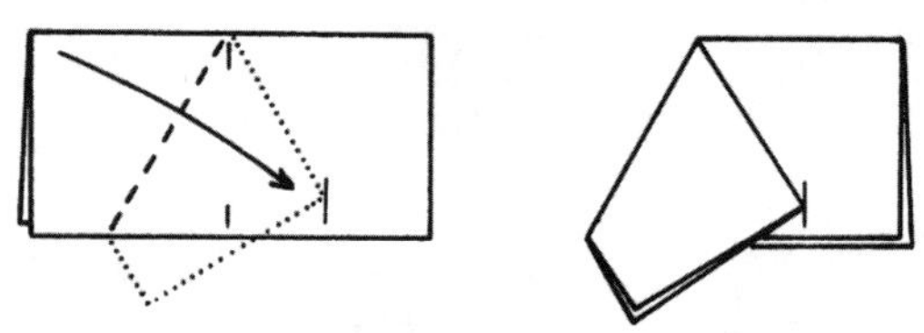

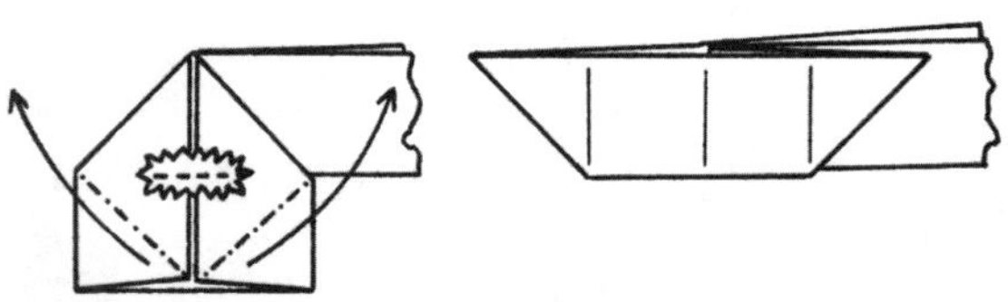

X-ray view of a hidden valley fold

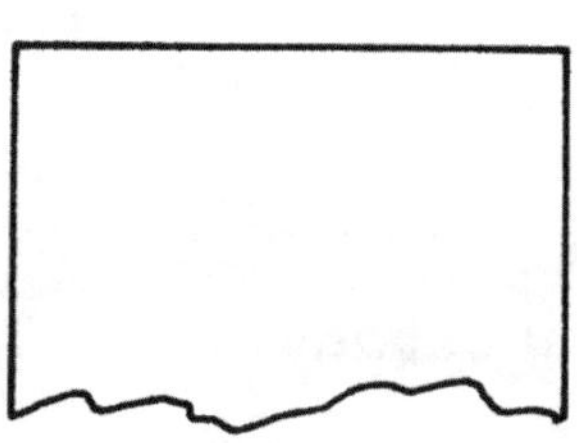

Miscellaneous Symbols

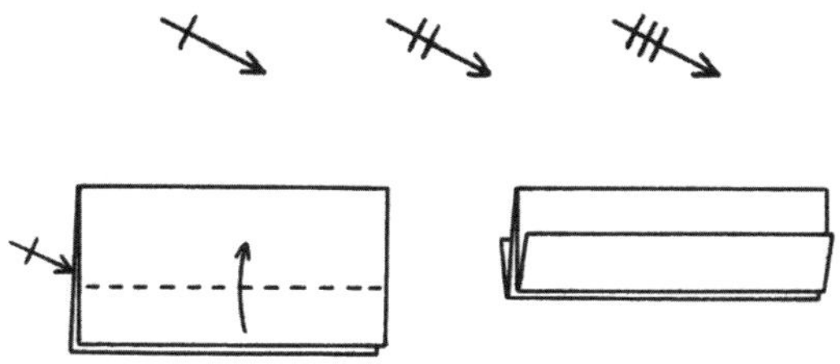

Repeat behind. Cross bars indicate number of repeats

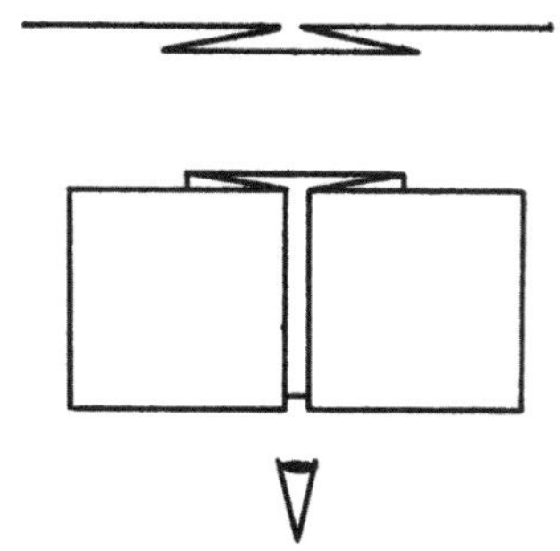

View of paper edge, showing layers
Often used with "eye" symbol

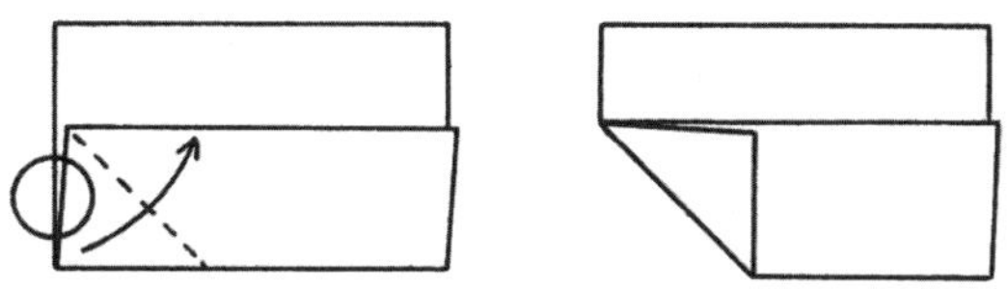

Hold where circled

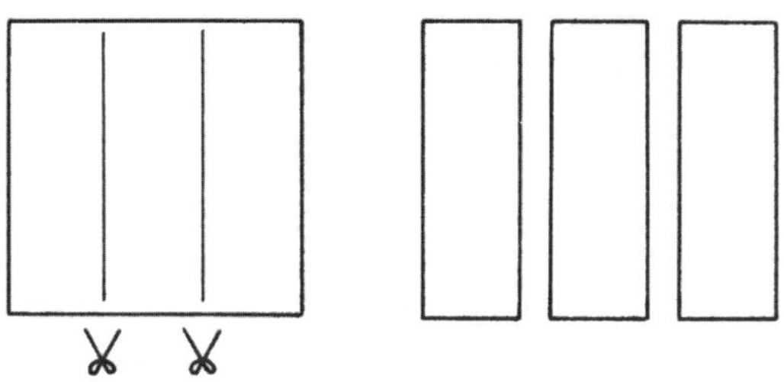

Use of Shading, "Color Side Up" and "Color

Origami diagrams commonly use a shade or color pattern to differentiate the paper's color surface from its "white" side. Some of the diagrams in this book use such shading. Others use text to indicate the proper position of the color or white surfaces.

Folding Techniques

Keep layers from slipping

Errors may occur when folding a flap or section of paper having more than one layer. The top layer of any two will tend to slide in the direction of movement. Prevent this by gripping the layers firmly as you move the paper section for the next crease. (See "Hold where circled" illustration.) This is always a good technique to use, but in this book, it is pointed out especially when slipping is very likely to occur.

Leave a small space

When narrowing a flap by folding edges to the center, leave a small space for "give." Otherwise, in a later step the flaps may cause resistance and bunching. The amount of space to leave is related to the model design **and** the thickness of the paper. This technique is sometimes referred to by the expression "Leave a fudge factor."

Edge curling for tensile strength

Some models benefit from this technique that strengthens and helps maintain shape. Examples include boxes, containers, ring models, and models with legs that need help to better support the weight of the paper. The technique is to form an inward curve along, and parallel to an edge.

Rearrange flaps, like turning pages of a book.

Some models have multiple flaps extending out from a central axis. The diagram may instruct to perform the same fold or folding sequence on each of the flaps. Rearrange the flaps as needed to bring the working flap to a front surface to perform the step.

PUZZLE CUBE

This 12-piece cube uses two different, and simple, modules which hold together with overlapping flaps and friction.

It was named Puzzle Cube because friends said it was like a puzzle to put it together.

Using 6 inch squares produces a cube 3 inches along each edge. I always use twelve different sheets.

Begin Module "A" with the paper color side down.

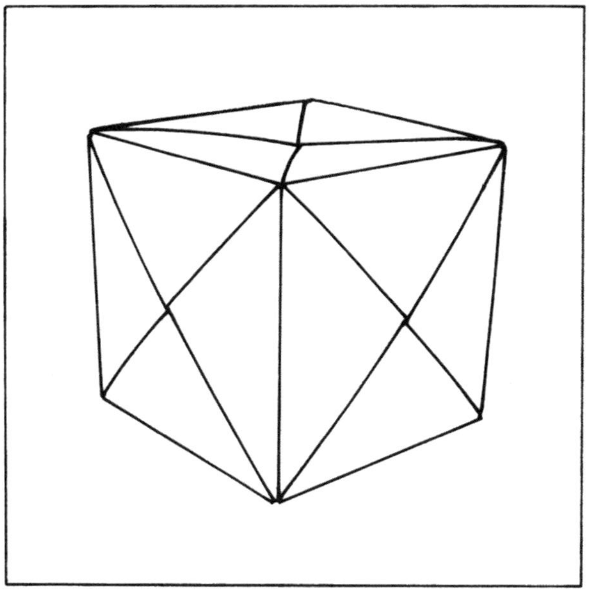

1

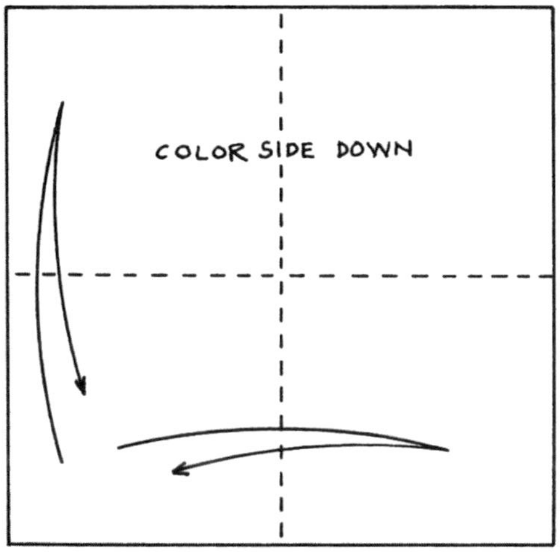

Fold in half and unfold in both directions.

2

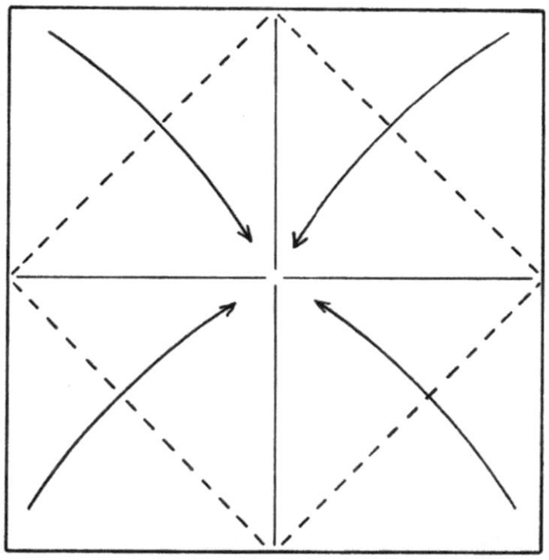

Valley fold corners to center, but allow small space so edges do not touch.

3

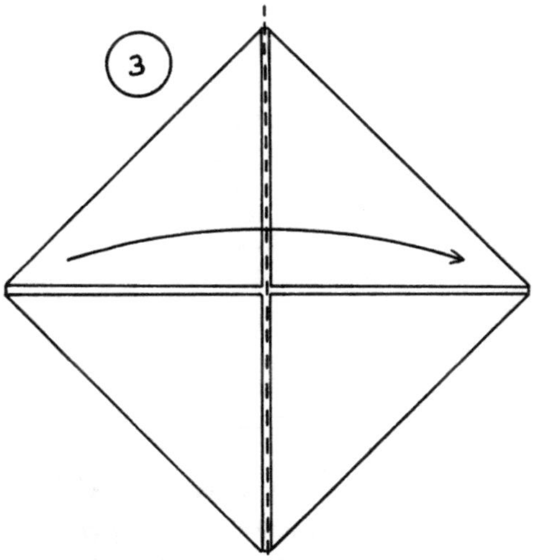

Valley fold to right.

4

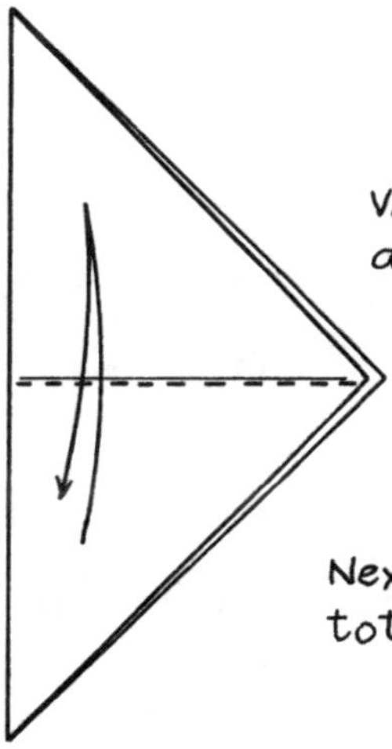

Valley fold and unfold along existing crease.

Next, finish making a total of 8 "A" modules.

Folding Module "B"

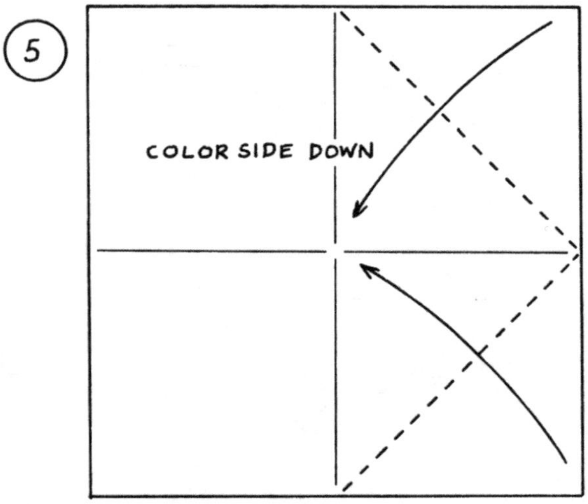

Begin at step 2 of Module "A."
Valley fold two corners, but allow a small space so edges do not touch.

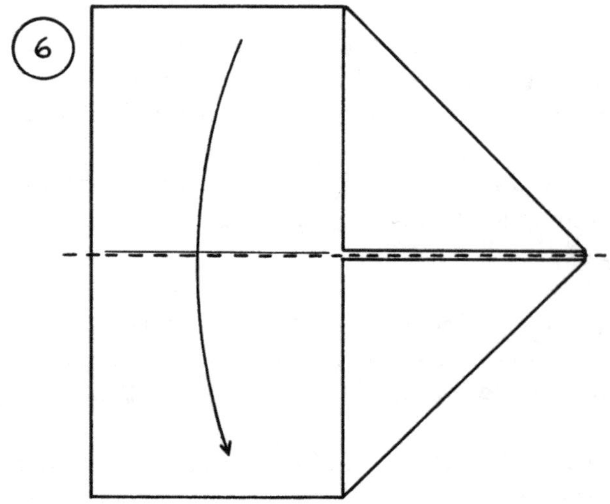

Valley fold top to bottom along existing crease.

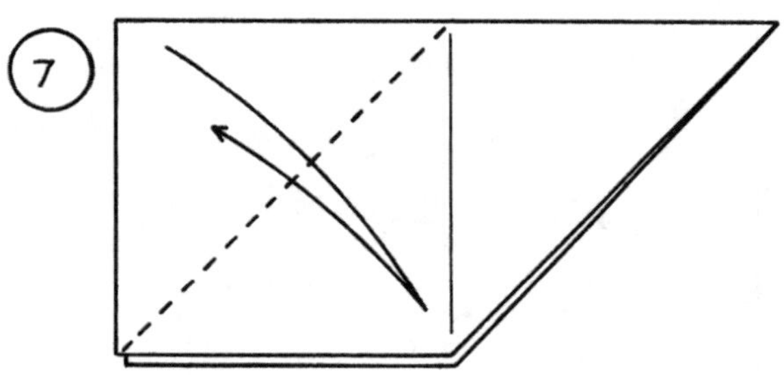

Valley fold and unfold the diagonal of the square area.

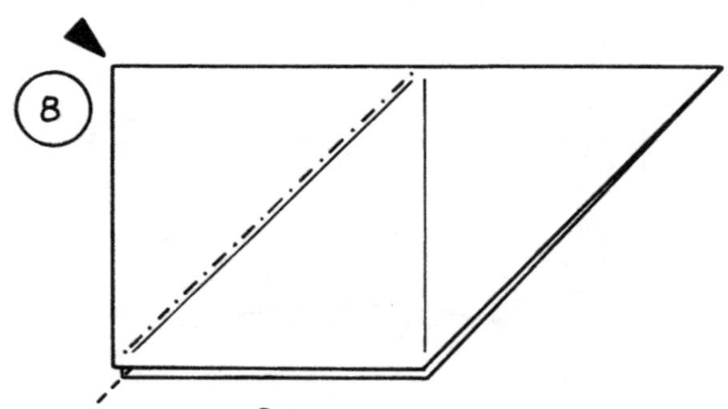

Reverse fold the corner inside, using creases made in step 7.

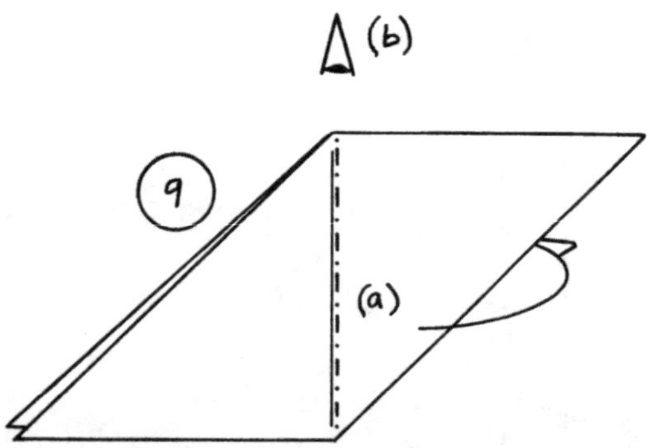

(a) Mountain fold right half behind to form a 90° angle.
(b) Look this way to see view of top edges.

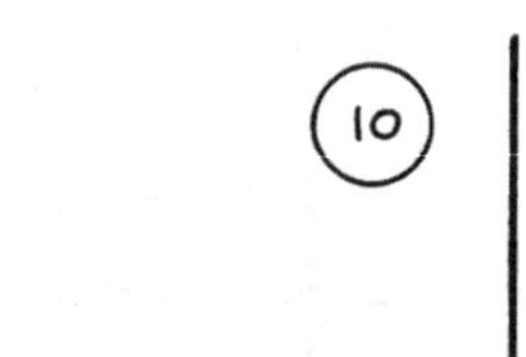

View of Top Edges Only.
Next, finish making a total of 4 "B" Modules.

Assembling the Puzzle Cube

Choose 4 "A" Modules. Position them on a surface as shown, including with the tip of each piece inserted part way into pocket of adjacent piece.

Then, carefully slide the 4 modules together.

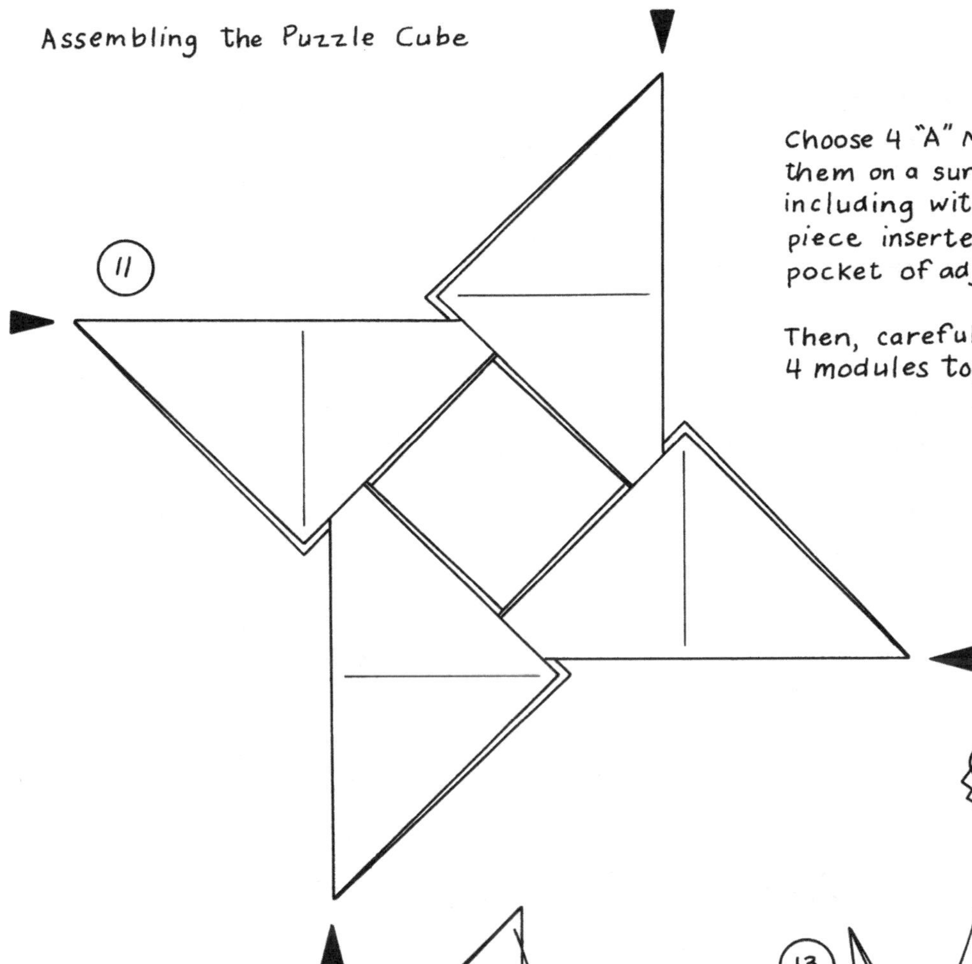

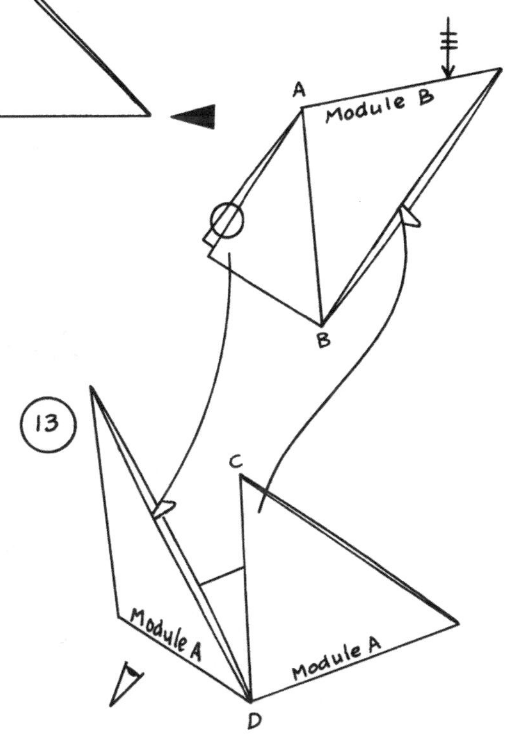

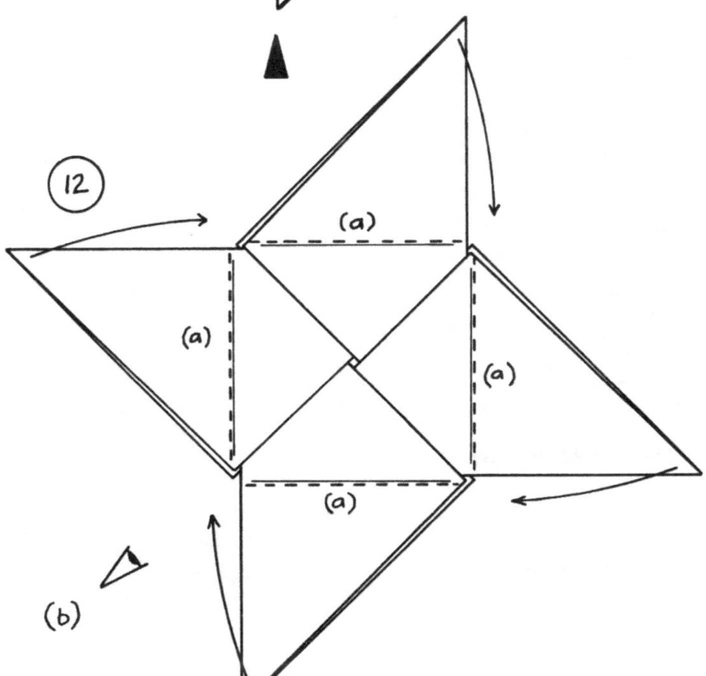

Side Corner View with Module "B."

Choose a "B" module. Hold left flaps together and insert both into pocket of module "A," while at same time inserting tip "C" into pocket of module "B." Edge CD will be inside, and allign with, mountain-folded corner AB.

Repeat steps on other 3 corners. Then, see side view.

(a) Raise the four flaps to a standing position by valley folding along existing creases.
(b) Look this way for side-corner view.

Final Assembly

1. Make a Top Assembly by repeating steps 11 and 12, using the remaining 4 "A" modules.

2. Pick up the Top Assembly, turn it over and position it above the base and side surfaces completed in step 13.

3. Insert tip of Module "A" from Top Assembly into pocket of Module "B" at same time tip of adjacent Module "B" is inserted in pocket of Module "A."

4. Repeat on other 3 sides.

5. Push all assembled surfaces snugly together.

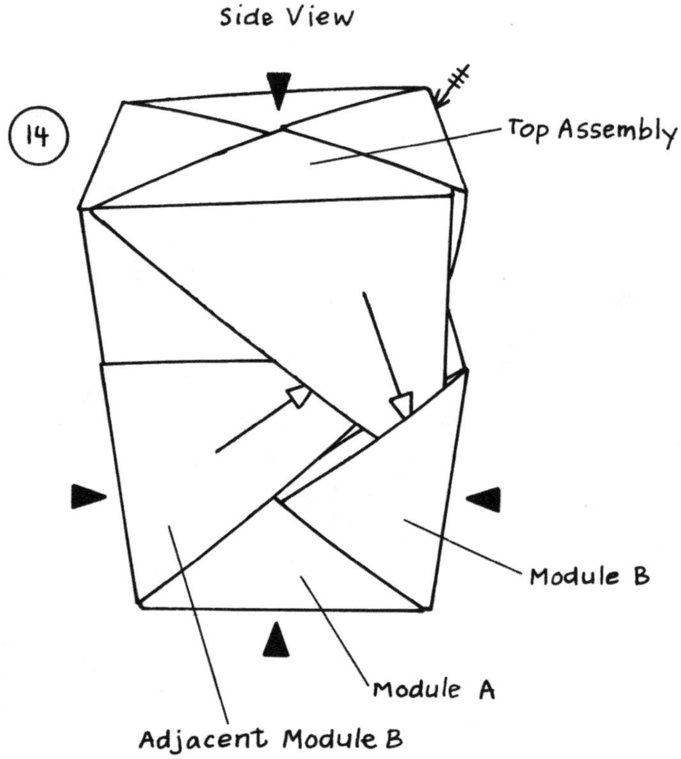

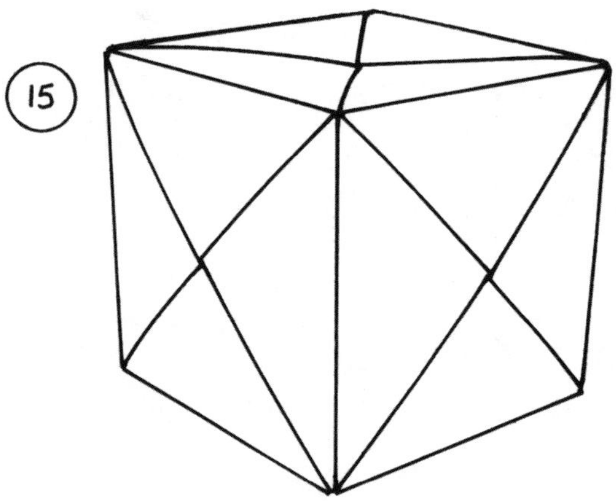

Finished Puzzle Cube

PAPER CHAIN

Try a 6" square for a large chain link, and a 3" square for a small one.

Preparing the Paper:

1

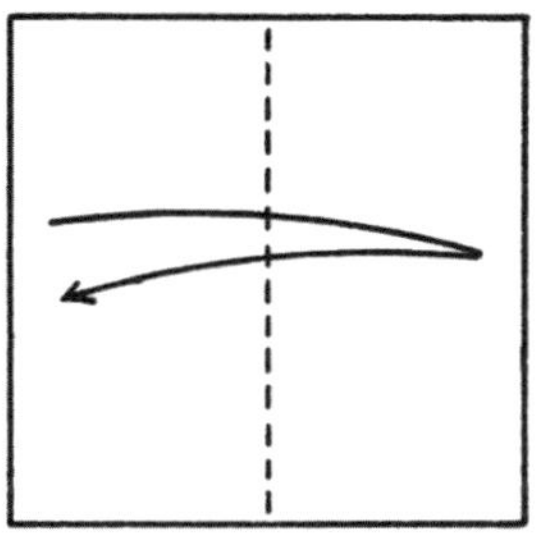

Bookfold in half and unfold.

2

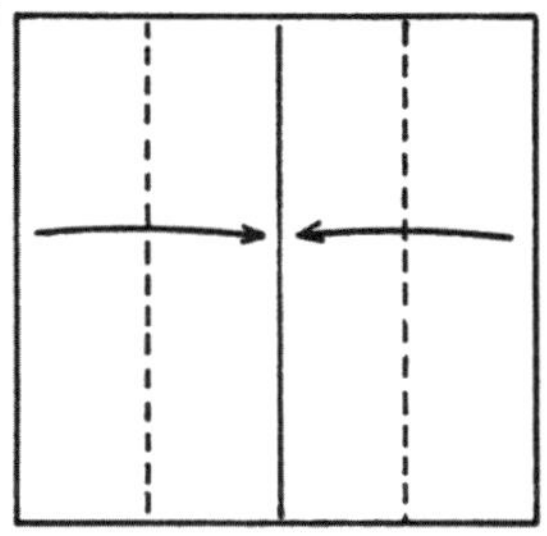

Cupboard fold side edges to center line.

3

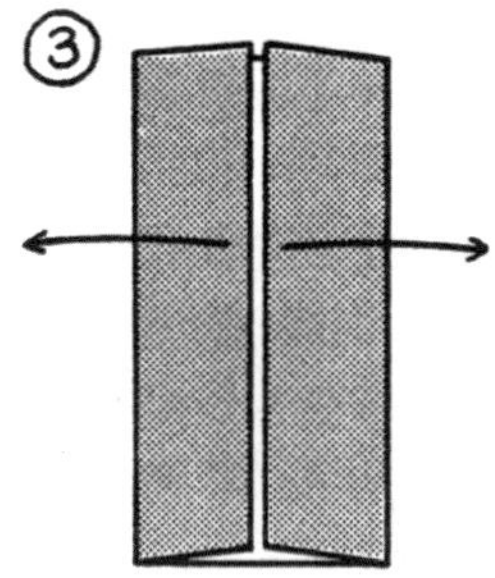

Unfold.

4

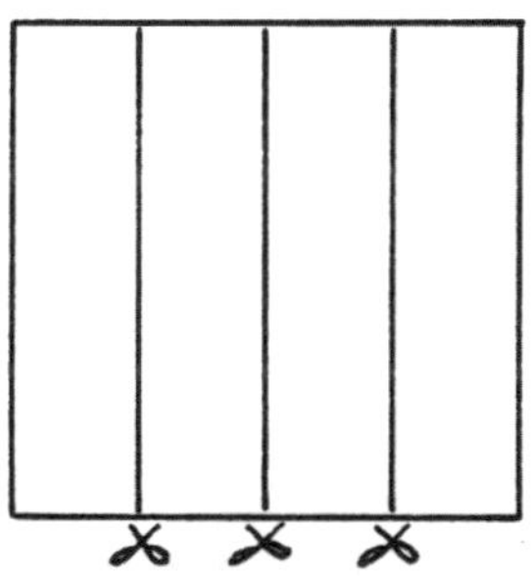

Cut along the three crease lines, . . .

5

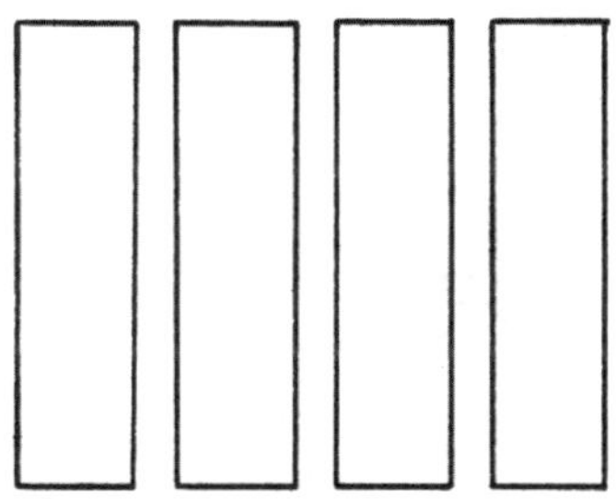

. . . making four rectangular strips (4x1 proportion) from each square used. Picture gets larger.

Making One Link - Connect as many as you like. Begin white side up.

6

Bring end corners together and pinch to make a landmark.

7

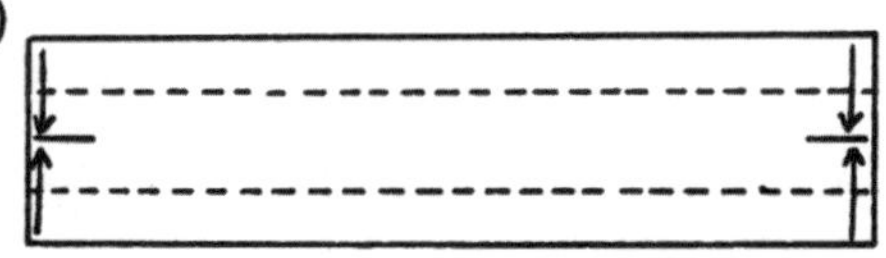

Fold long edges to the landmarks.

8

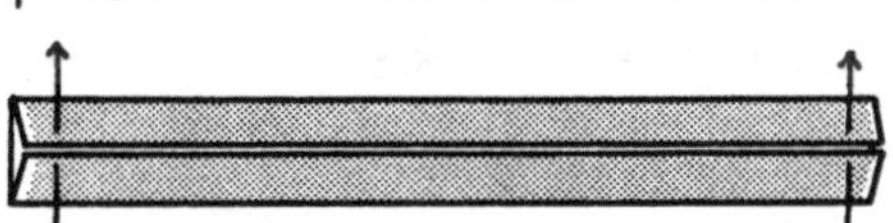

Unfold.

9

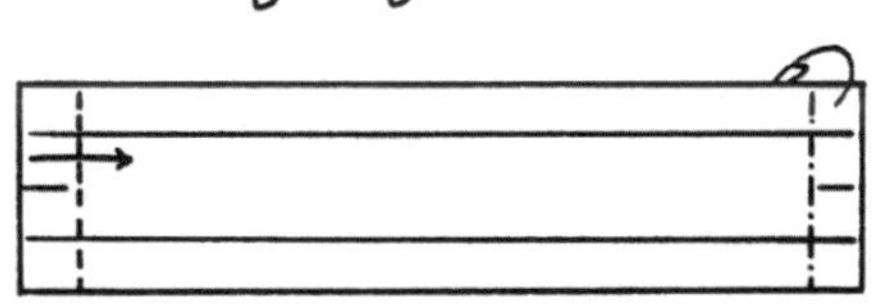

Valley fold the left end to the right. Mountain fold an equal amount of the right end behind.

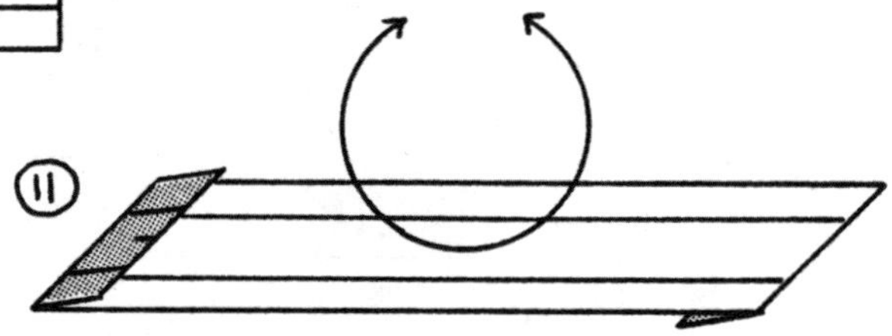

Side View
Curl to bring ends together.
Picture gets larger.

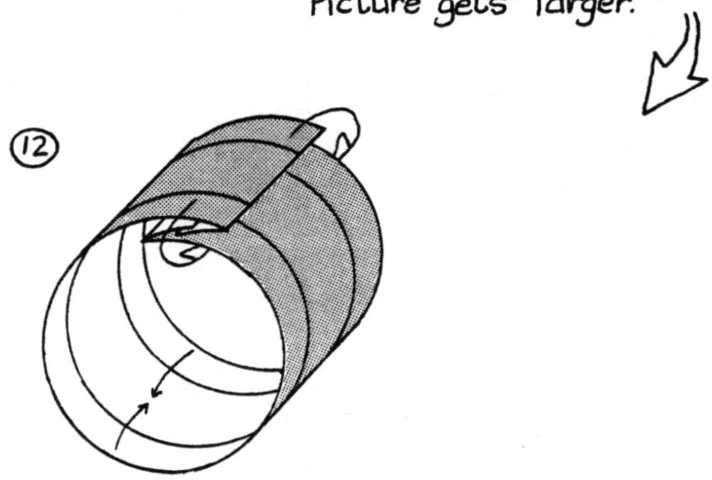

Link the left end flap over and into the "V" formed by the right end flap. Line up the edges and creases, hold the overlapped area tightly, and fold the edges of both sides to the inside, using existing creases from step 7.

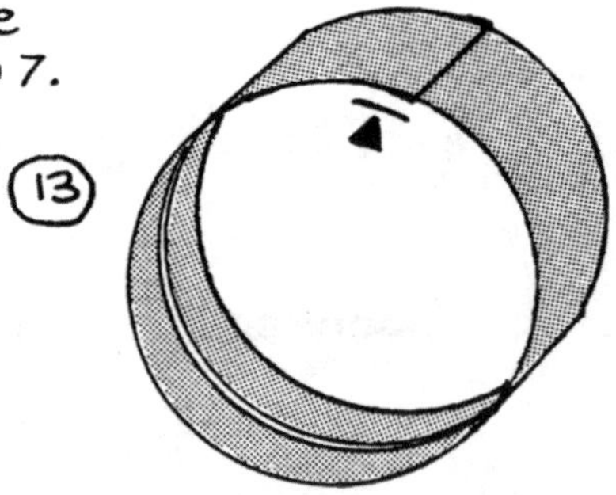

Beginning with the overlapped area, curl and smooth to give the link a nice round shape.

Now, add more links!

WRISTWATCH

Use foil paper. Color side up.
10" square for adults.
8" square for children.

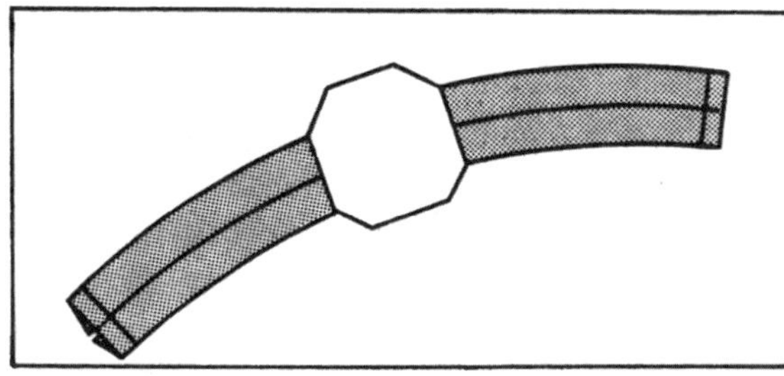

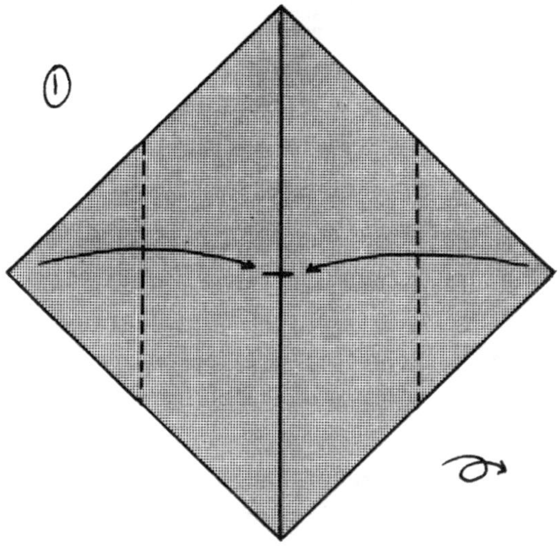

Fold side corners to the center.
Turn over.

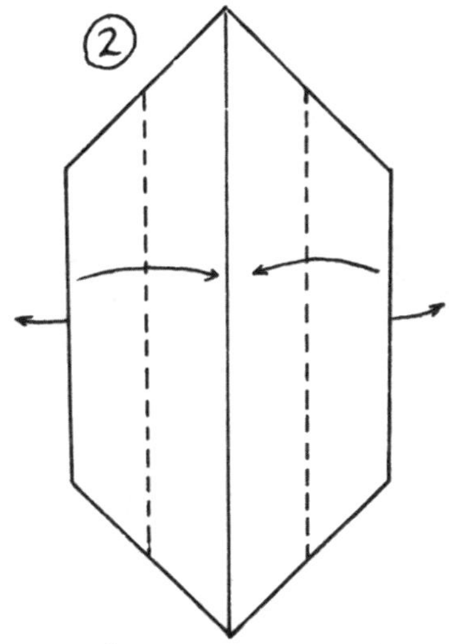

Bring sides to center line, folding top surface only, while allowing the flaps behind to swing around to the front.

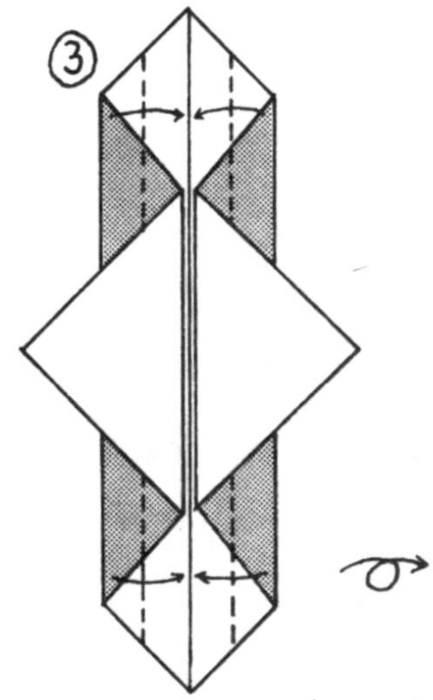

Raise each triangular flap, and fold both long edges to the center line.

Turn over.

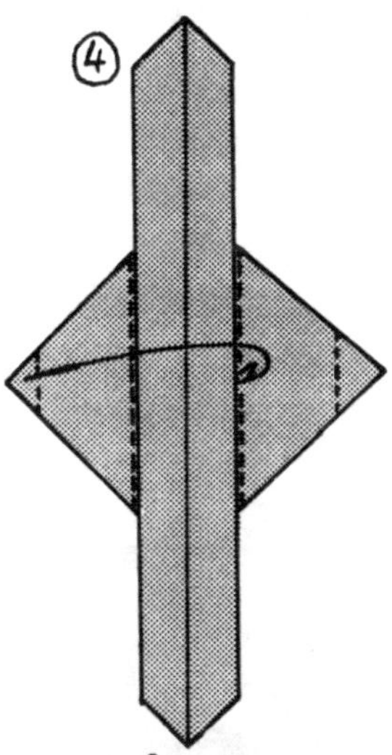

Wrap left flap snugly around and behind material in center. Repeat with right flap.

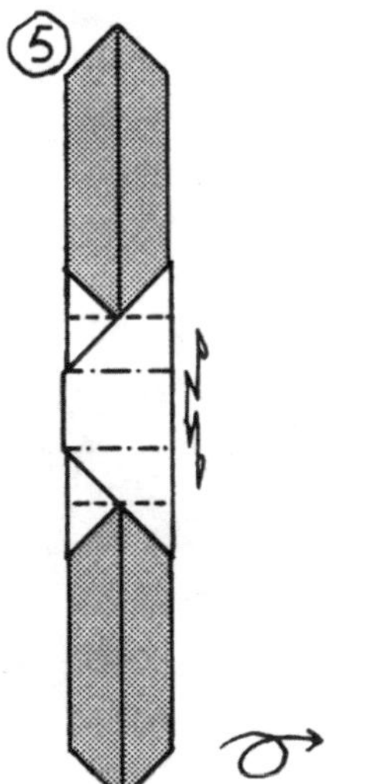

Pleat fold as shown on each side of the center.
Turn over.
Picture gets larger.

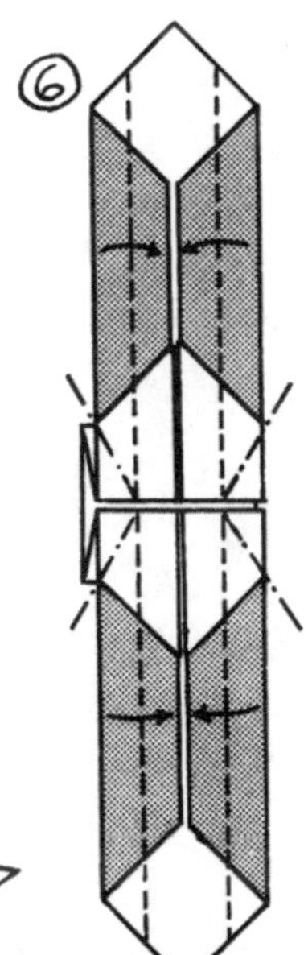

Narrow each end of watch-band by forming the four valley and squash folds shown.

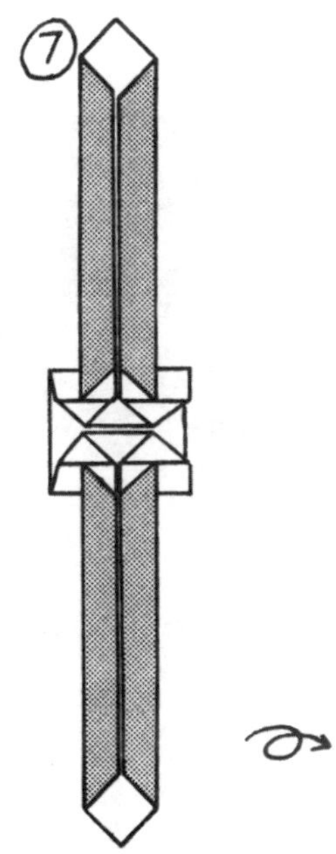

Turn over.

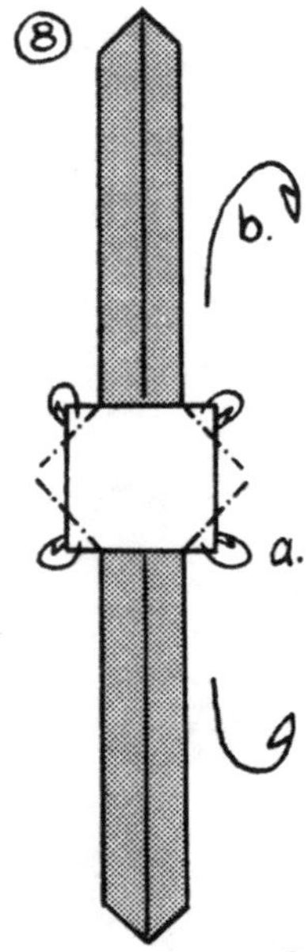

a. Mountain fold the four corners underneath.
b. Curl the band halves behind.
Turn over.

Fitting the watch around your wrist:

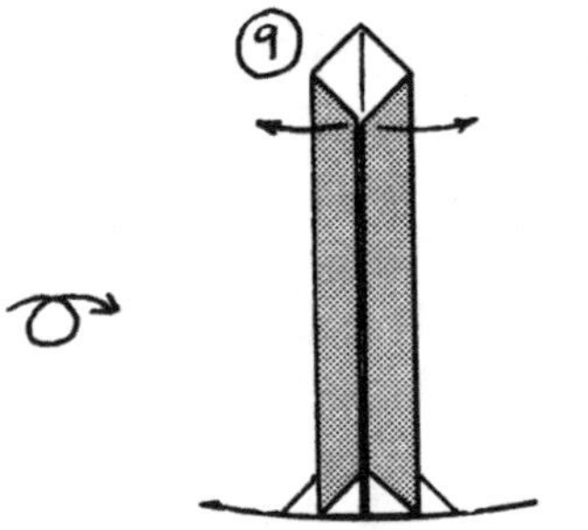

Open out top flaps just enough for the next fold.

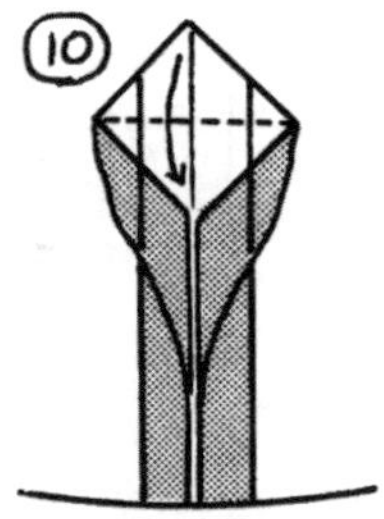

Valley fold the point downward, then re-close the flaps opened in step 9.

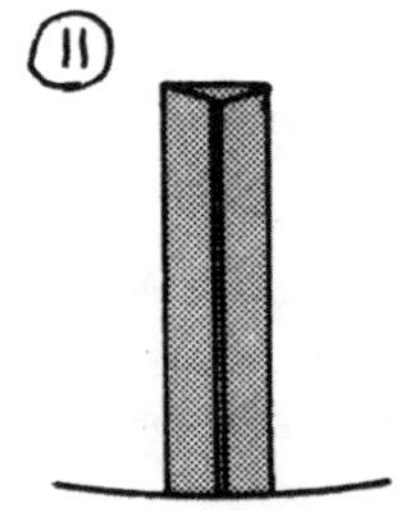

End of band completed. Repeat steps 9 and 10 on other end.

a. Lay face of watch on flat surface. Place wrist over top and wrap band around, bringing ends together. Position of matching folds shown is about ½ inch above the skin with the watch fitting loosely.

b. Open out inside flaps enough to make the folds in step 13.

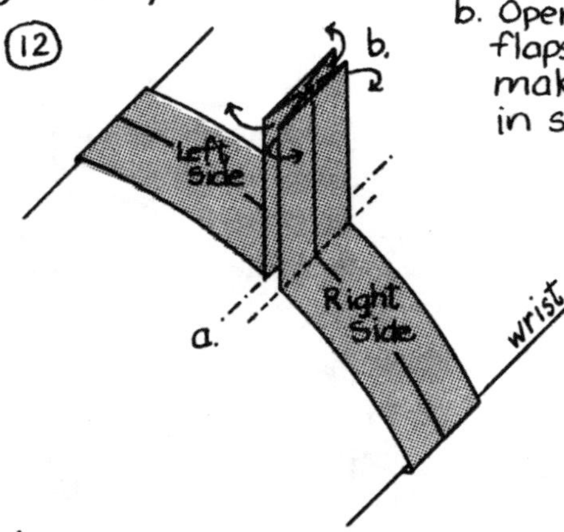

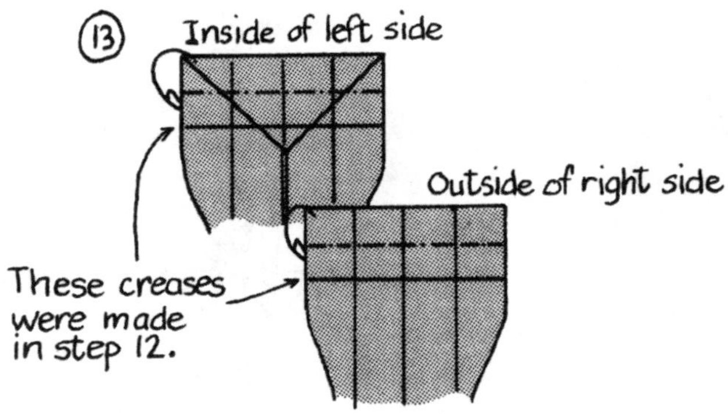

This shows the ends opened. Mountain fold each end to the crease made in step 12.

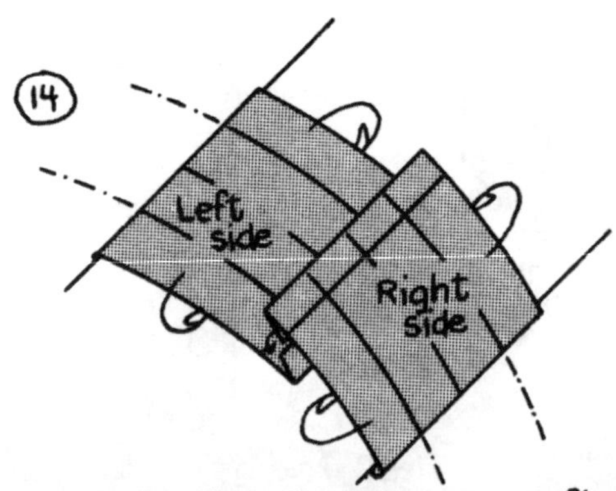

Flatten left side to skin. Link flap of right side over and into the "V" of the left side. Hold this linkage tightly and mountain fold sides of band underneath. Have someone help.

LETTERFOLD

Use 8½" X 11" paper. Start message side up.

1

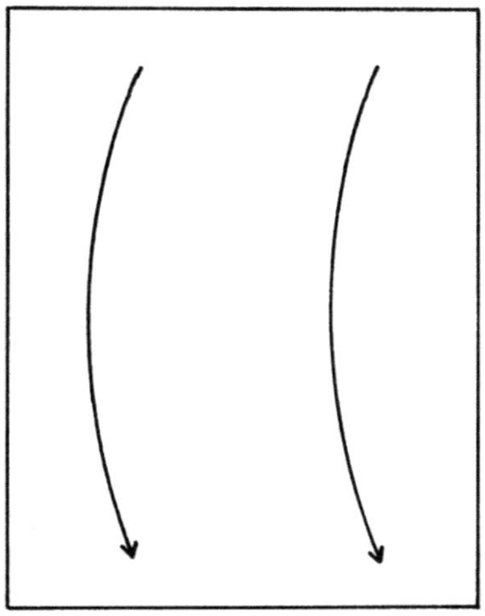

Bring ends together, but don't fold.

2

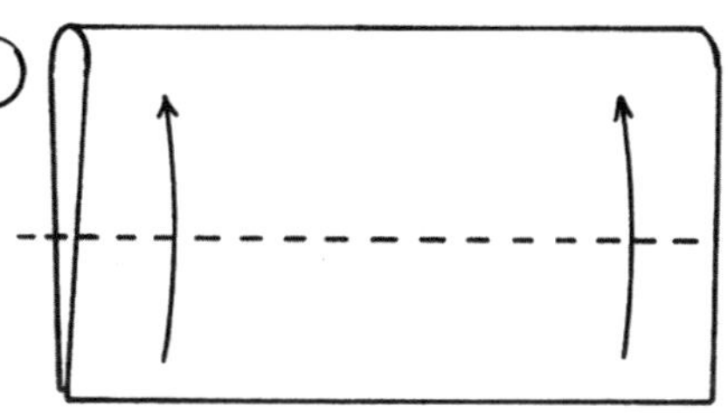

½" to 1"

3

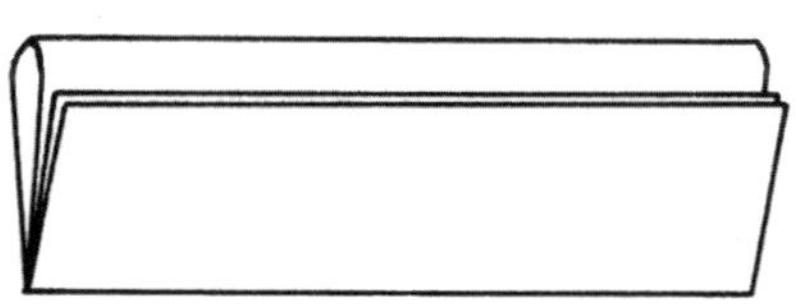

½" to 1"

Next, unfold and position paper as in step 4, with valley fold at top.

4

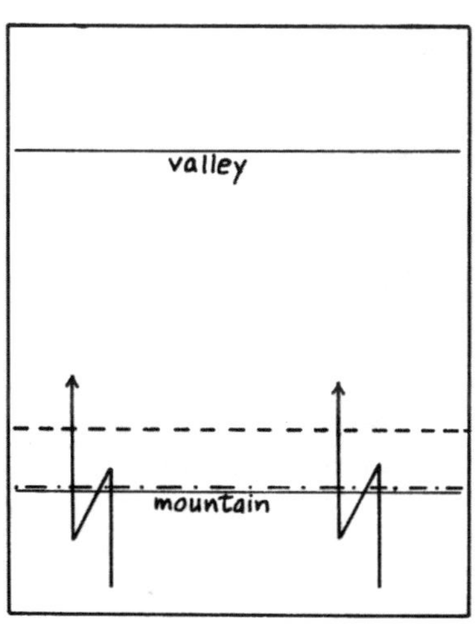

5

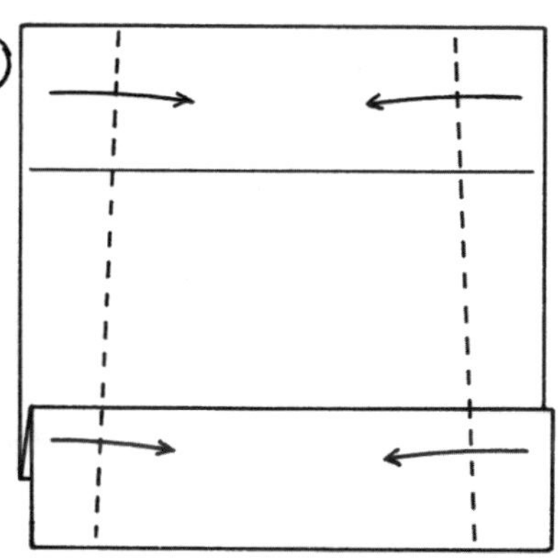

Valley folds are slanted just a little.

6

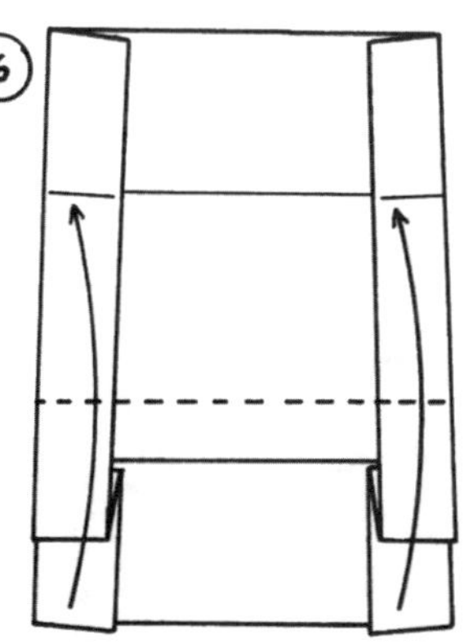

Place bottom edge at top crease and valley fold.

7

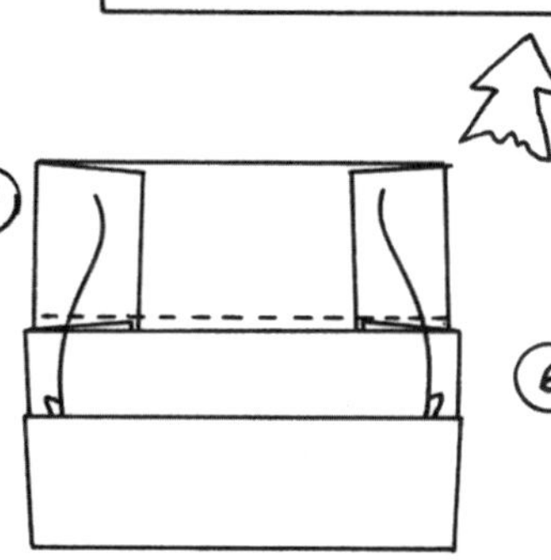

Valley fold flap down and insert into pocket, sealing the letterfold closed.

8

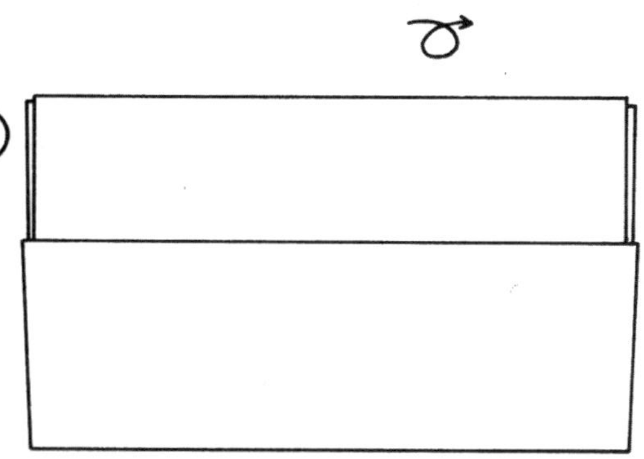

9

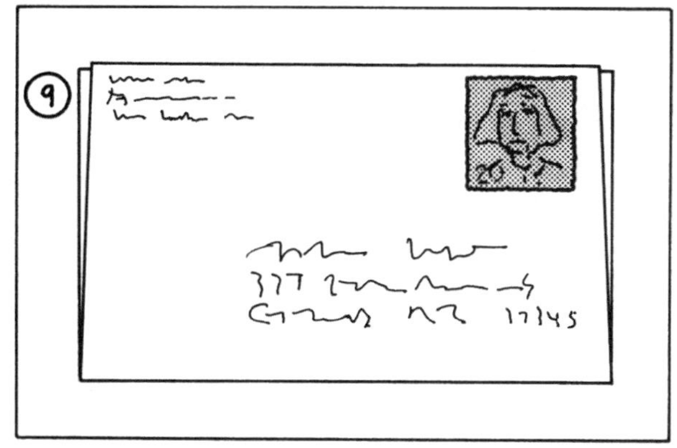

MOUSE

Square paper, foil.

White side up, pre-creased diagonally.

5" square makes life-size mouse.

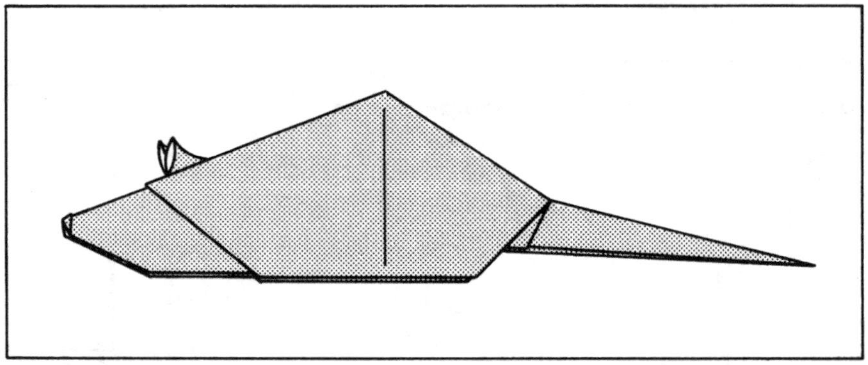

1

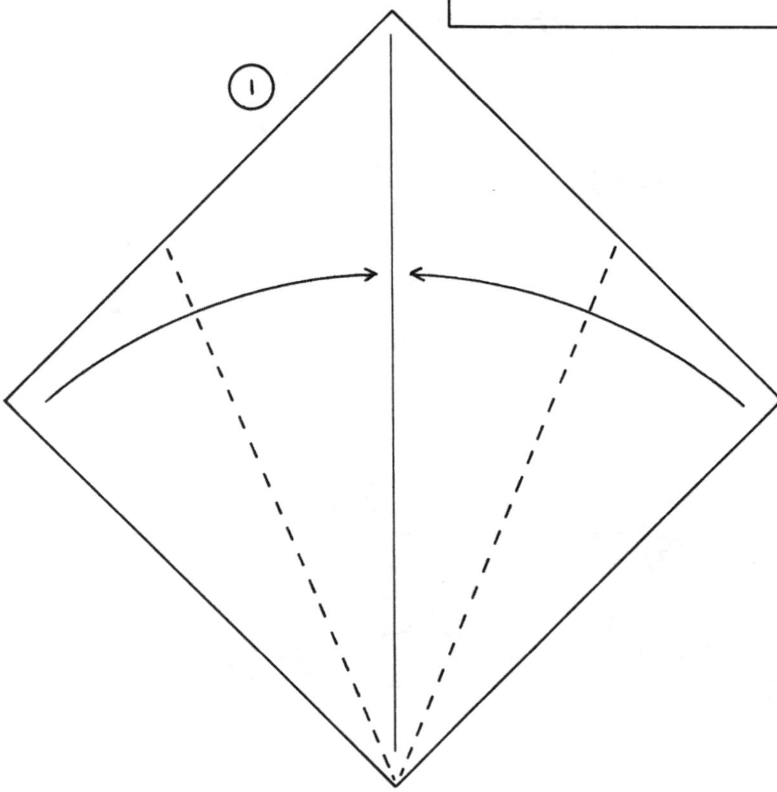

2

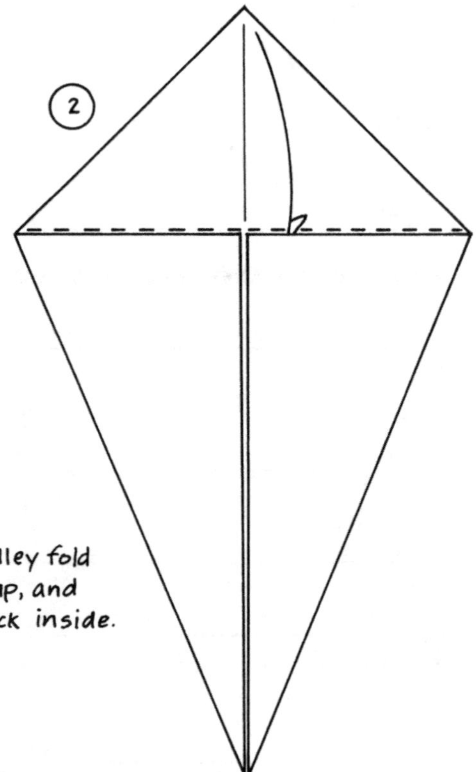

Valley fold flap, and tuck inside.

3

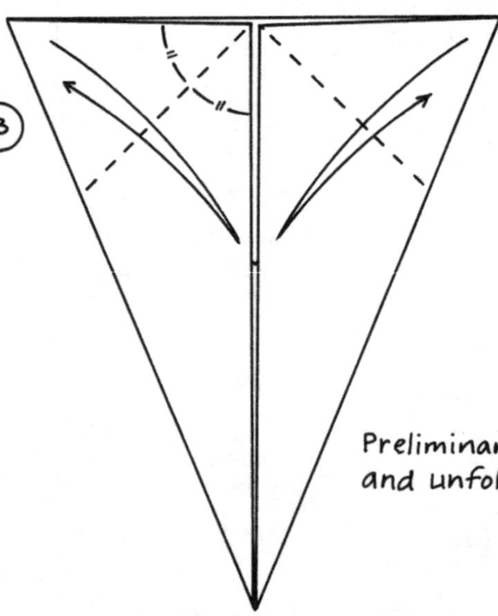

Preliminary fold and unfold.

4

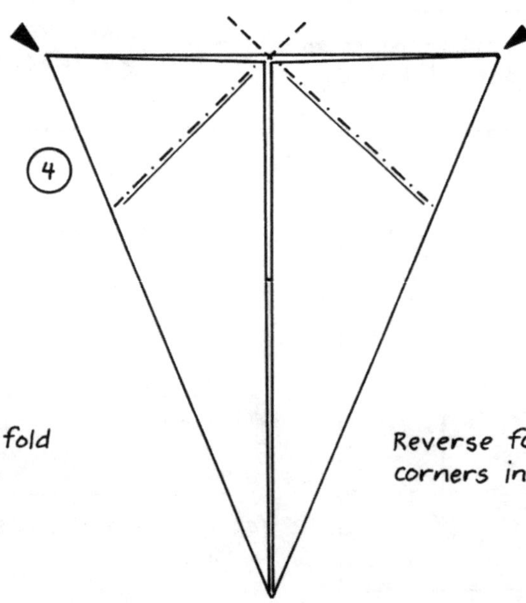

Reverse fold corners inside.

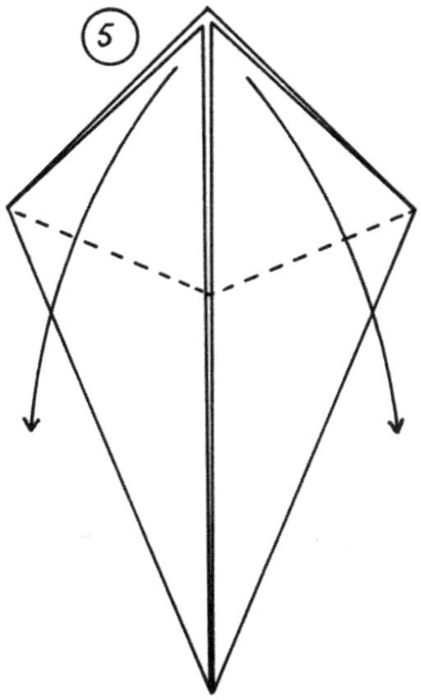

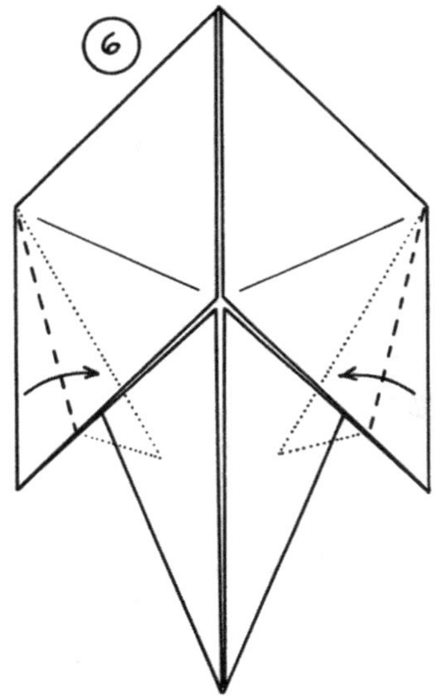

Valley fold each flap. Dotted lines show resulting position.

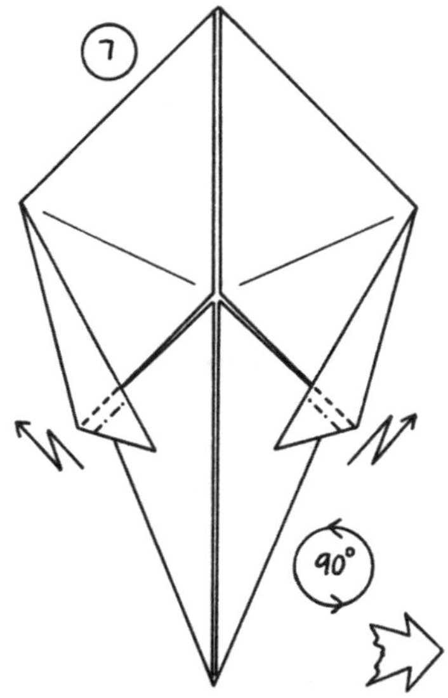

Pleat fold end of each flap. Rotate 90° counterclockwise. Picture gets larger.

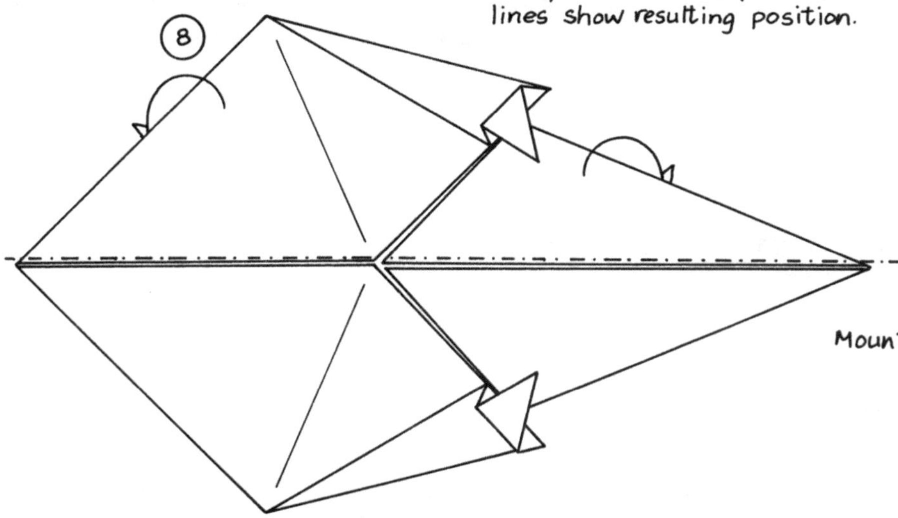

Mountain fold top half behind.

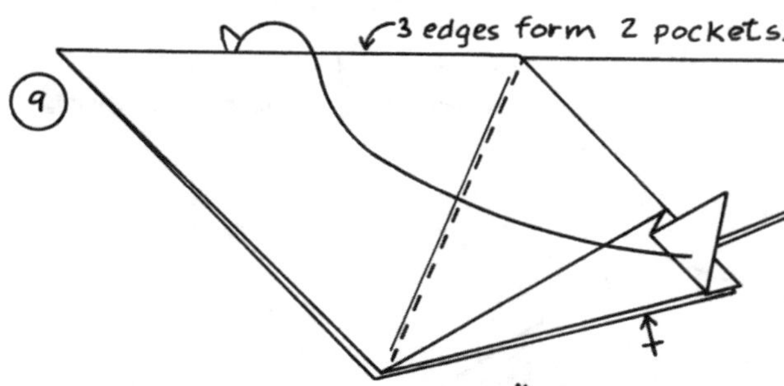

Fold flap along existing crease, and insert flap of pleat into pocket along top edge. Repeat behind.

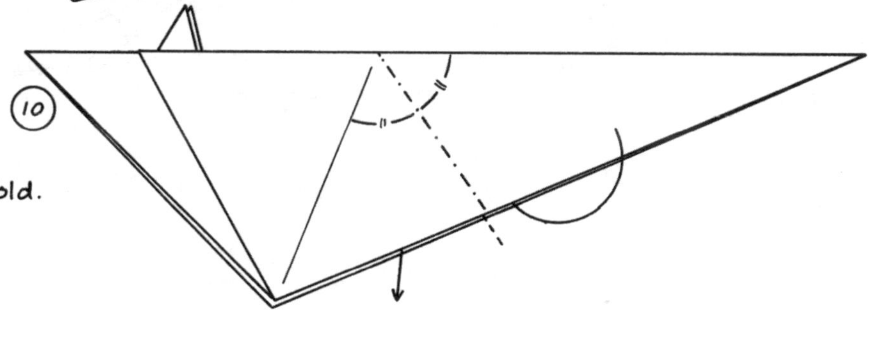

Reverse fold.

11

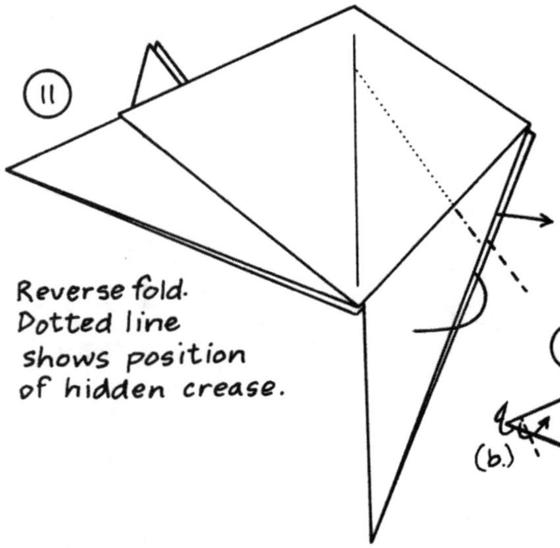

Reverse fold.
Dotted line
shows position
of hidden crease.

12

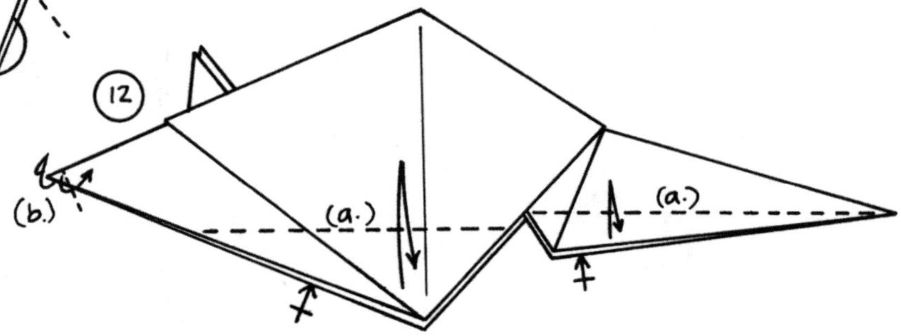

(a.) Pre-crease flaps and unfold. Repeat behind.
(b.) Outside reverse fold to form nose.

13

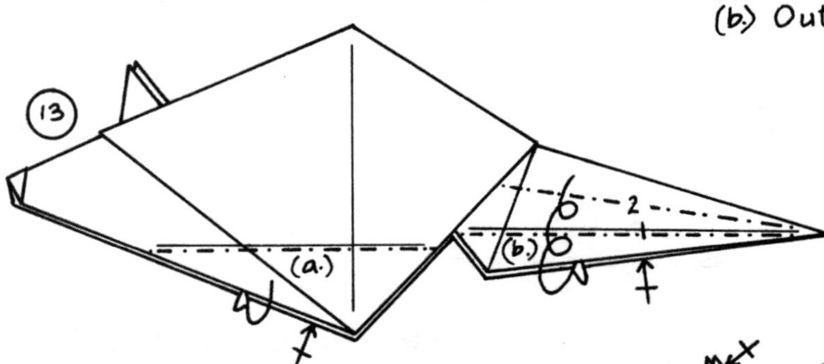

(a.) Fold front and rear flaps inside.
(b.) Roll over twice, inside.
Repeat behind.

14

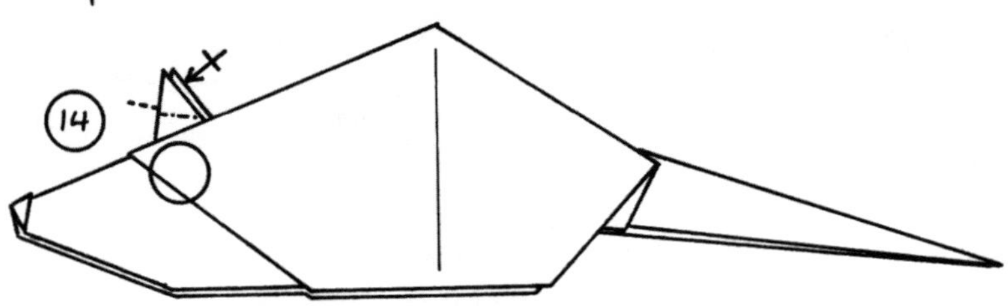

Hold circled area.
Open and flare the ears.

15

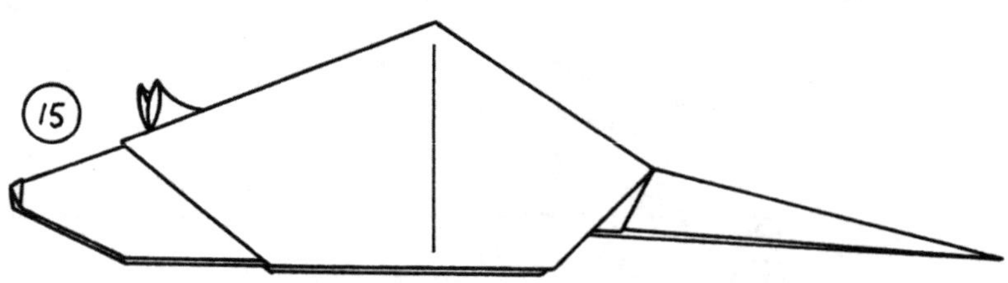

ROWBOAT

Use a square
Begin white side up.

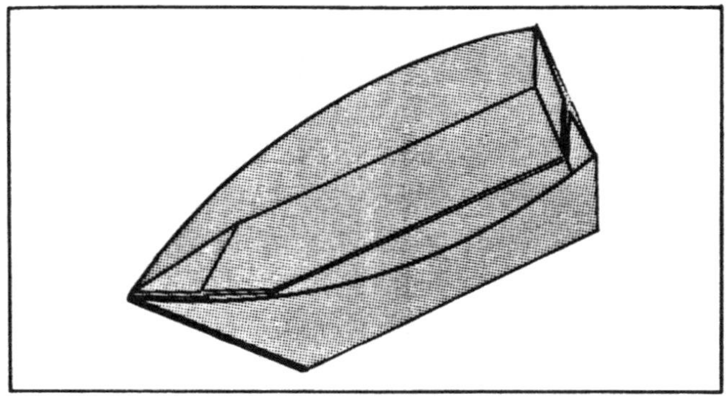

1

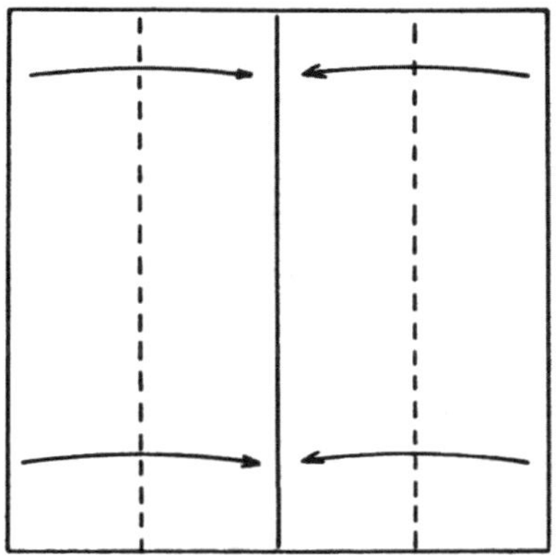

Start with a square folded in half, then cupboard-fold side edges to center.

2

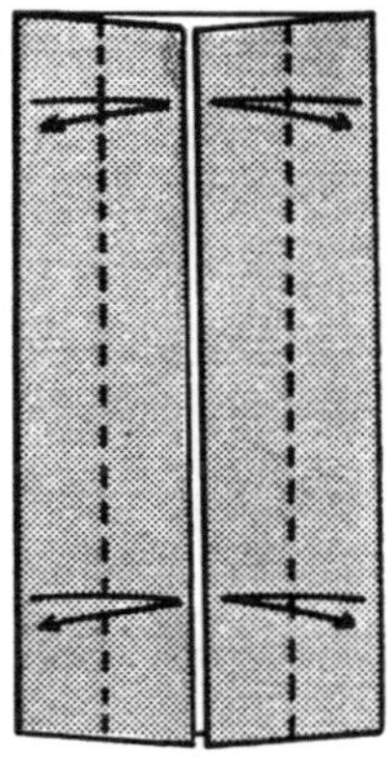

Cupboard-fold again, and unfold.

3

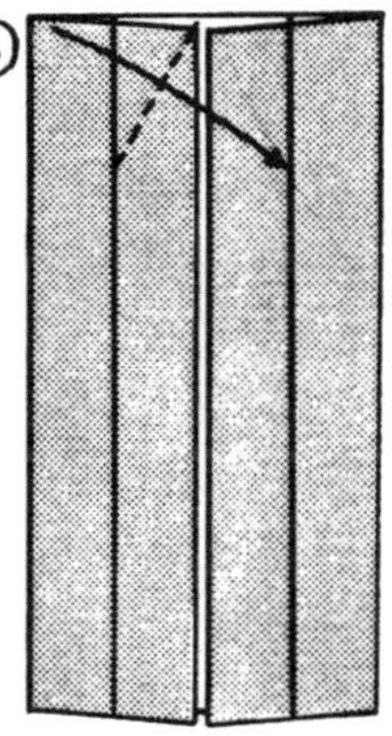

Start this fold at center of top edge and bring left corner over to touch crease. Fold only in area shown.

4

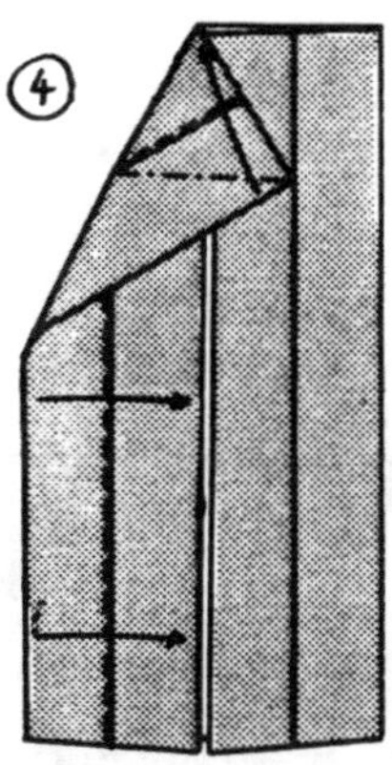

Starting at top of model, valley fold along existing crease, then form mountain fold through corner, as shown. Swing this corner to the top center of model, while folding lower left edge to center line.

5

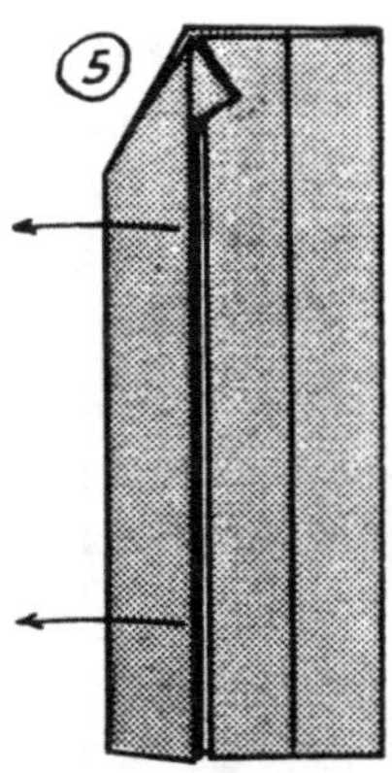

Unfold left flap.

6

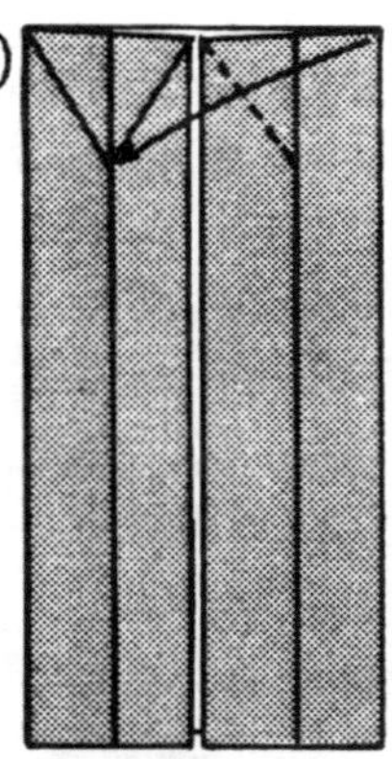

Steps 6, 7, 8 are the same as steps 3,4,5, but on the right side of model.

7

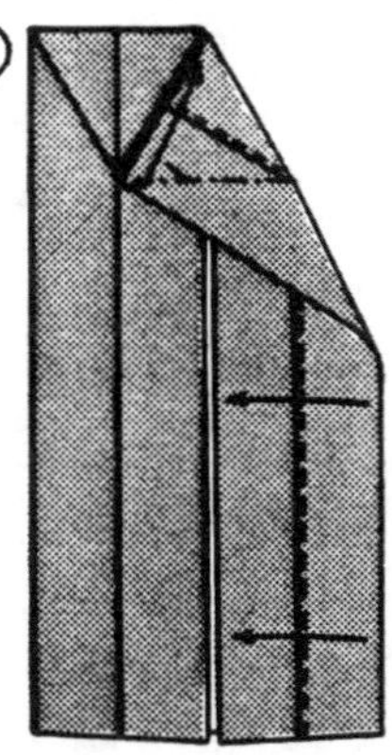

Opposite of step 4.

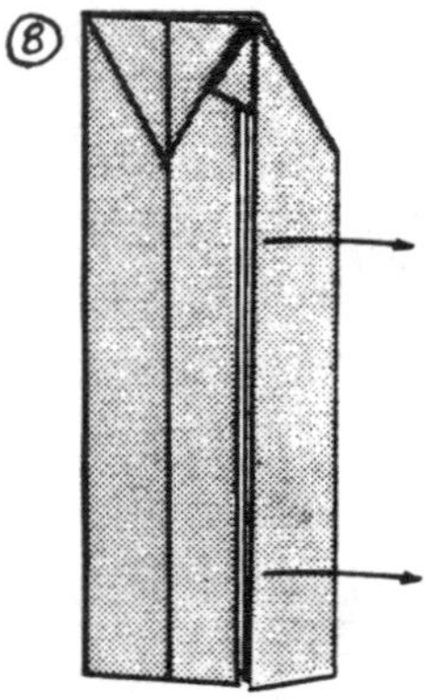

Unfold right flap.

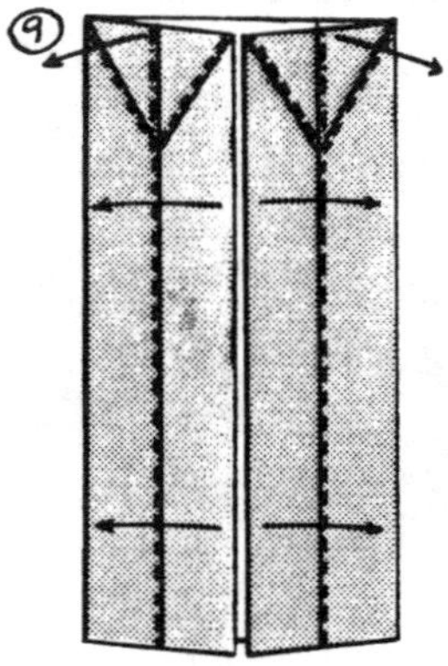

Fold as shown along existing creases, bringing center edges to sides while reversing folds at top to form tabs.

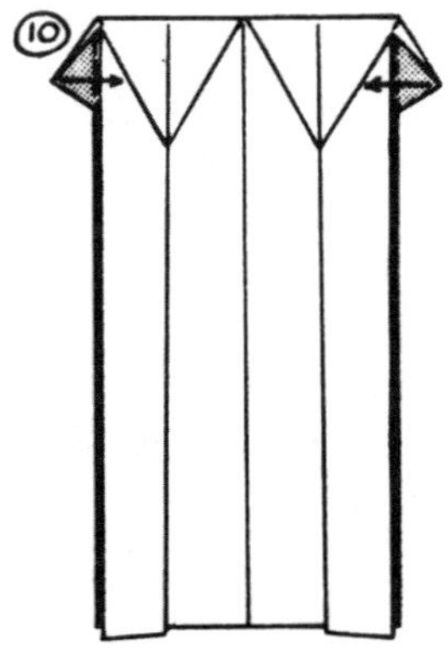

Fold tabs in. Next picture becomes larger.

Detail of Bow:

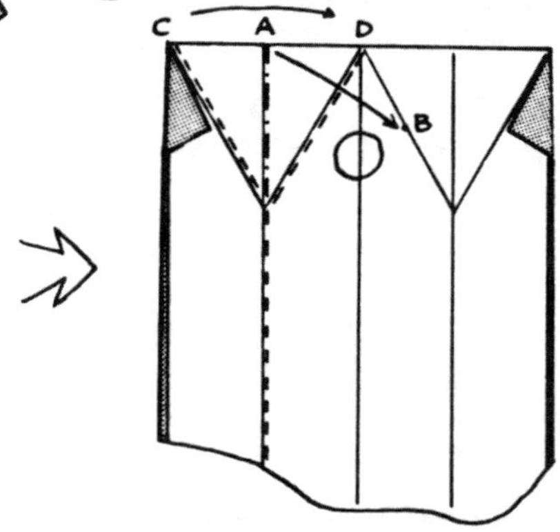

Area marked with circle should be raised toward you; then using existing creases, valley and mountain fold to bring point A to meet point B and point C to meet point D. This step begins to shape the bow and raises the left side of boat to upright position.

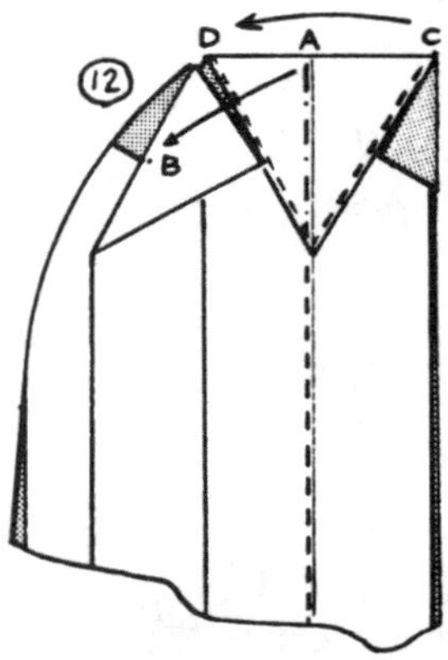

Repeat step 11 to shape right side of bow and raise right side of boat into upright position.

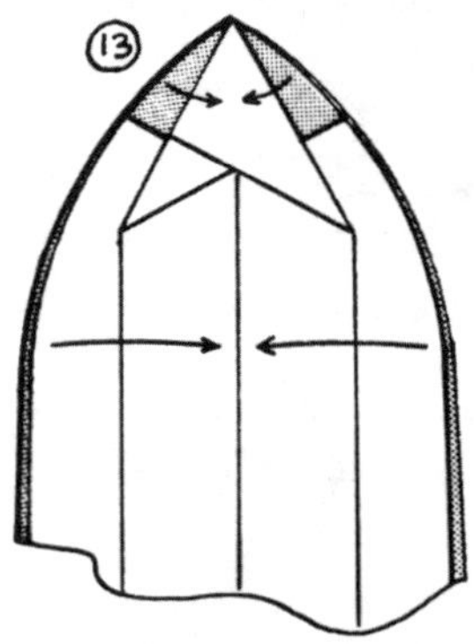

Notice the rim of the boat has two edges all around. While holding the overlapped area tightly, fold down the inner edge to the center line.

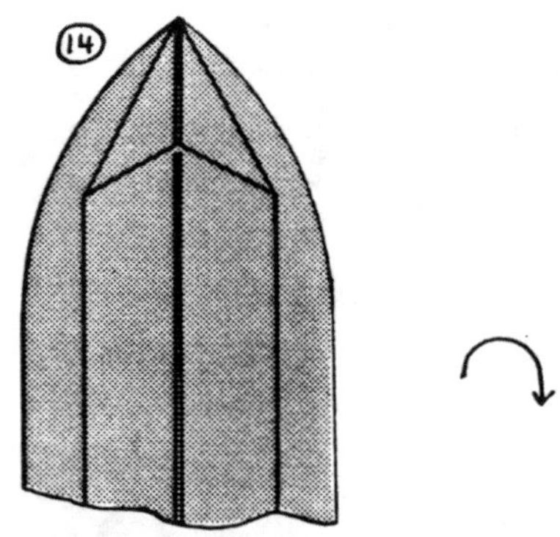

Bow completed. Rotate to work on other end.

Detail of Stern:

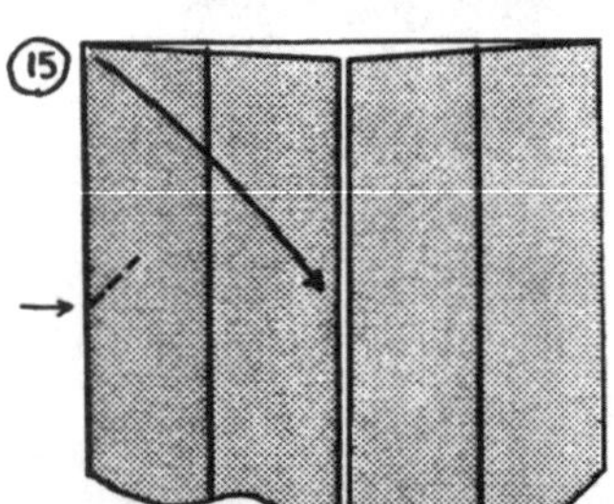

Bring left corner to center line and pinch a landmark on side.

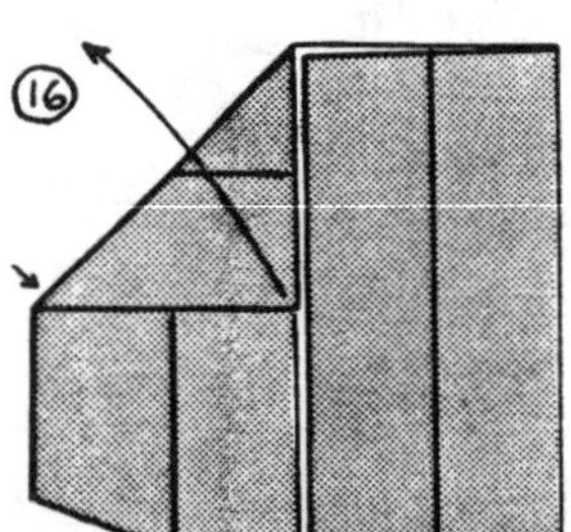

Unfold.

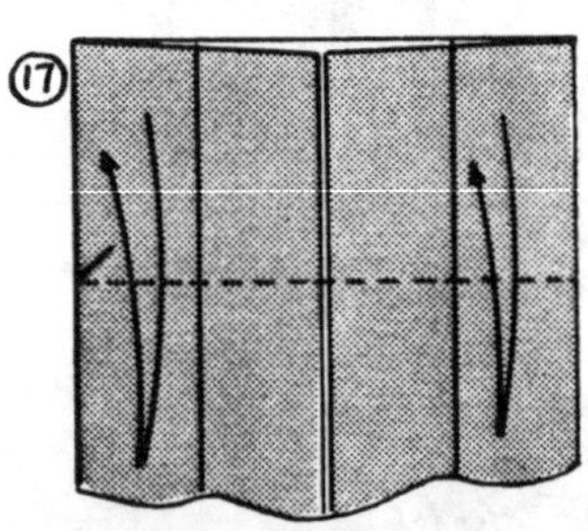

Fold straight across at landmark and unfold.

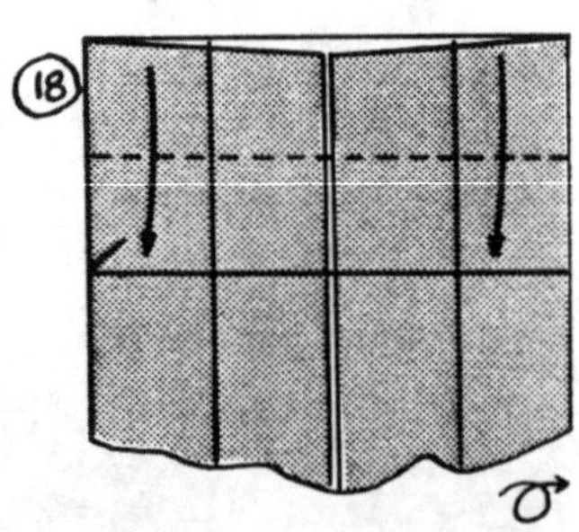

Fold end to the new crease. Turn over.

19

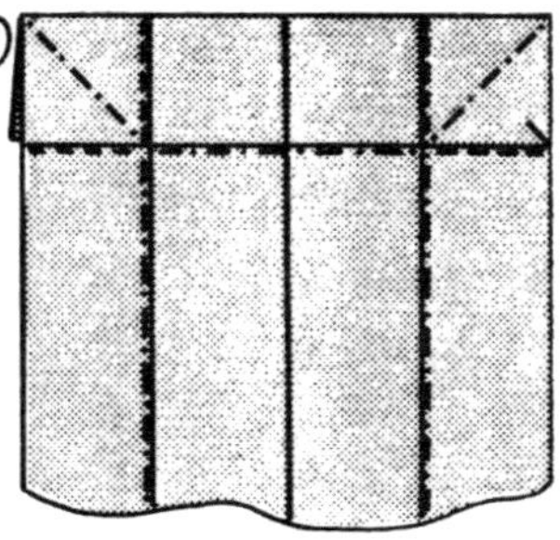

Mountain fold as shown in each corner square.

20

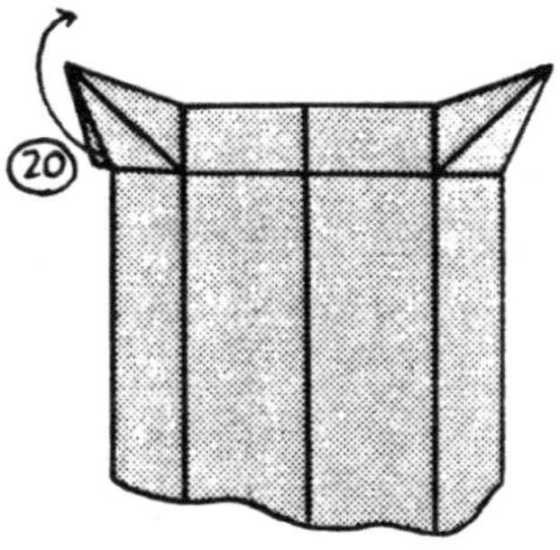

Unfold rear flap upward.

21

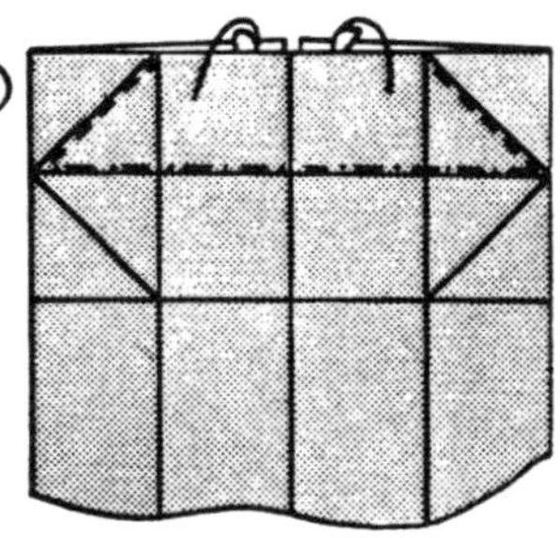

Mountain and valley fold as shown as you push the top center area down between the front surface and rear flaps.

22

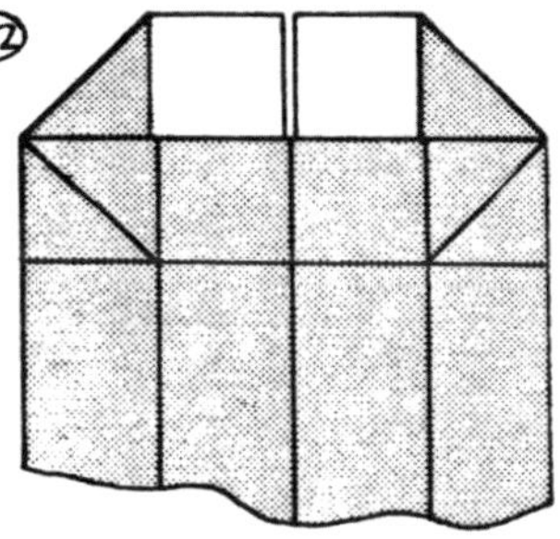

Step 21 completed. Turn over.

23

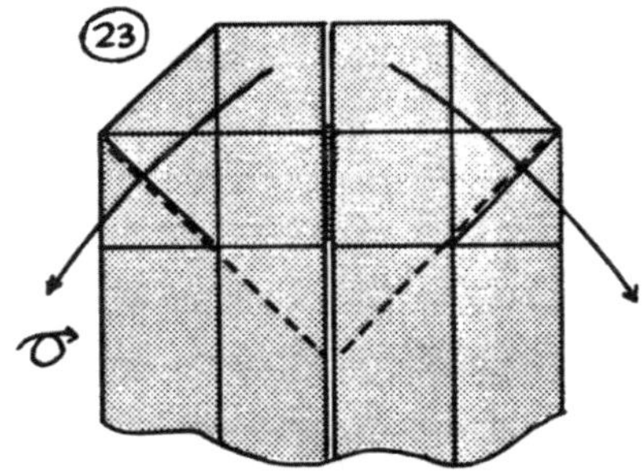

Fold each flap down and to the side.

24

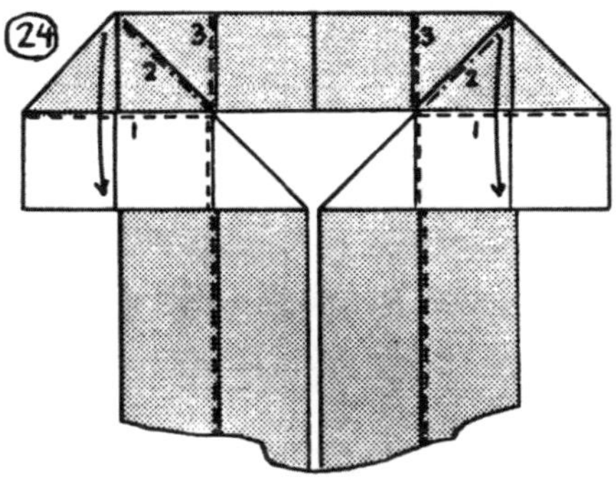

This step shapes the stern. Do one corner at a time making folds in the order shown.

25

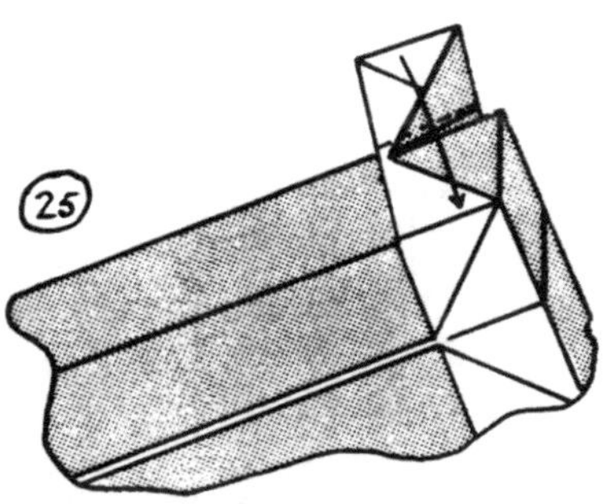

One corner shown
Fold square-shaped flap inside to touch bottom of boat. Repeat this step in other rear corner.

26

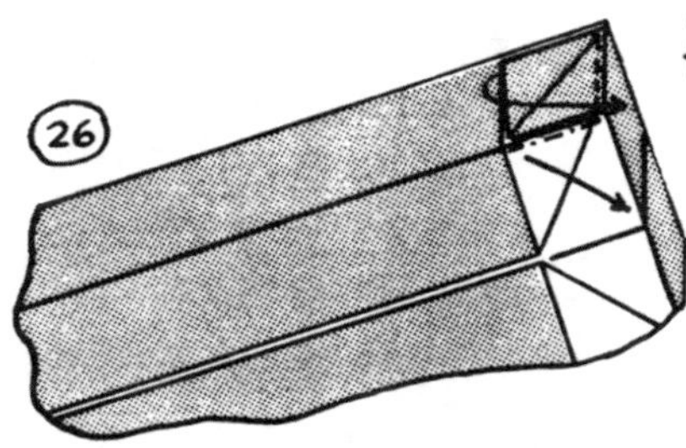

Swing the square-shaped flap like a door from the side to the stern. Some paper from bottom will follow and cover rear corner. Repeat on other side.

27

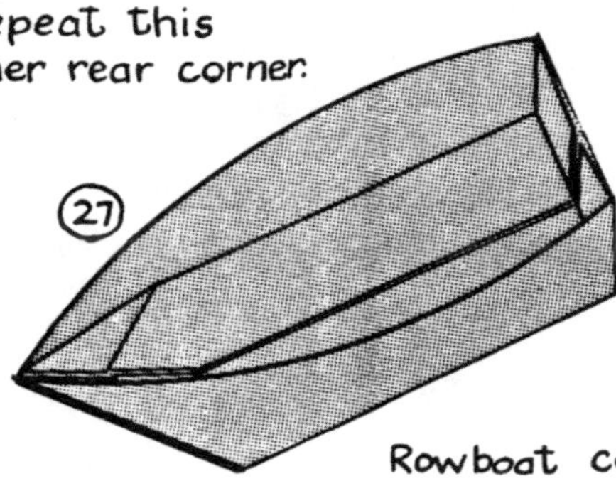

Rowboat completed.

MICHAEL SHALL'S COIN PURSE

Use two squares of equal size. A 7 inch square makes a coin purse approximately 3½" X 1¾" in size.

The purse that inspired this model was found, stuffed with coins, in Michael Shall's apartment after he passed away. His was made of woven reeds, hand-painted with Chinese characters.

Begin white side up.

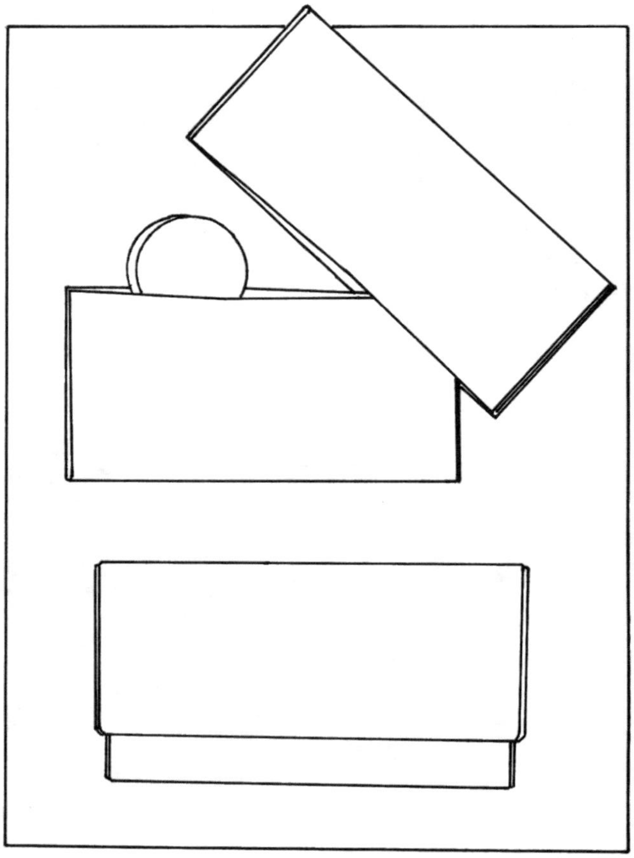

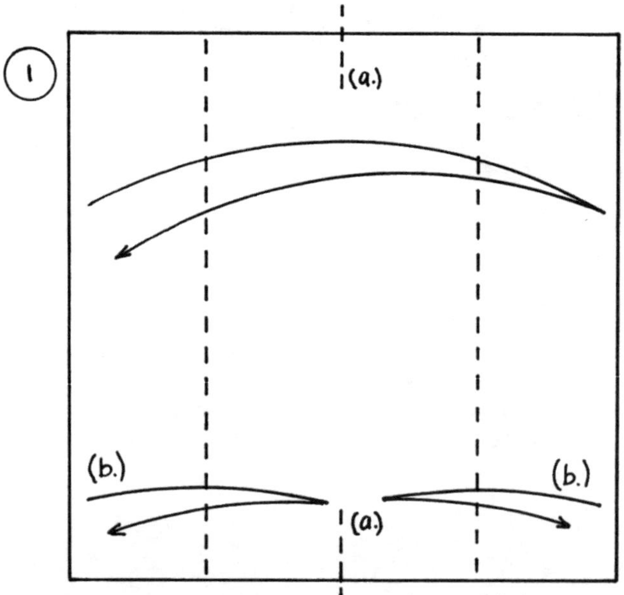

(a.) Landmark the midpoints of top and bottom edges.
(b.) Cupboard fold and unfold.

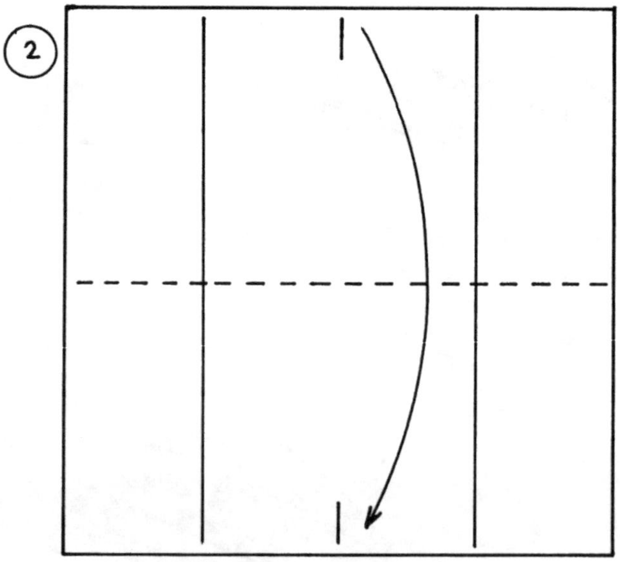

Fold in half downward.

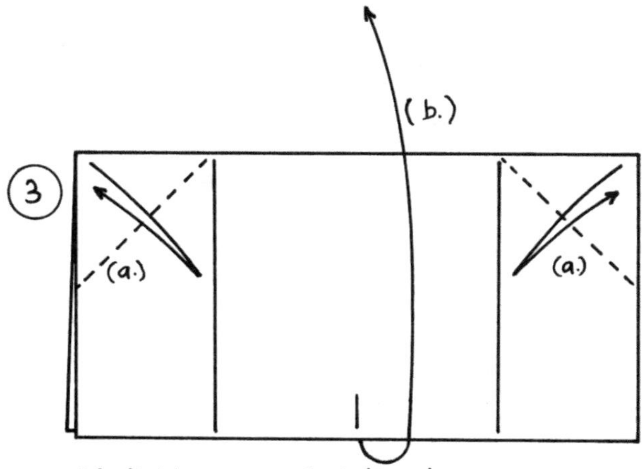

(a.) Fold and unfold the top corners
to the vertical creases.
(b.) Open out by unfolding top folded edge.

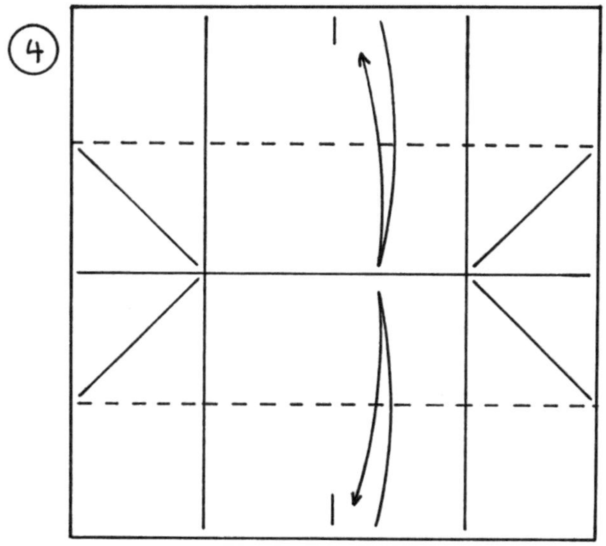

Fold and unfold top and bottom edges to the center crease.

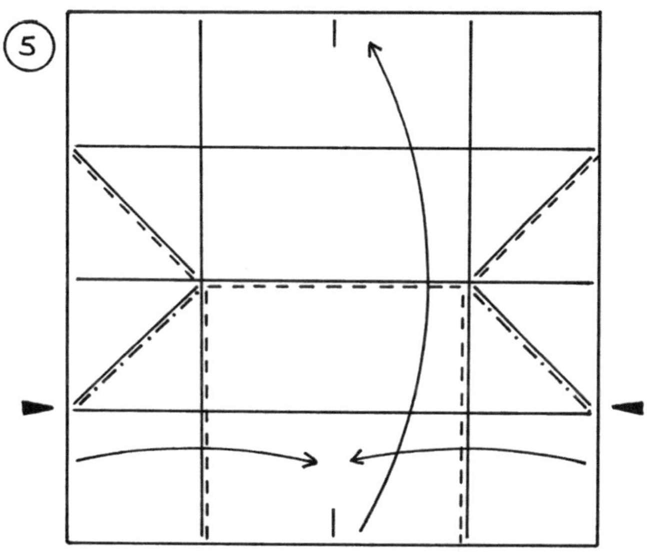

Begin this move by folding vertical valley folds shown. Push paper in (▶) and form mountain and valley folds as you bring bottom edge to top.

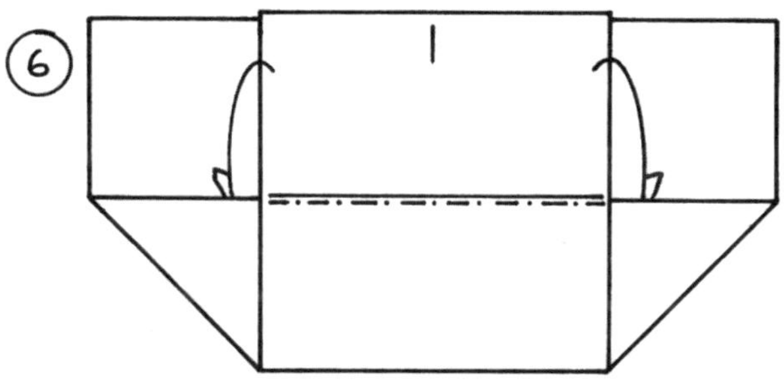

Mountain fold the top half of the front flap behind and inside the pocket.

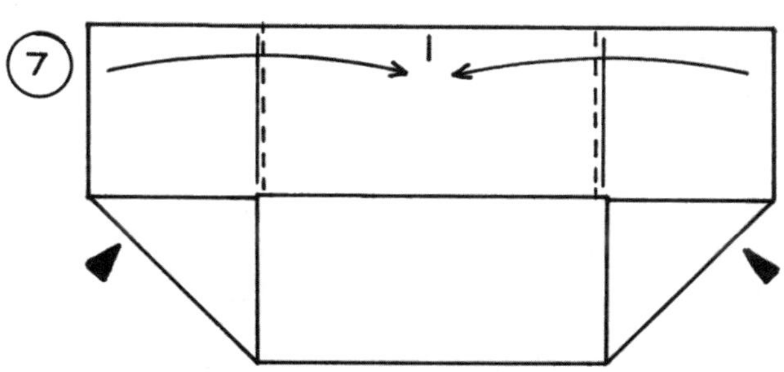

Push in (▶) and reverse fold diagonal edges to inside while folding sides to center.

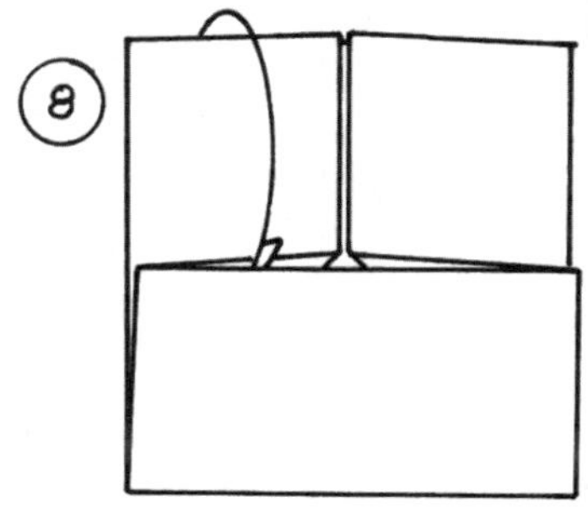

Curl top flap forward and slide all the way down inside.

Second Sheet: COVER

9

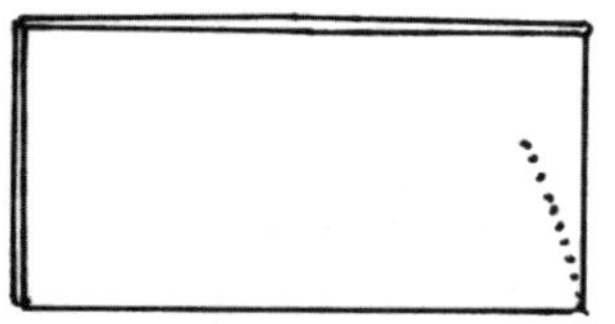

Finished purse;
Cover is next.

10

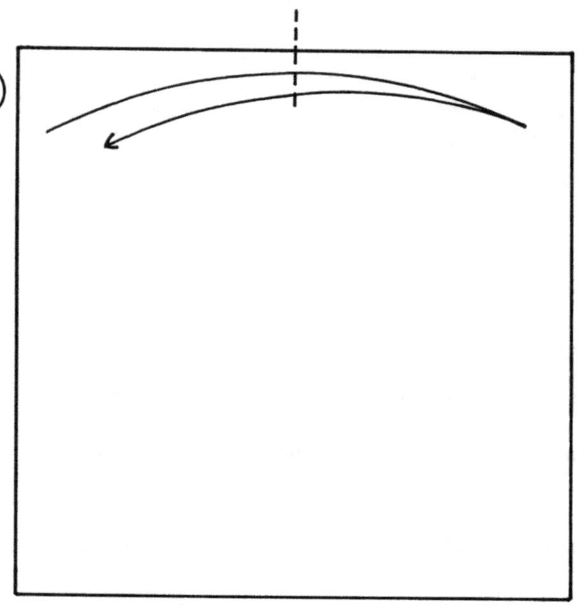

Landmark mid-point of the top edge.

11

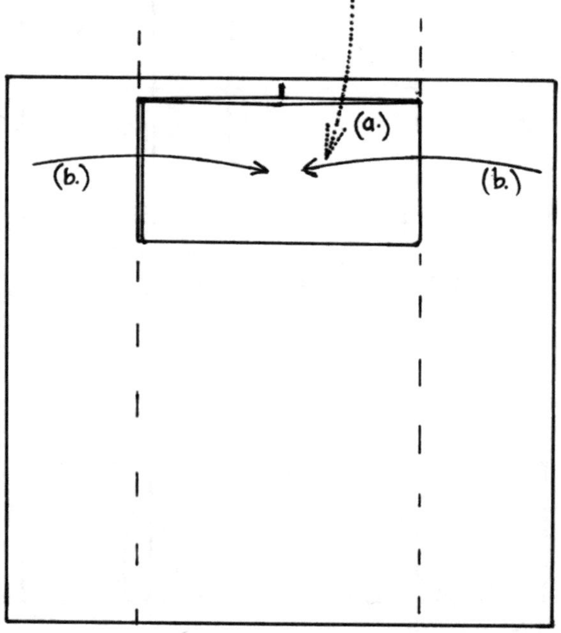

(a.) Center the purse near top edge, but still see landmark.
(b.) Wrap the side edges over the sides of purse.

12

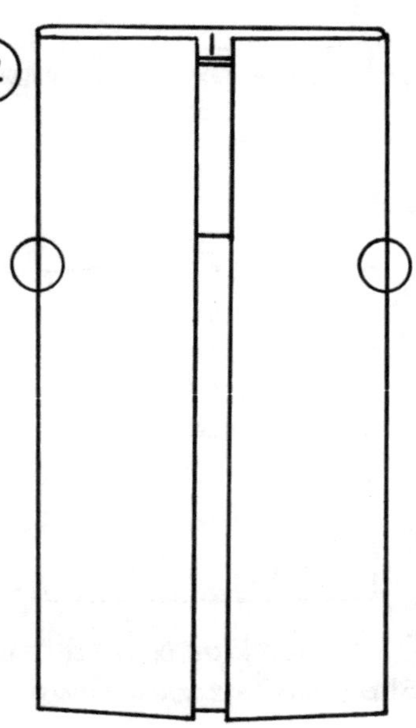

If needed, slide purse left or right until the landmark is centered.

At the circled spots, crease vertical landmarks. This move increases the width of the cover to fit over the purse.

REMOVE PURSE FROM INSIDE
Use the landmarks to fold long vertical creases.

13

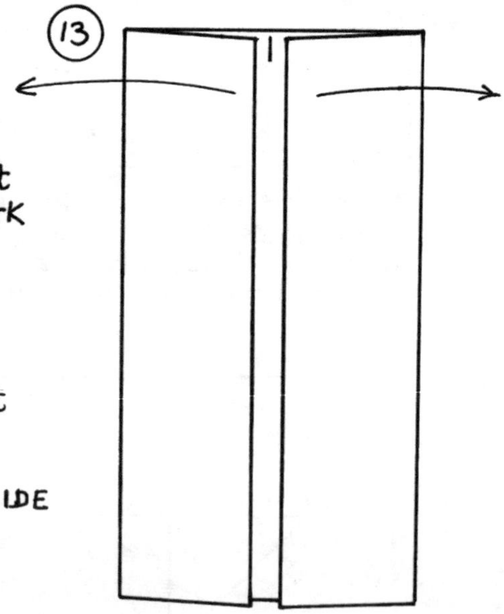

Unfold.... GO TO STEP 2, AND FOLD STEPS 2-9. Insert purse into cover.

SEAMLESS BOX AND LID

Use any size rectangle; differently shaped rectangles make differently shaped boxes. Length limited to less than twice the width.

To make the BOX AND LID two rectangles 6½" x 10" were used. (cut from photos of the "National Geographic"). One sheet for the box is cut to 6⅛" x 9". (BOX AND LID can be made from same-sized sheets - see end of instructions.)

To make box and lid from two sizes, begin box with the smaller sheet, white side up.

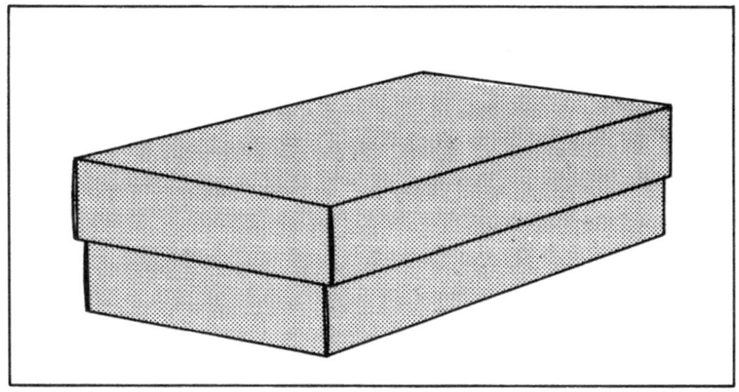

1

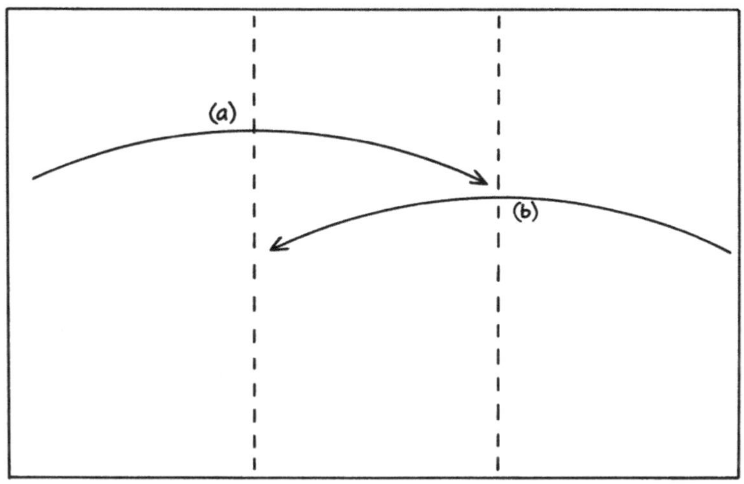

Fold in thirds.

2

Use top layer only and landmark center of top and bottom edges.

3

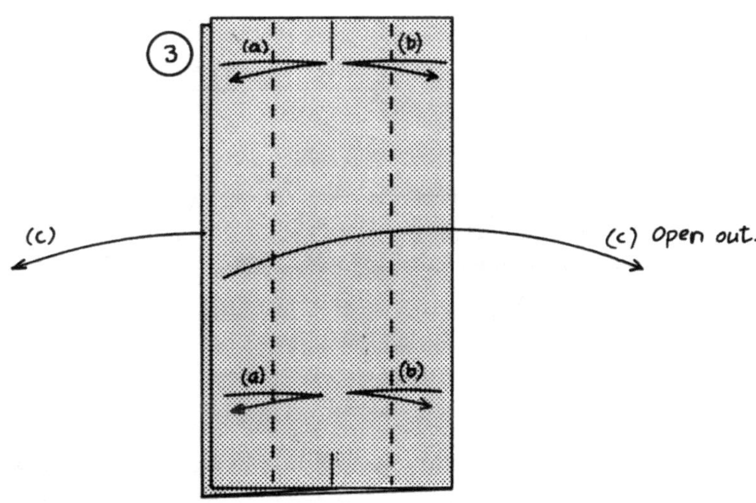

Cupboard fold, and unfold all layers to the landmarks, then open out.

4

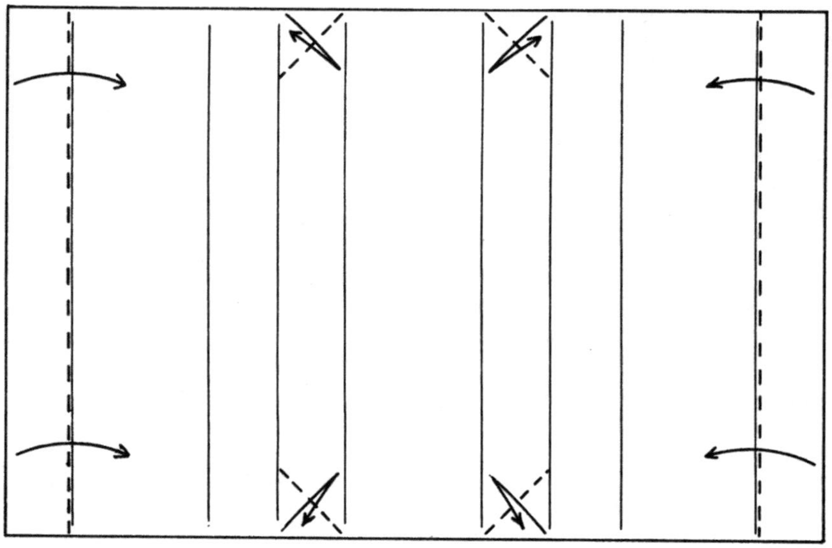

5

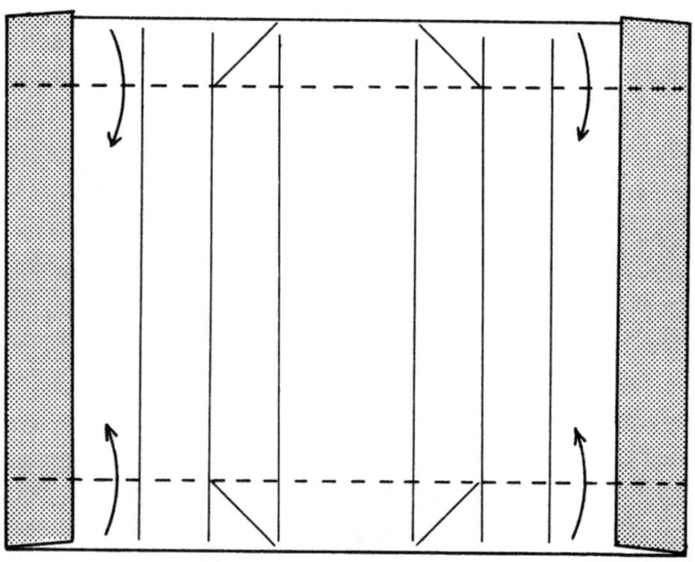

6

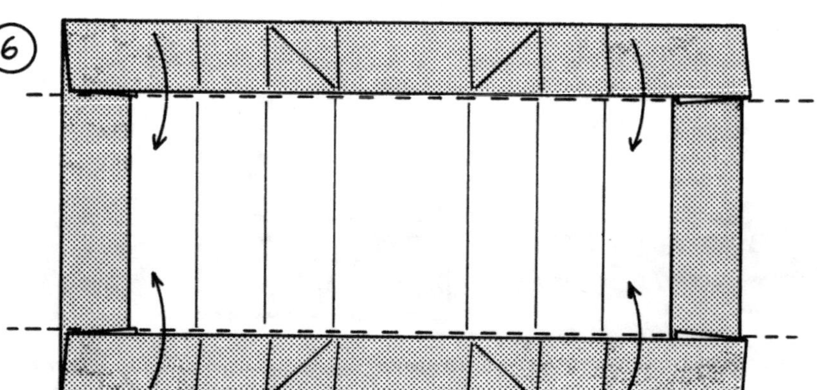

Picture gets larger.

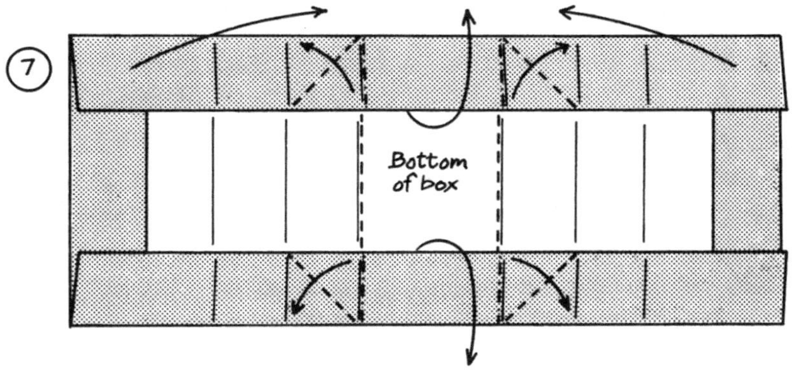

Shape and 3-D the box. Fold all the creases at the same time. Start with the valley folds along side of bottom of box, as you raise the end flaps 90°. The four diagonal valley folds in the corners will form along hidden creases inside.

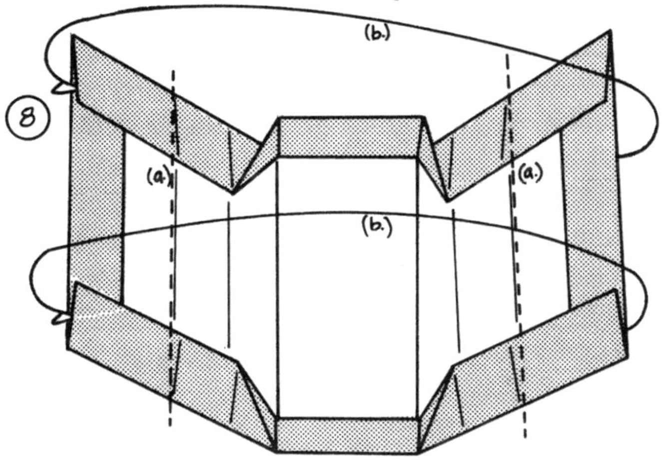

(a.) Valley fold each flap along existing creases, at a 90° angle.
(b.) Insert one end into slots of other end, all the way to crease "a."

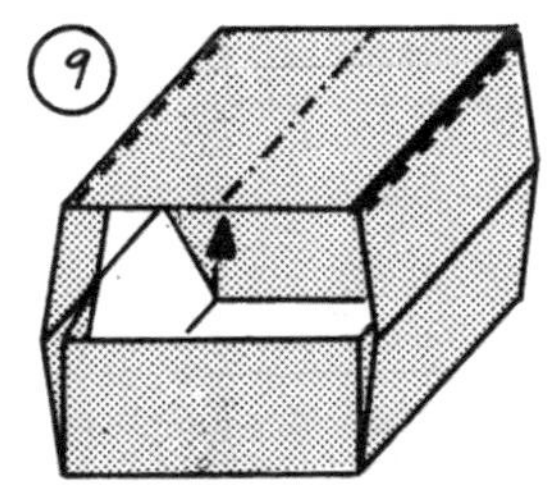

END VIEW: Push up to form a soft, rounded mountain fold; Do not crease sharply.

Pinch top softly as you push paper down inside the box.

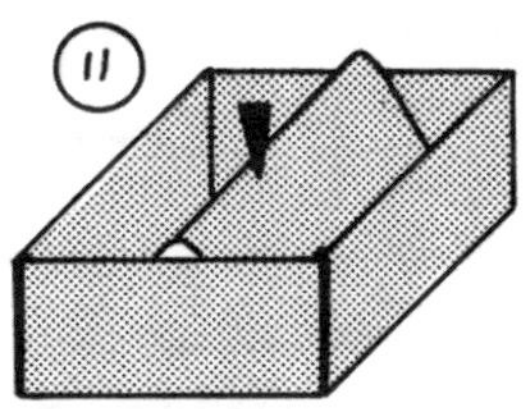

Push down and flatten the bottom.

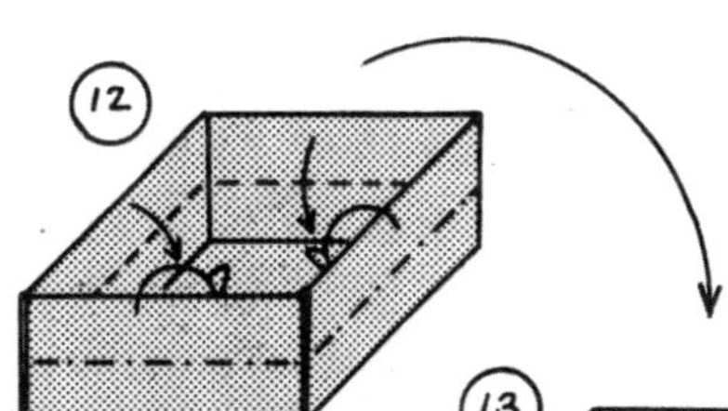

BOX COMPLETED. Repeat with lid sheet. Fold edges all around to inside.

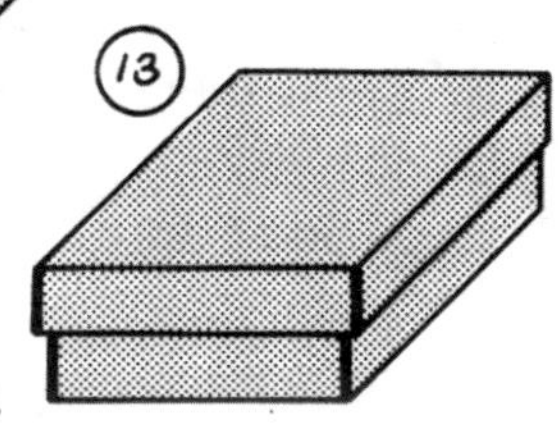

INSTRUCTIONS FOR SAME-SIZE SHEETS (6½" X 10")

Fold model steps 1 and 2. Then in step 3, cupboard fold long edges only part way toward landmarks on short edges. Allow about 1/16" space between edges and landmarks. All other steps are the same. You may need to experiment to obtain proper fit of the lid.

FRIENDS' LOGO

Use a 4 x 1 proportioned rectangle of foil paper. Try a 16" x 4" piece.

Begin white side up.

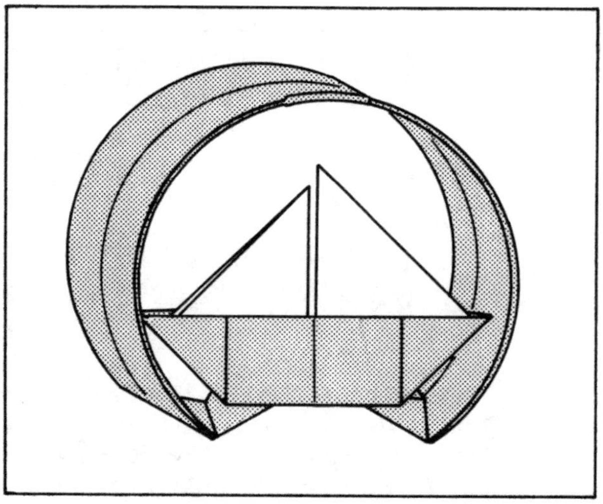

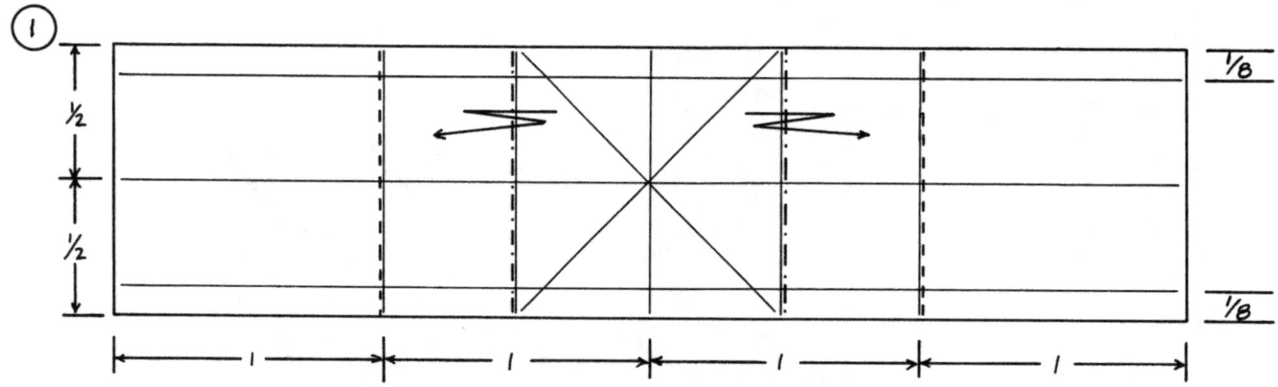

PRECREASE FIRST, then pleat-fold along existing creases.

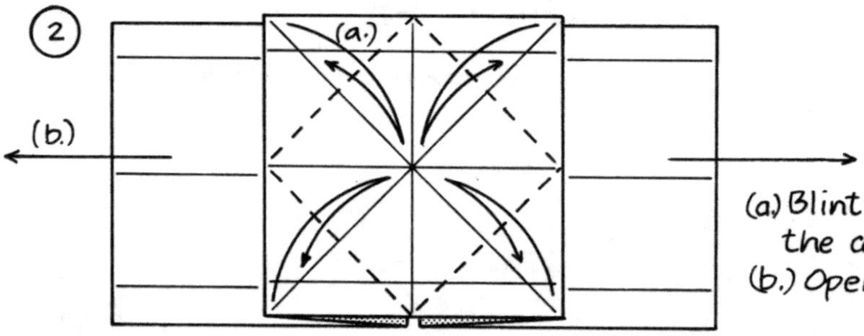

(a.) Blintz fold, and unfold the center square.
(b.) Open out flat.

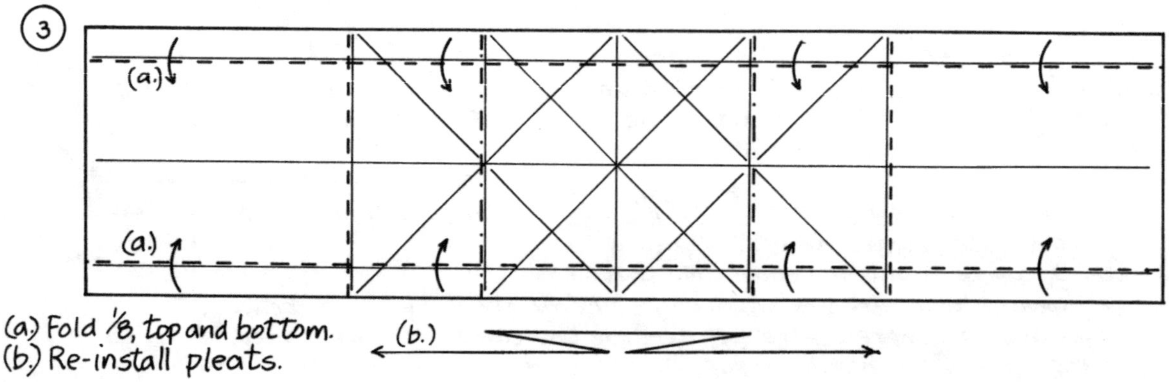

(a.) Fold 1/8, top and bottom.
(b.) Re-install pleats.

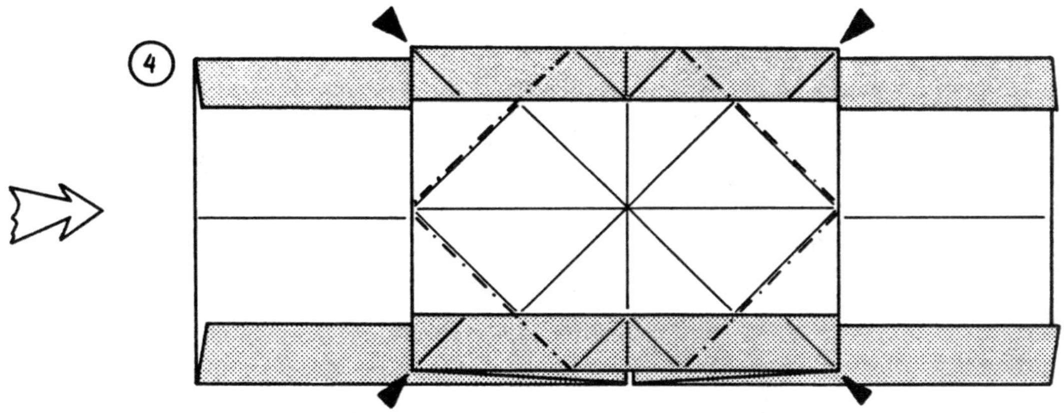

PICTURE GETS LARGER. Reverse fold the four corners along existing creases.

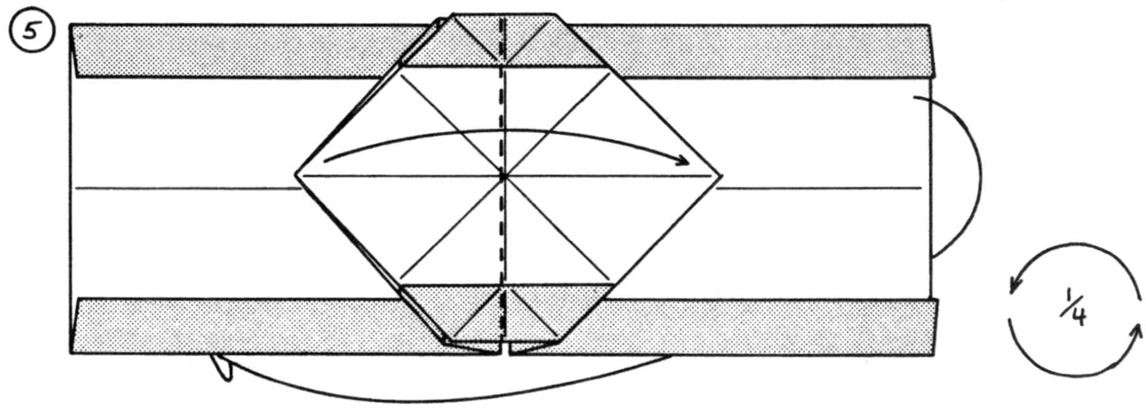

Minor Miracle- Left top flap to right and right rear flap behind and to the left.
Then, rotate ¼ turn.

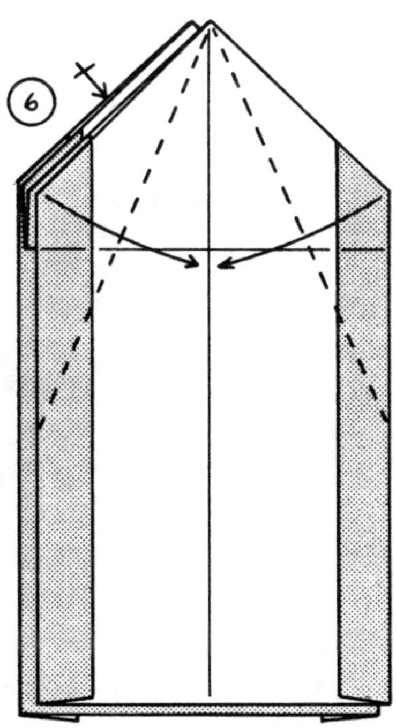

Fold corners to center. Repeat behind.

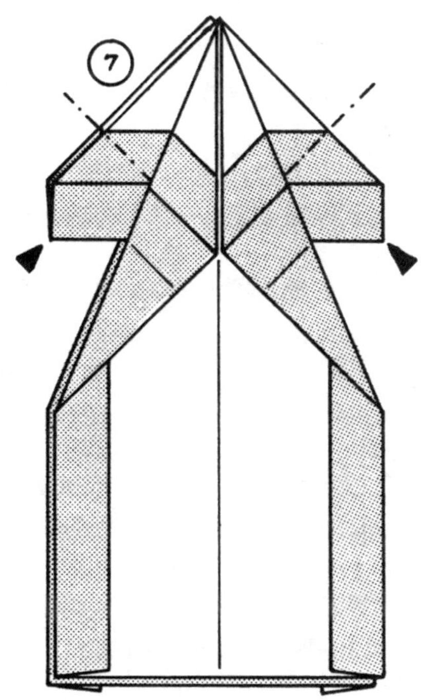

Reverse the corners inside, using existing creases.

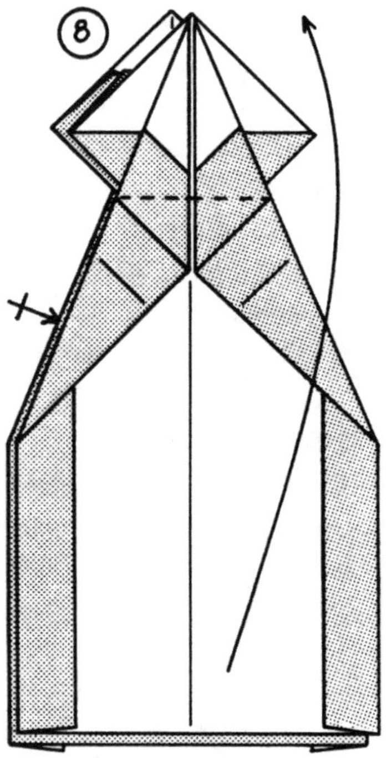

Valley fold long front and rear flaps upward.

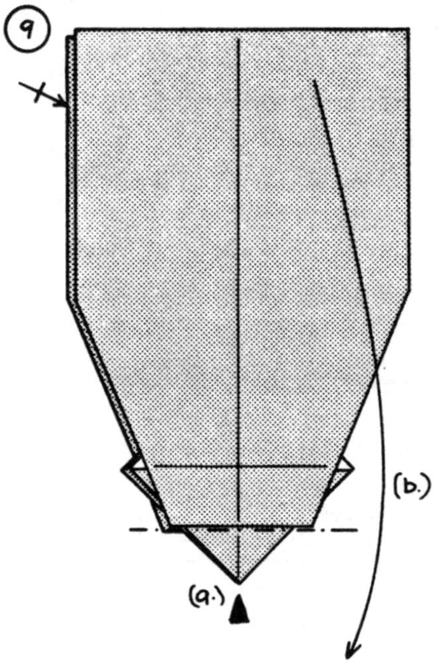

(a.) Sink triangular area.
(b.) Fold long front and rear flaps down.

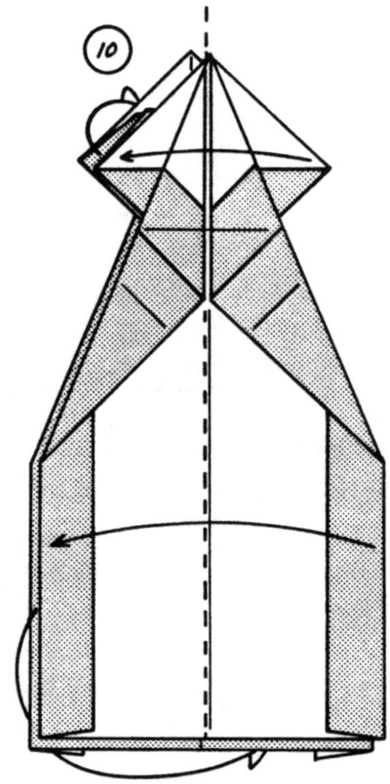

Minor Miracle: Front right flaps to left; rear left flaps behind and to the right.

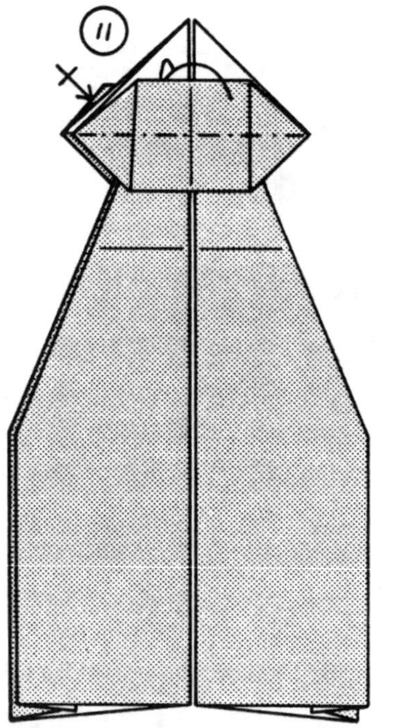

Mountain fold small flap behind into pocket. Repeat behind.

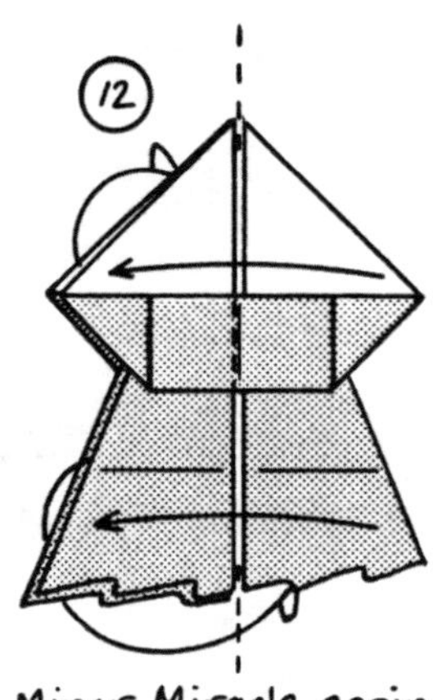

Minor Miracle again.

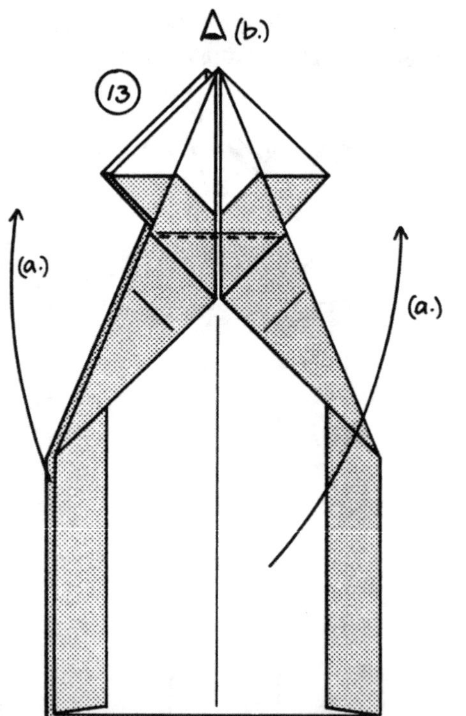

(a.) Fold long front and rear flaps up at 90° angle, along existing creases; (b.) Look down from here - top view next.

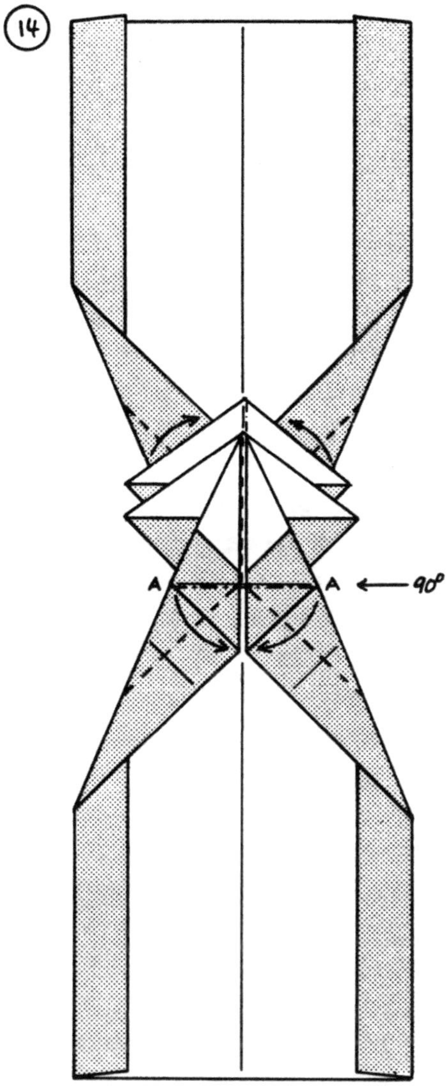

Top view, with sailboat section at center tilted back to show this step. Fold points "A" to center line. Repeat other end.

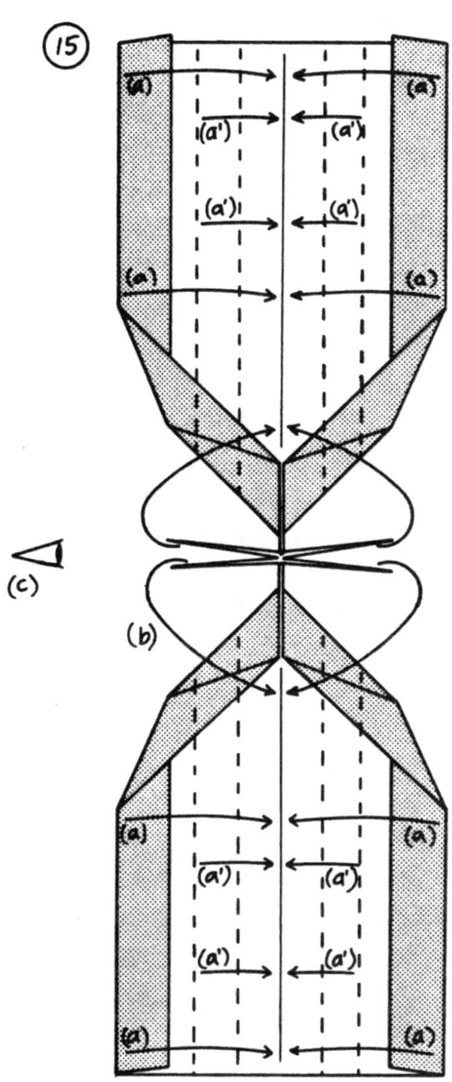

Top View
(a.) Cupboard fold outside edges to center.
(a'.) Cupboard fold, again to center.
(b.) Swing pairs of sail flaps to center.
(c.) Look from side.

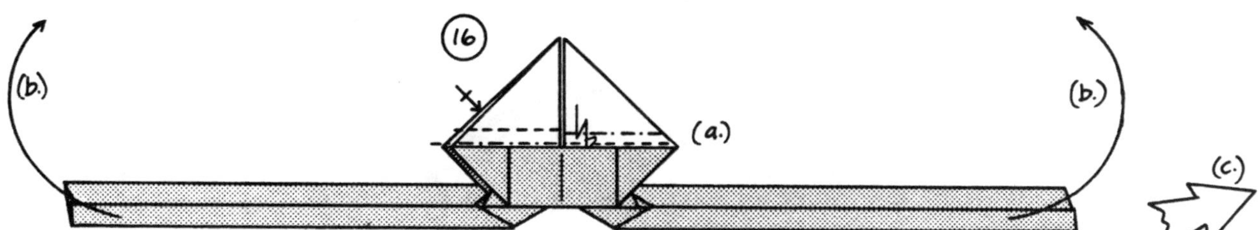

(a.) Pleat each sail, BUT, make the finished sails of uneven height by using a wider pleat on the left than on the right. Also, pleat one sail toward front surface and the other toward the rear surface. Each pleated flap should be tucked underneath top edge of boat. This step also loosely locks the bow and stern closed.

(b.) Curl each long strip with numerous small bends. (c.) Picture gets larger.

(17)

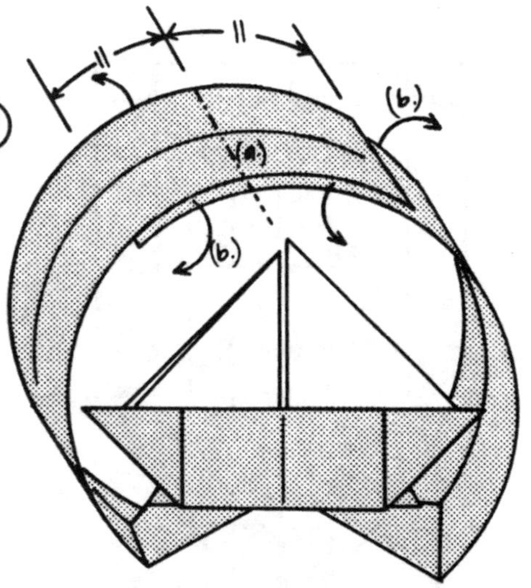

Overlap ends. Amount of overlap depends on size of ring desired. (a.) Determine mid-point between ends, and precrease and uncrease across both ends. (b.) Open out first layers from underside of each end.

(18) TOP VIEW OF EACH END:

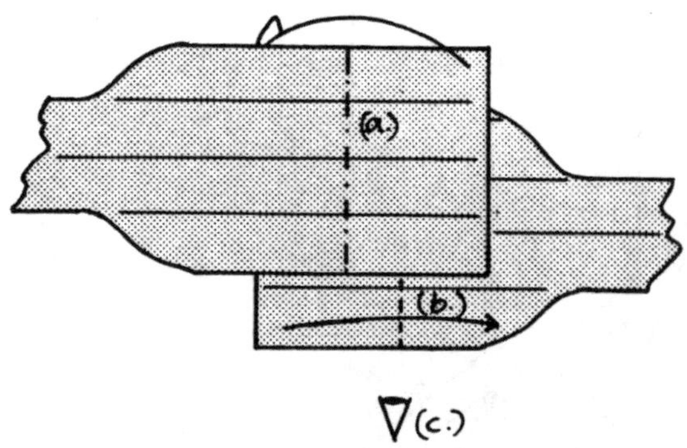

(a.) Mountain fold end underneath along precrease made in step 17.
(b) Valley fold this end
OVERLAP AND LINK THE END FLAPS, and...
(c) Look from front view.

(19)

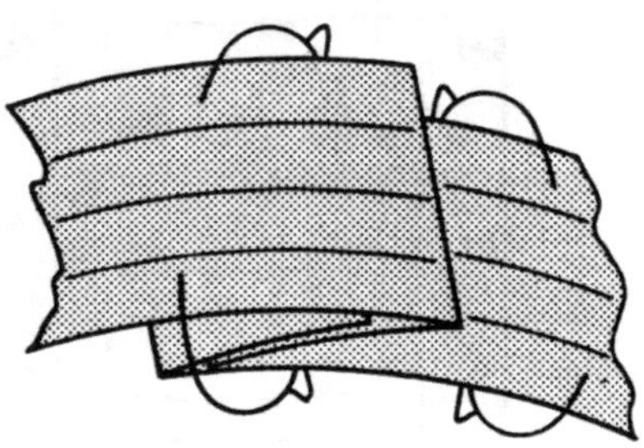

Link overlapped flaps snugly, allign the side edges and parallel creases, and fold the outer edges underneath to the center crease of the ring.
SHAPE THE RING, especially rounding the area where the overlapped ends are locked.

(20)

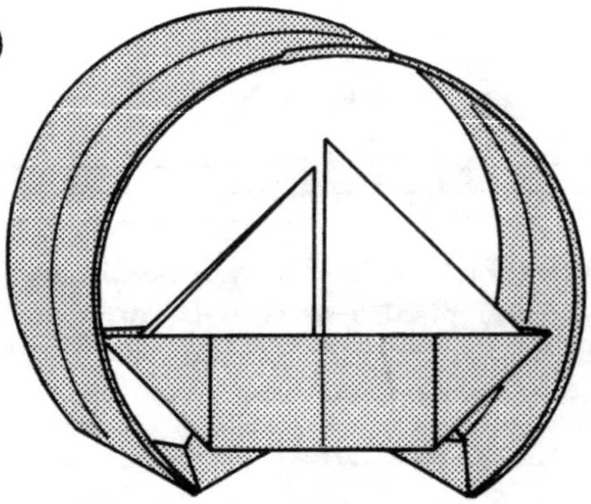

CRANE STICKPIN

Use a foil paper square, edge length from 4½" to 6."

Begin white side up, and precrease the diagonal.

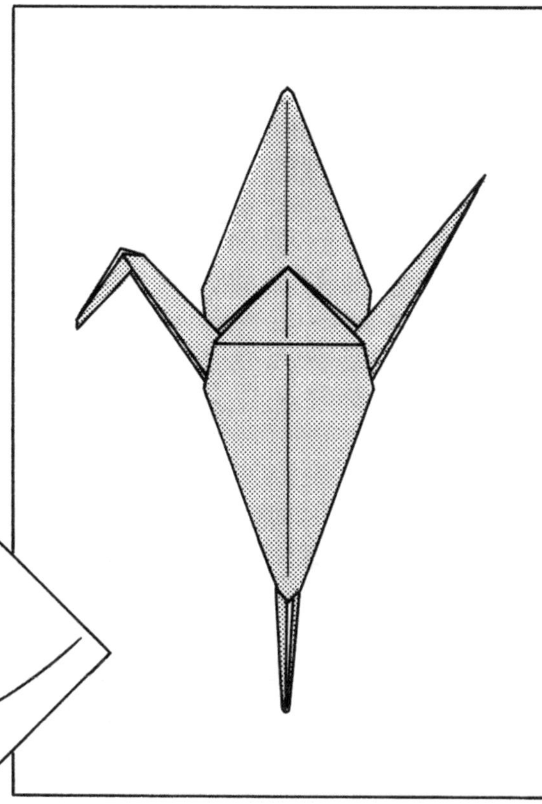

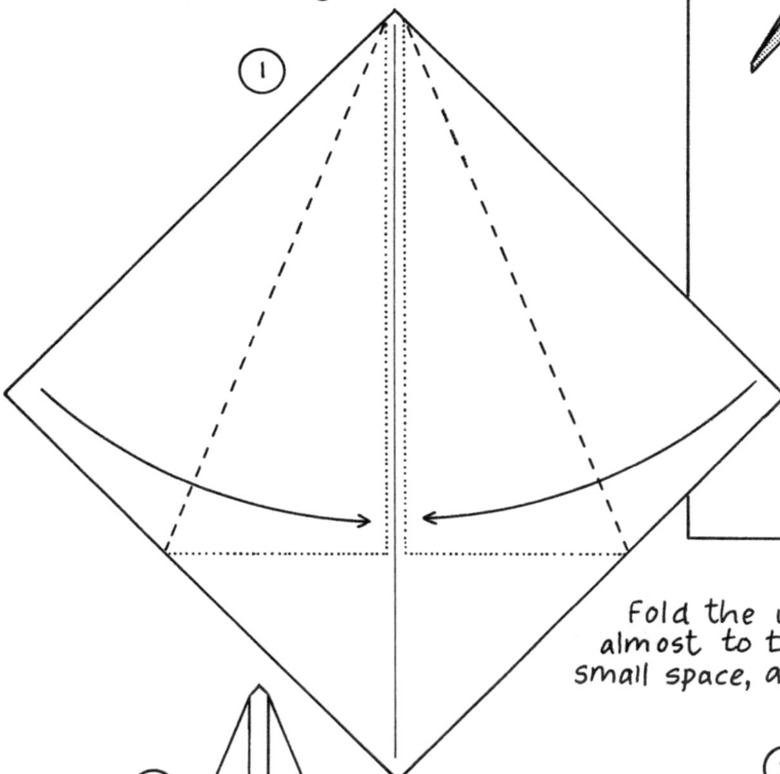

Fold the upper left and right edges almost to the center line, leaving a small space, as shown by dotted lines.

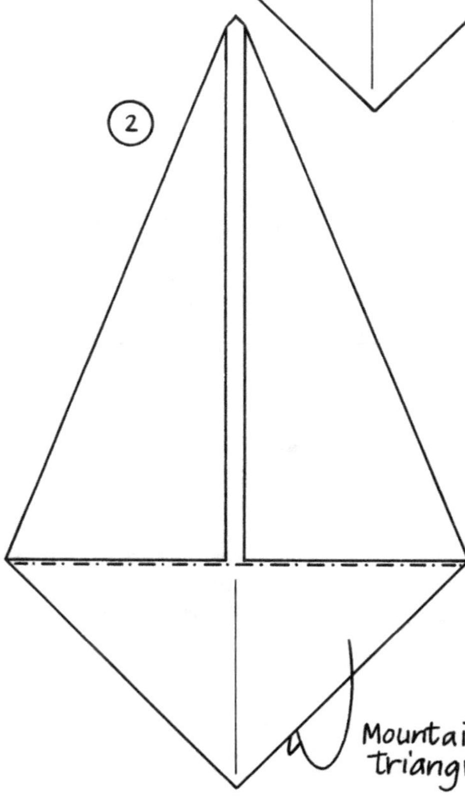

Mountain fold triangular flap behind.

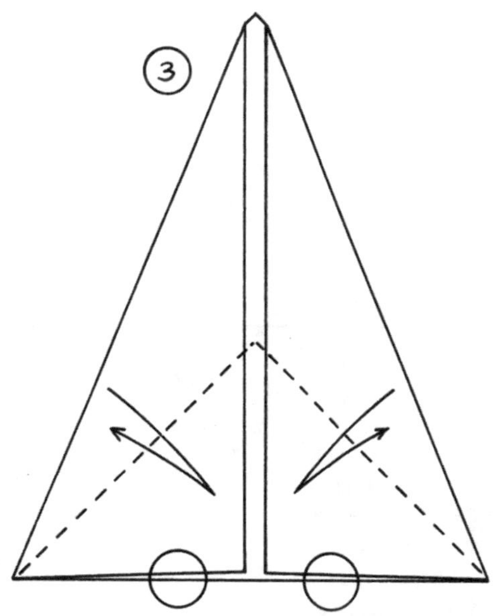

Hold layers at circled locations to prevent layers from slipping. Then, valley fold and unfold — matching the edges of the triangular flap behind.

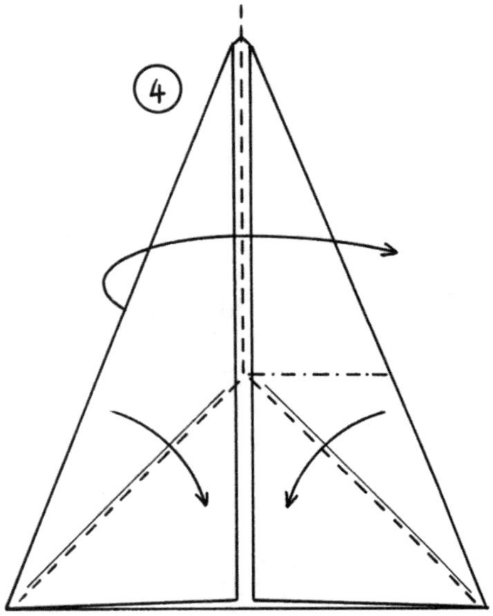

Rabbit ear.

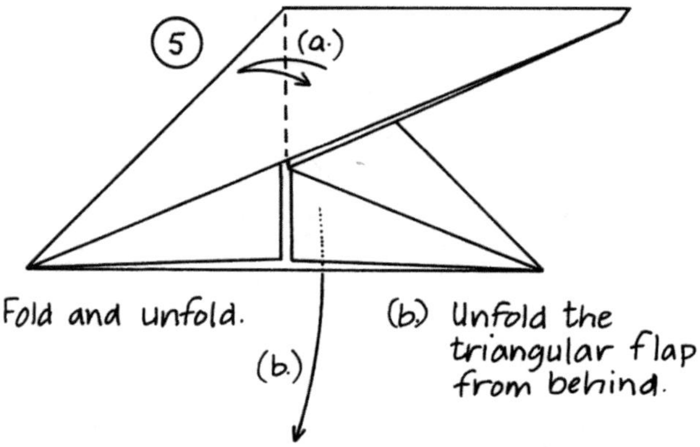

(a.) Fold and unfold.

(b.) Unfold the triangular flap from behind.

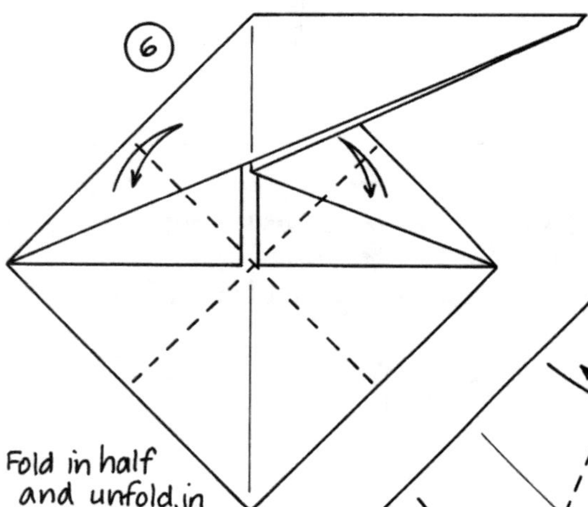

Fold in half and unfold, in both directions.

Picture gets larger.

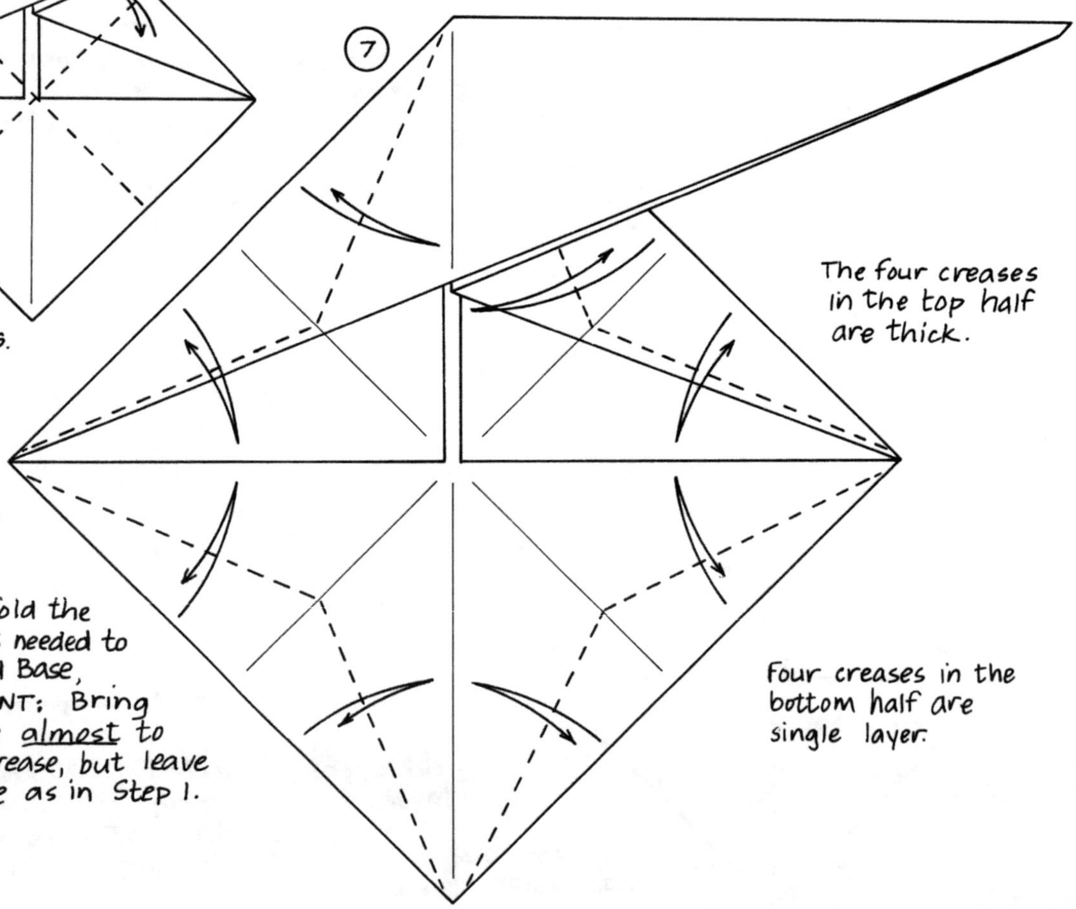

The four creases in the top half are thick.

Fold and unfold the eight creases needed to make a Bird Base, BUT IMPORTANT: Bring each edge almost to the center crease, but leave as much space as in Step 1.

Four creases in the bottom half are single layer.

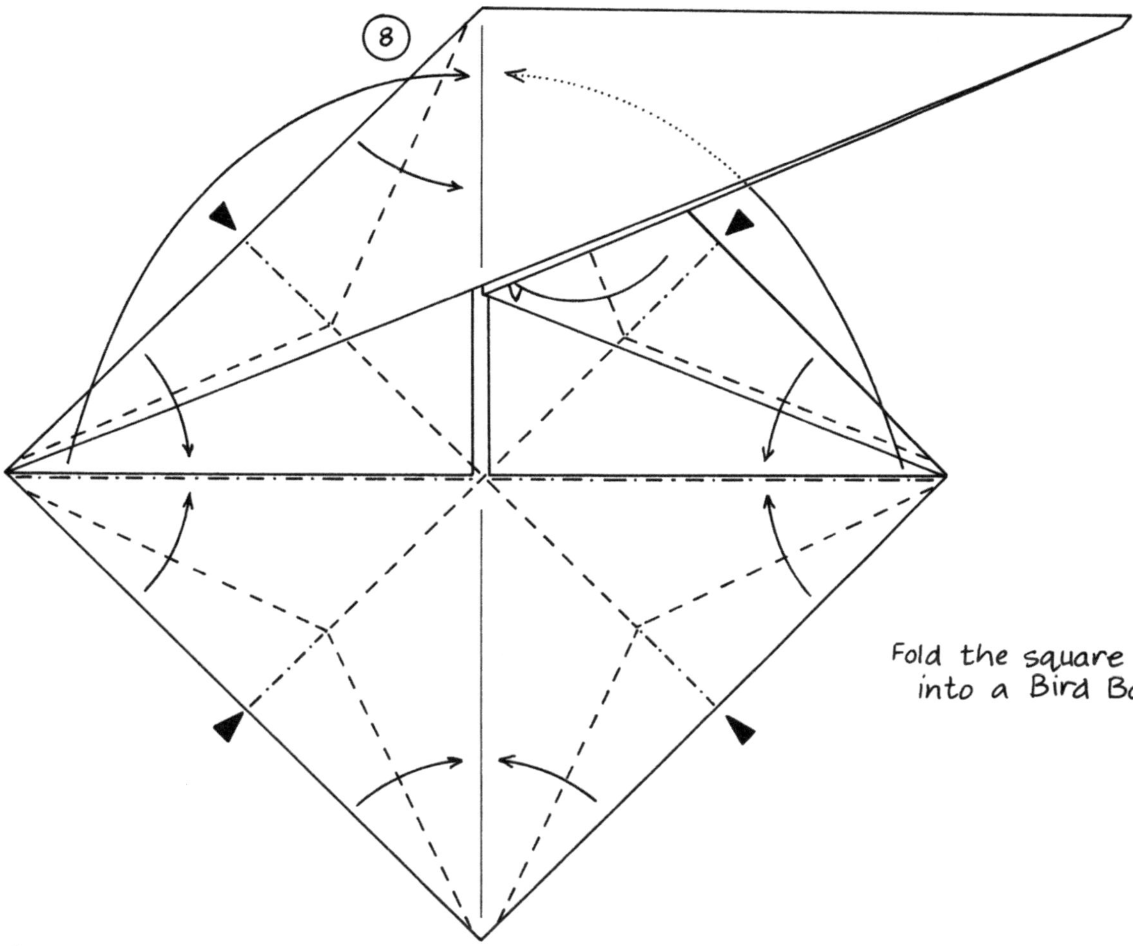

Fold the square area into a Bird Base.

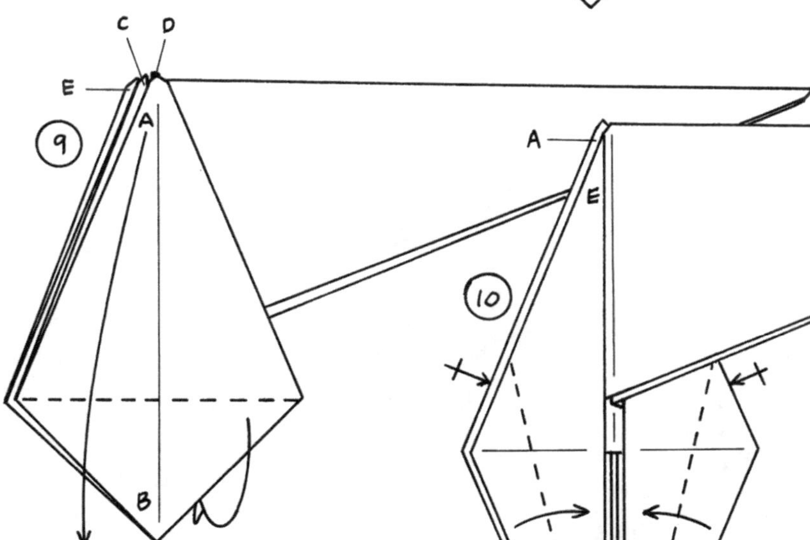

Fold flap A down, then B up behind, then C and D down, and lastly, A up behind.

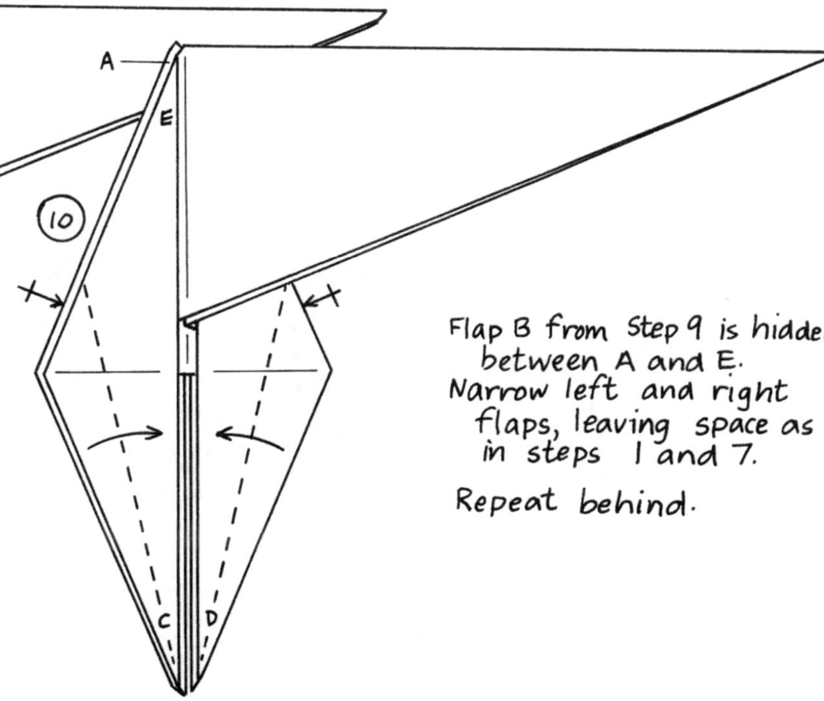

Flap B from Step 9 is hidden between A and E.
Narrow left and right flaps, leaving space as in steps 1 and 7.

Repeat behind.

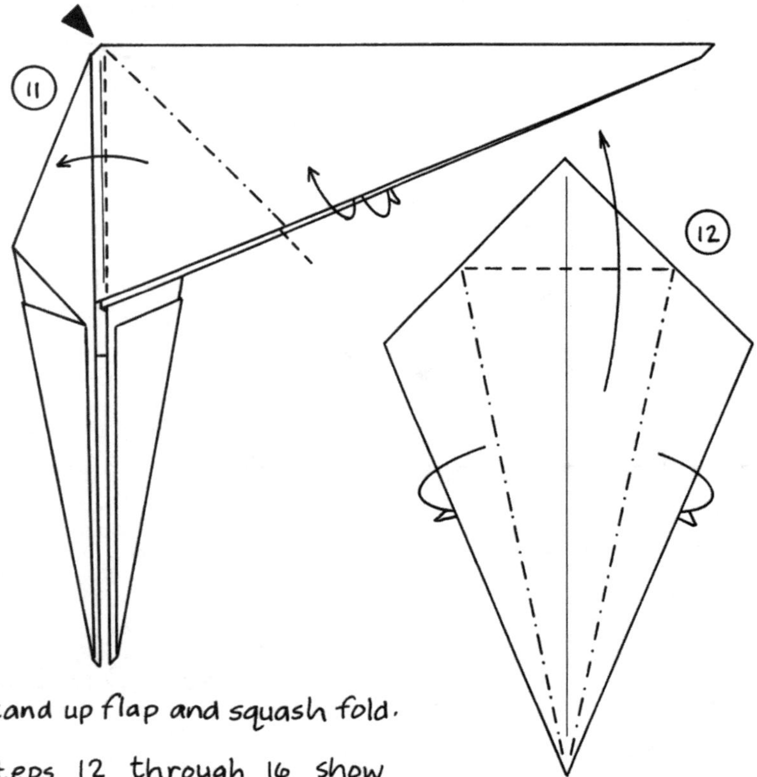

Stand up flap and squash fold.

Steps 12 through 16 show only this flap to completion.

Raise flap from bottom – curl along the valley crease line but do not fold.
Petal fold the long edges to the inside, underneath.

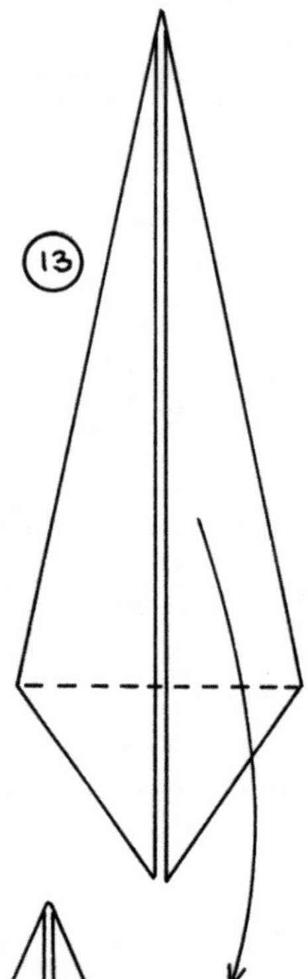

Underside finished.

Fold flap down.

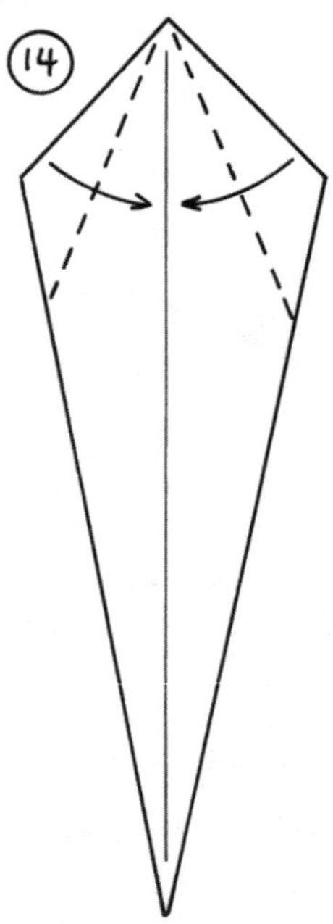

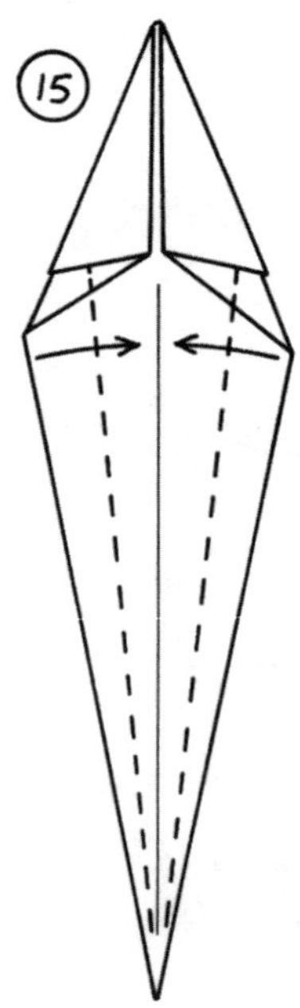

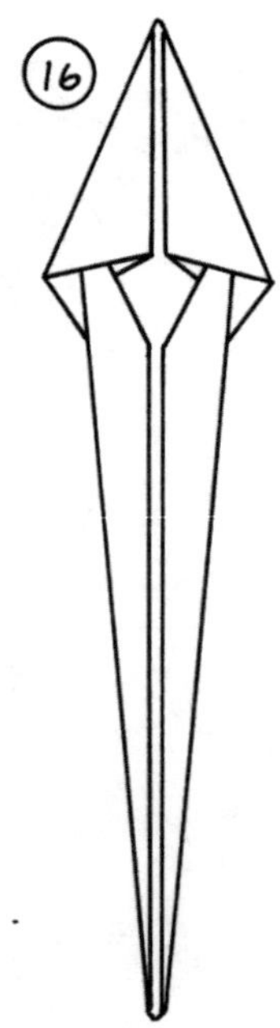

Turn model over

Stick pin flap finished.

Basket

Candlestick

Claw Hammer

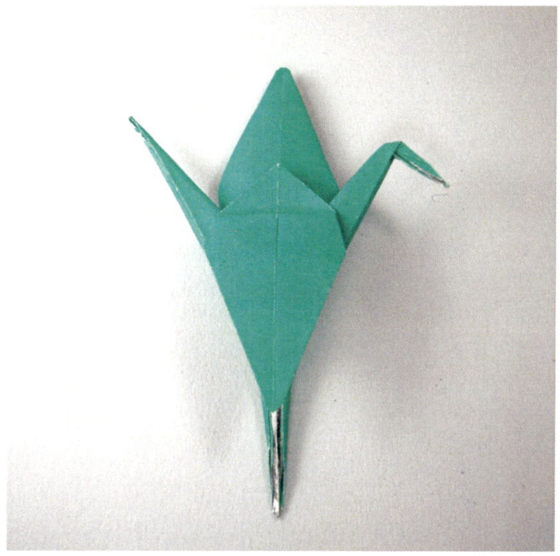
Crane Stickpin

Cross-Shaped Dish

Daffodil

Dodecadedron

Expanding Ball

Flying Crane on a Stand

Friends' Logo

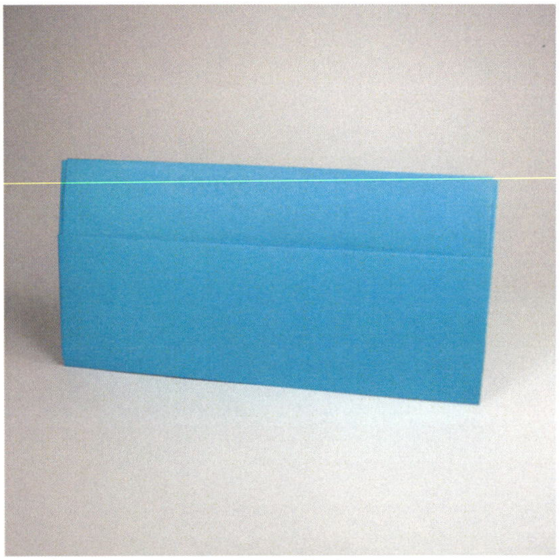

Letterfold

Lily

Mat

Michael's Coin Purse

Mouse

Paper Chain

Puzzle Cube

Rabbit

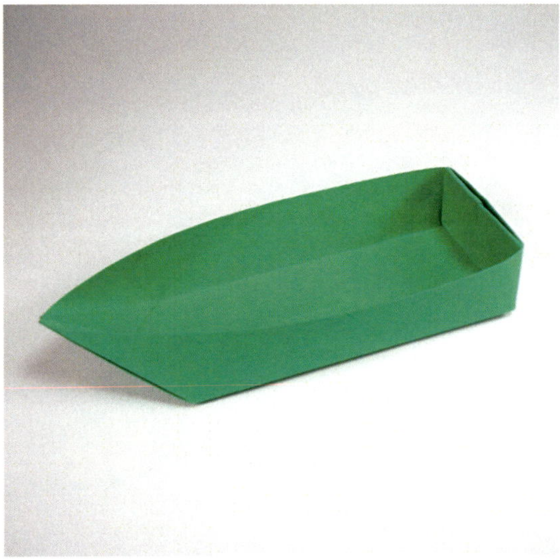

Rowboat

Seamless Box

Soccer Ball

Triangular Solid

Truncated Icosahedron

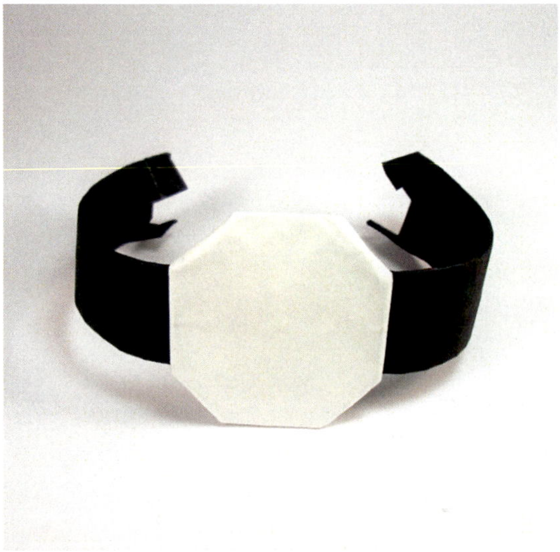

Wristwatch

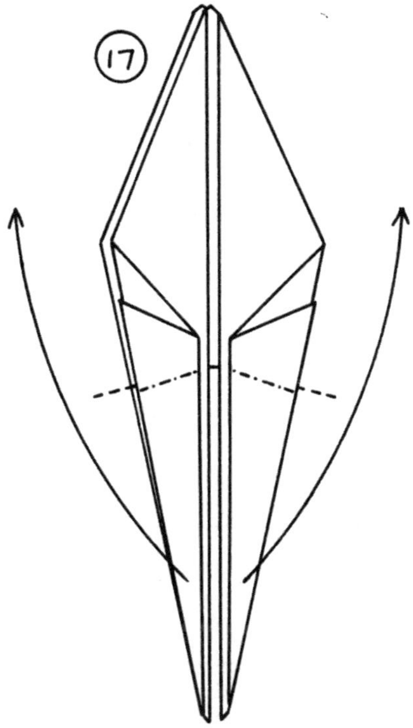

Reverse fold left and right flaps upward.

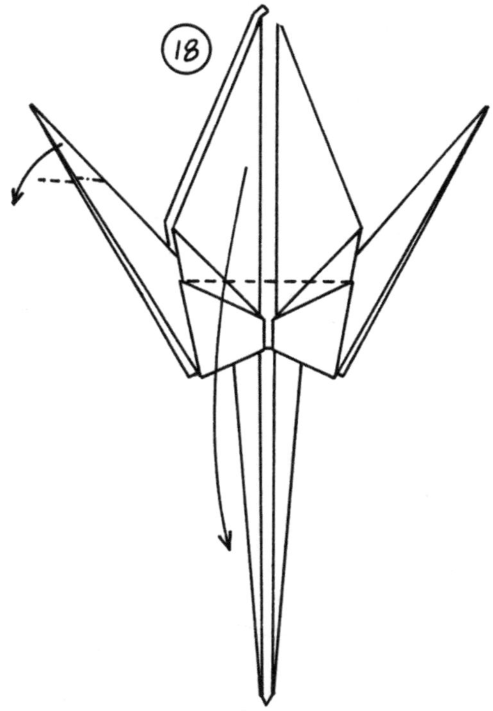

Reverse fold to form the head, and fold wing down.

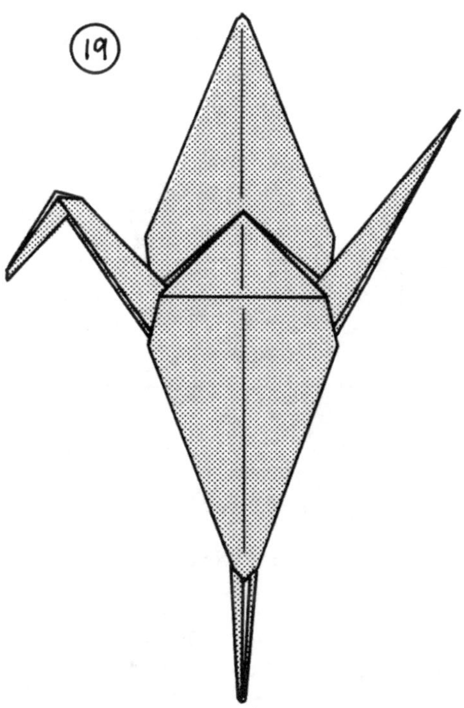

CROSS-SHAPED DISH

A 6 inch square makes a dish 3 3/4 inches across and 1 1/8 inches high.

A 10 inch square makes a dish 6 1/4 inches across and 1 3/4 inches high.

The model works well with a wide variety of papers including thicker paper such as certain wallpapers, Canson paper or paper with bonded layers.

Begin color side up.

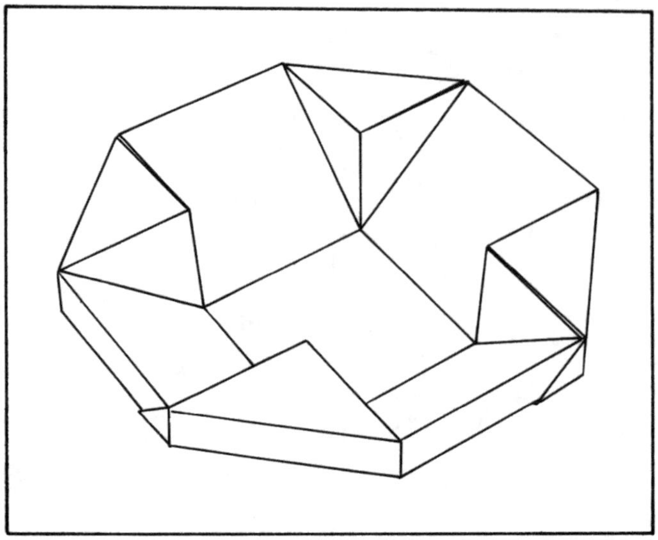

1
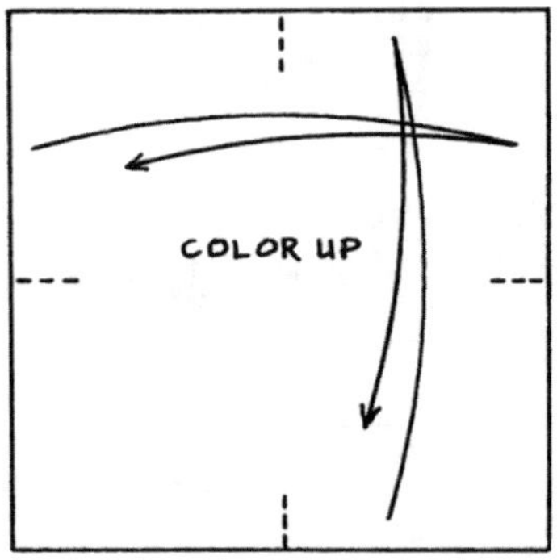

Landmark the midpoint of each edge.

2
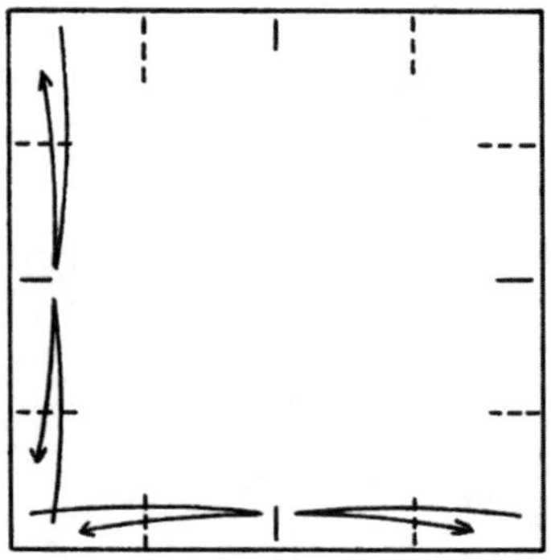

Landmark again to divide each edge into fourths.

3
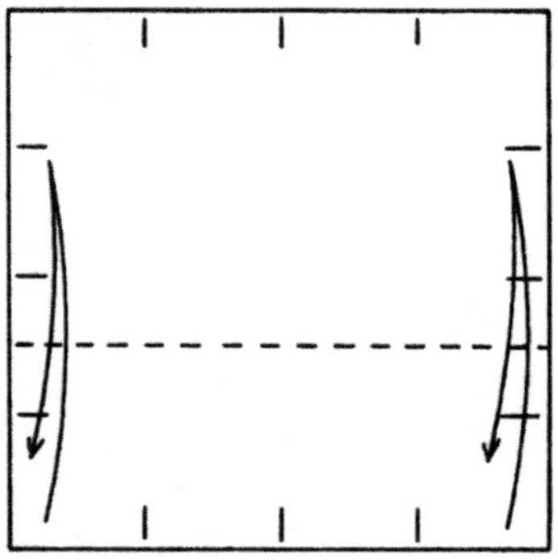

Fold bottom corners to farthest landmarks, and unfold.

4
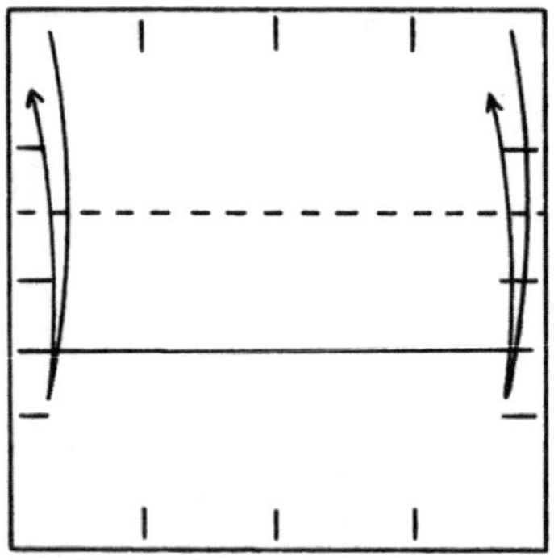

Fold top corners to farthest landmarks, and unfold.

5
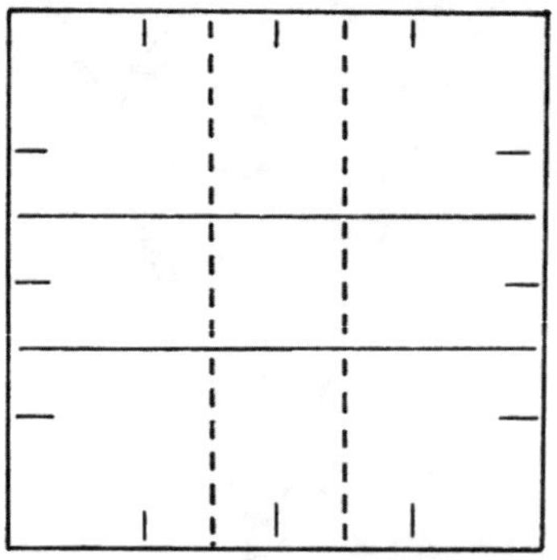

Rotate paper 90° and repeat steps 3 and 4.

6
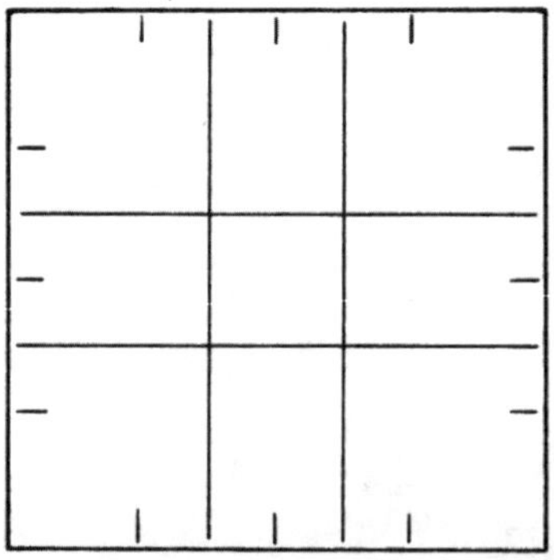

View of step 5 finished. Turn paper over.

7

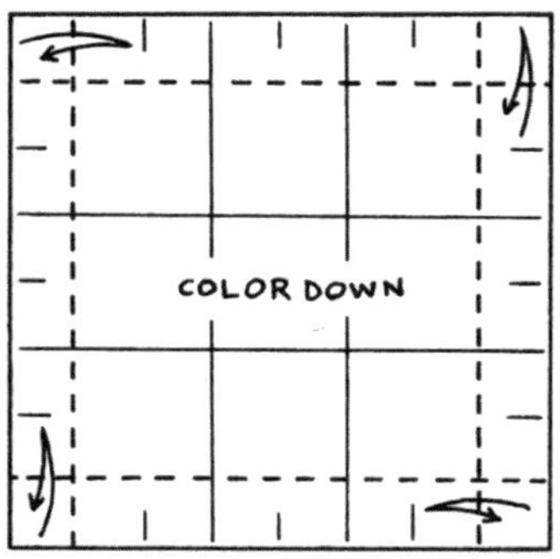

Fold each edge to closest landmarks, and unfold.

8

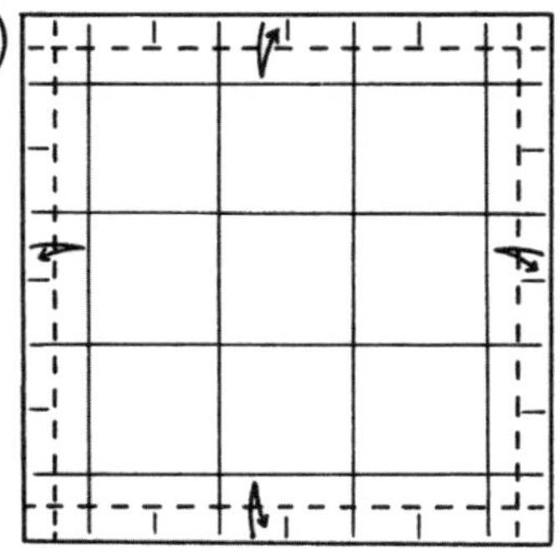

Fold each edge to nearest crease, and unfold.

9

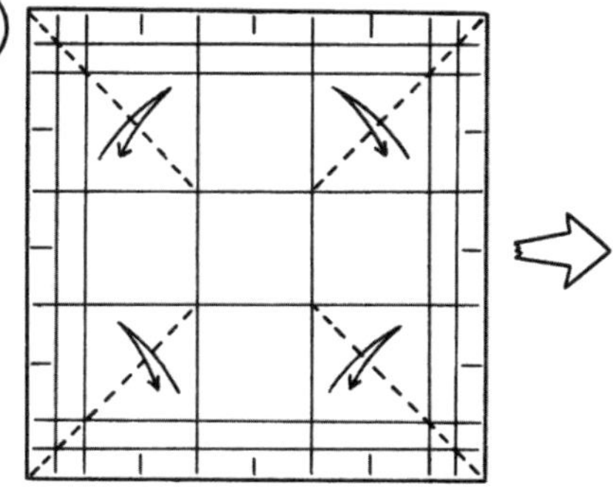

Valley fold and unfold the diagonal creases, only where shown. Picture gets larger.

10

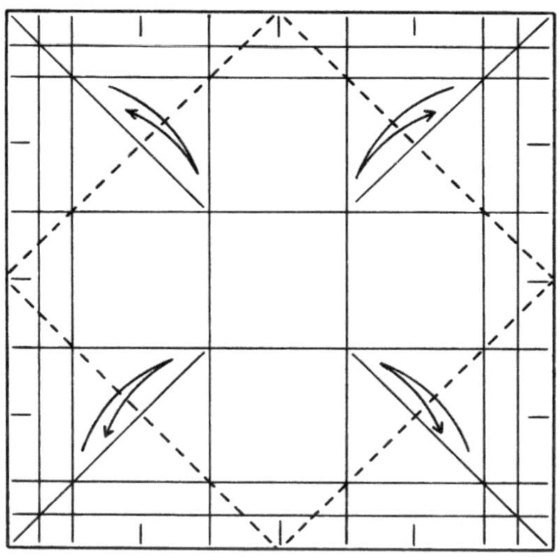

Valley fold between the midpoints of each two adjacent edges, and unfold. Turn model over to color side up.

11

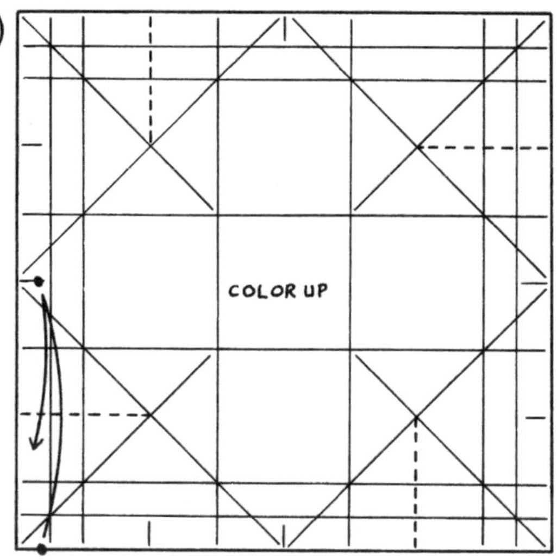

Place lower left corner at midpoint and valley fold and unfold only where shown. Repeat on other 3 corners.

12

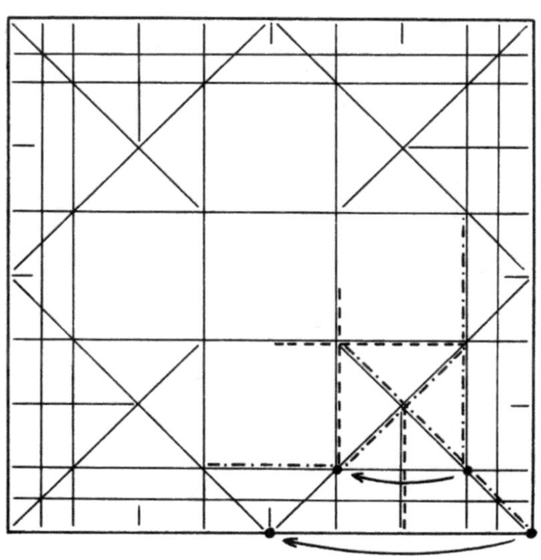

First, work on the lower right corner. Check that all mountain and valley folds are in place. Refer to finished model picture to see desired shape. Fold dot-to-dot as shown to 3-D the corner. Then, let the corner loose temporarily. Rotate in turn to each remaining corner, and repeat. You are "training the paper" for the final steps.

13

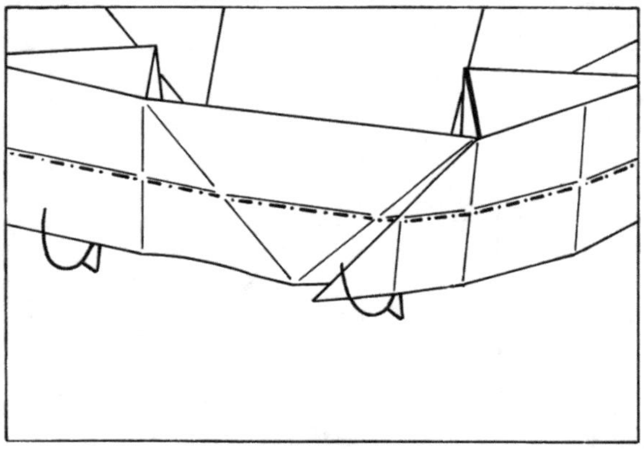

This is an enlarged view of one corner folded 3-D. Wait until the end to do the mountain fold, which goes all the way around, and locks the model. Turn model upside down.

14

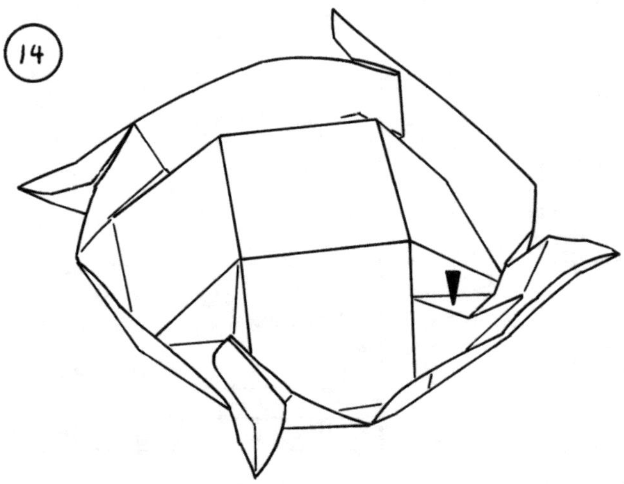

View of underside. Push down flat where shown. Repeat on other 3 corners. Locking fold is done from underside position. See explanation next.

Locking Fold: Place model upside down on a surface. Before mountain folding, notice that edges of the cross shape are in the way. Avoid damaging these edges. It helps to curl the paper a little as you begin the mountain fold, using the existing crease shown in step 13.

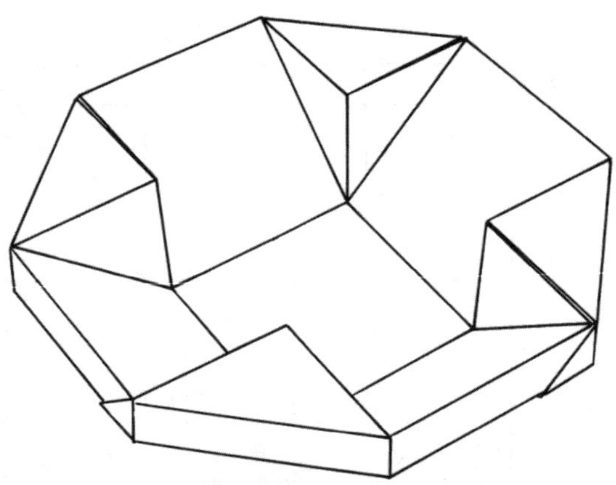

BASKET

Use a foil paper rectangle proportioned 1 x 3.

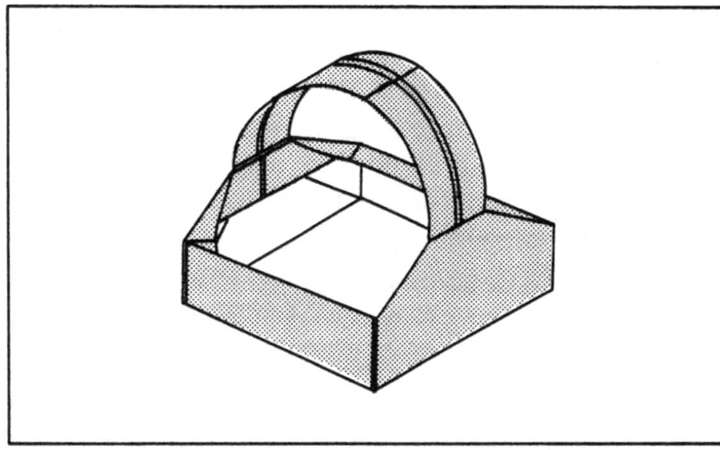

1
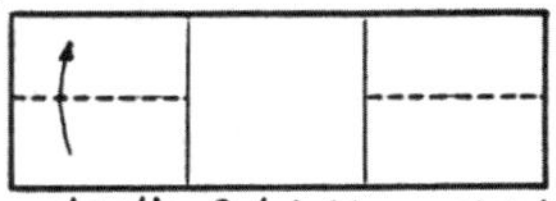
don't fold the middle

2
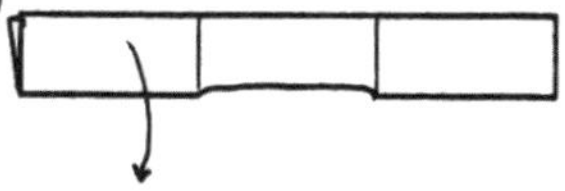

3
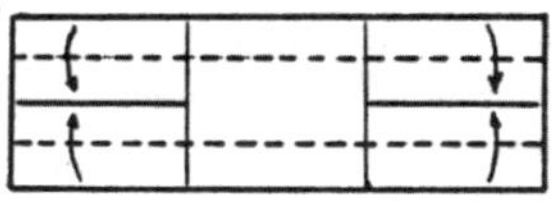

4

The next sequence of steps shows only one end. Repeat each step on other end.

5
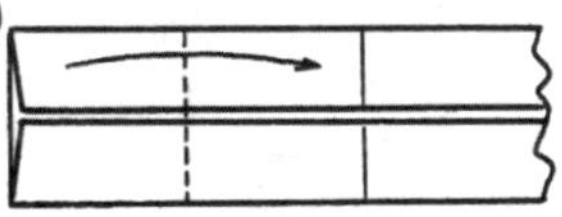

6
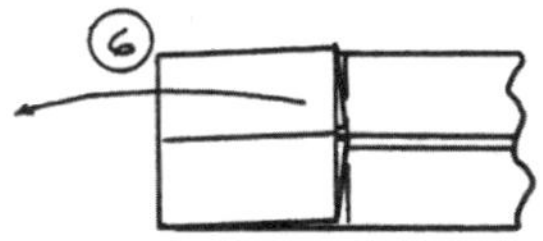

7
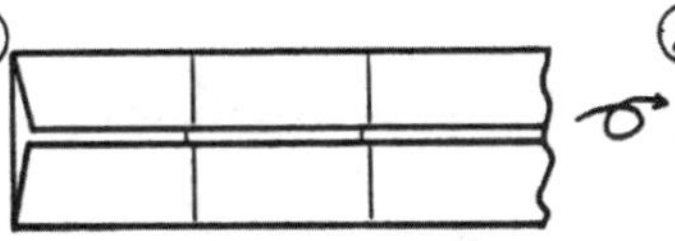

8
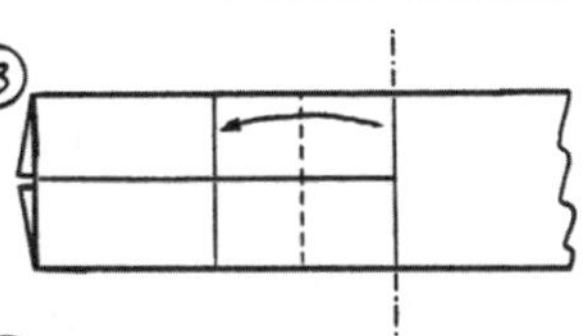

9

10
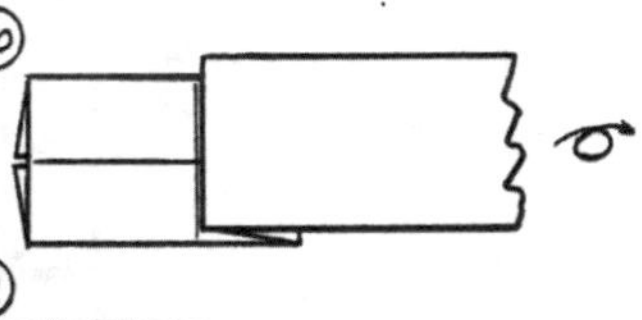

11
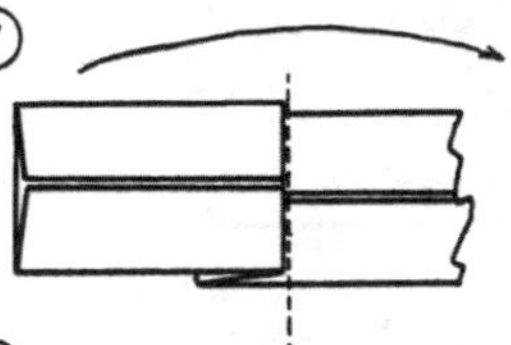

12
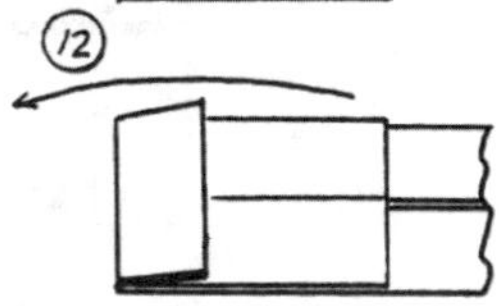

13 Shows whole model completed through step 12.

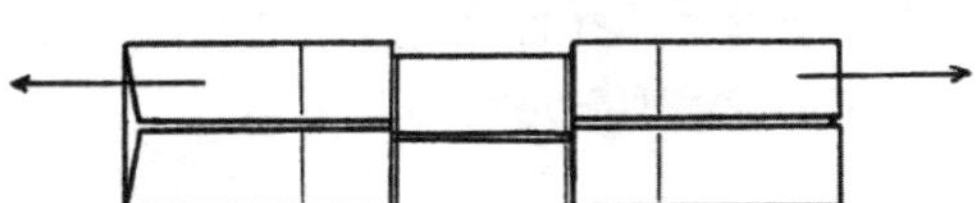

Pull out flat

14
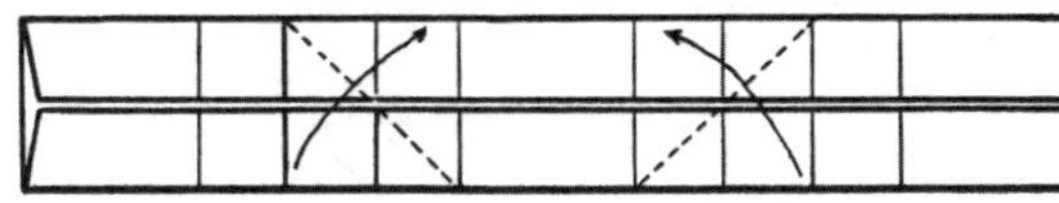

15
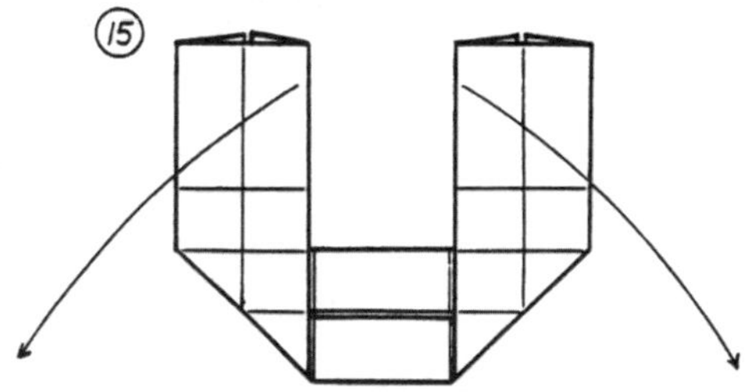

16
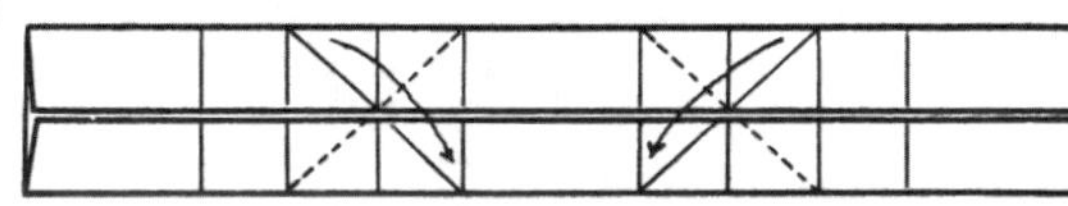

17
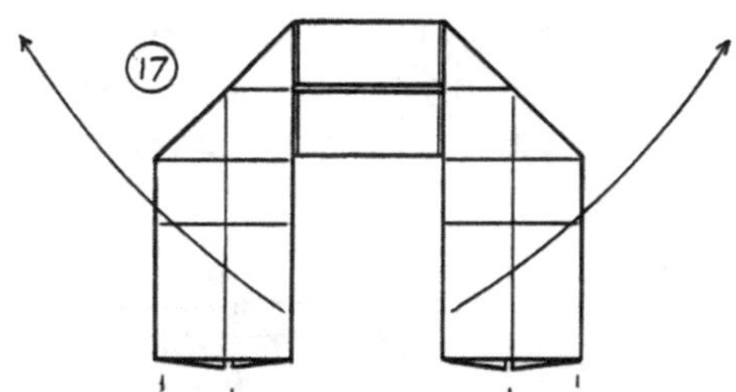

18
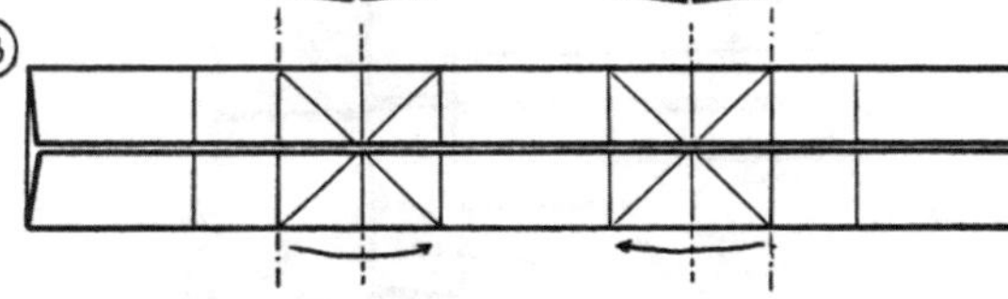

Return model to position shown in step 13.

19
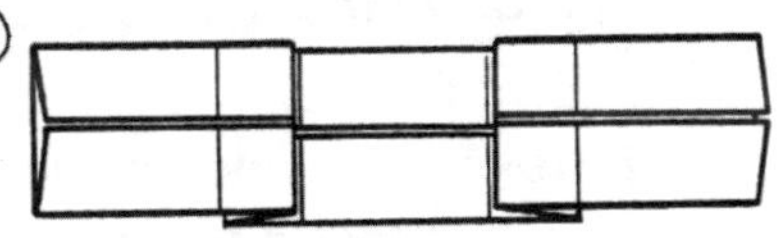

In next sequence, picture becomes larger and shows only one end.
Repeat each step on other end.

20

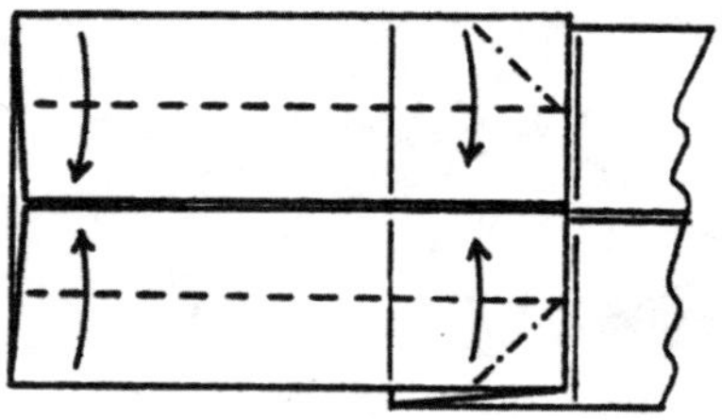

21

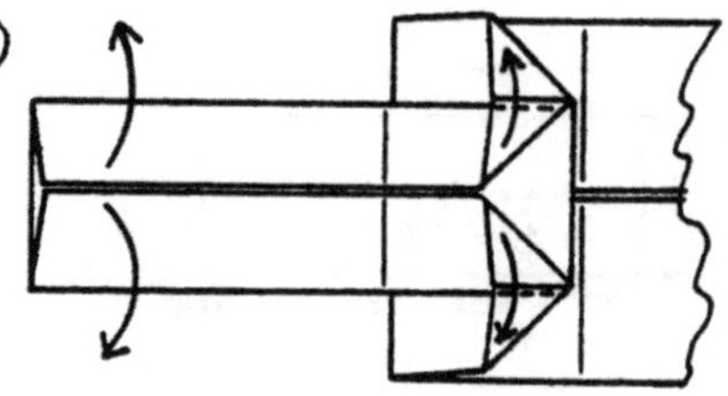

22

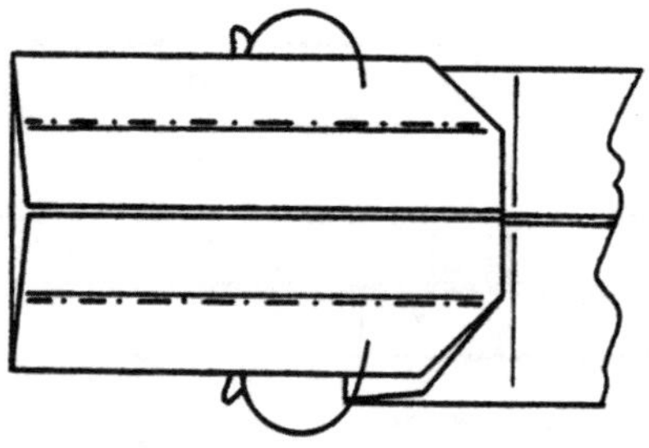

23

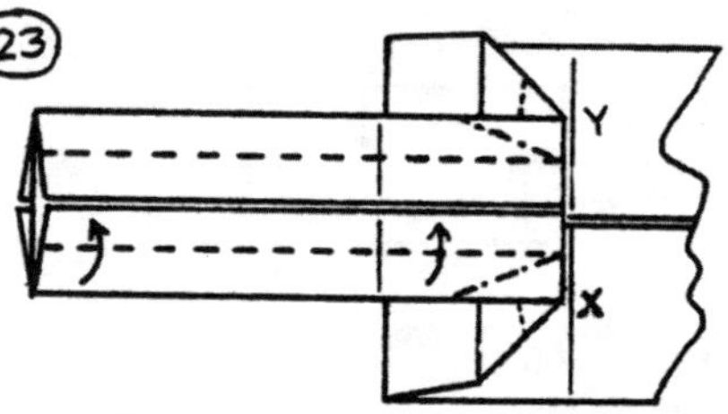

Points X and Y will become centers of spread-squash folds.

24

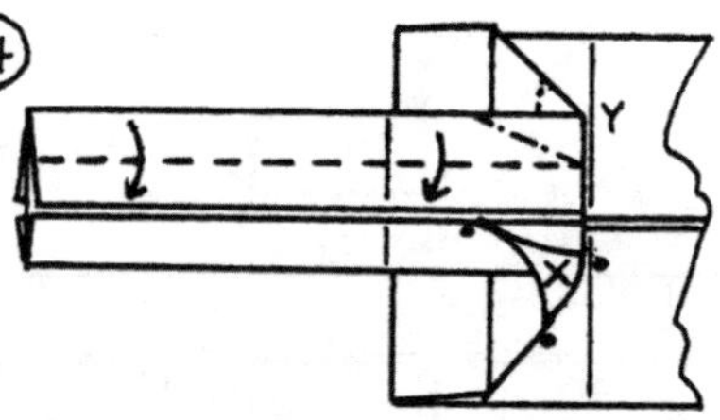

Spread simultaneously from three points •, forming a triangle shaped area. Flatten. Repeat on top half, spreading Y.

25

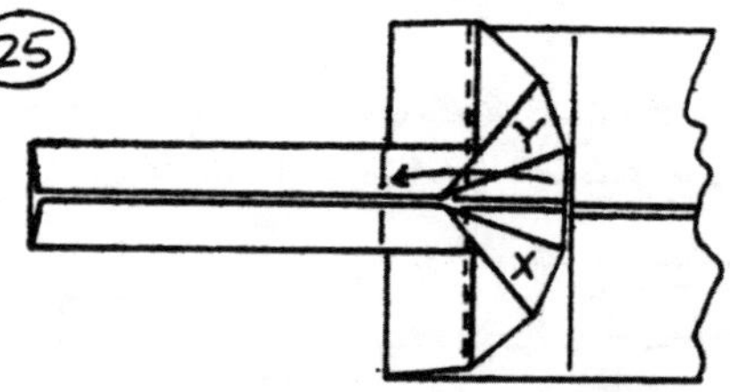

Fold right end to left; prevent narrow handle from sliding out of position.

26

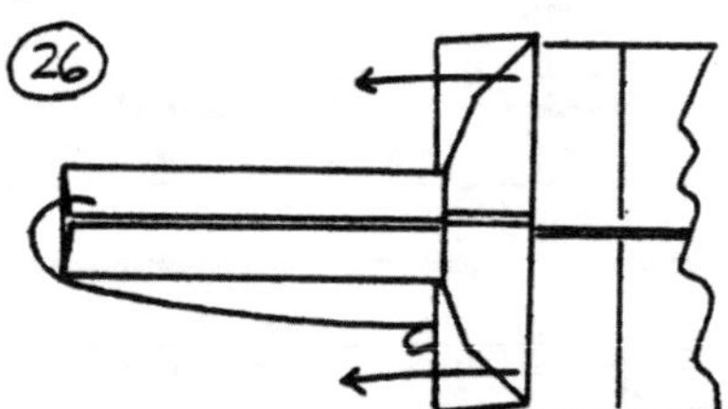

Unfold whole flap to left while allowing handle to swing behind.

IMPORTANT: Model must be raised from folding surface for next step.

27

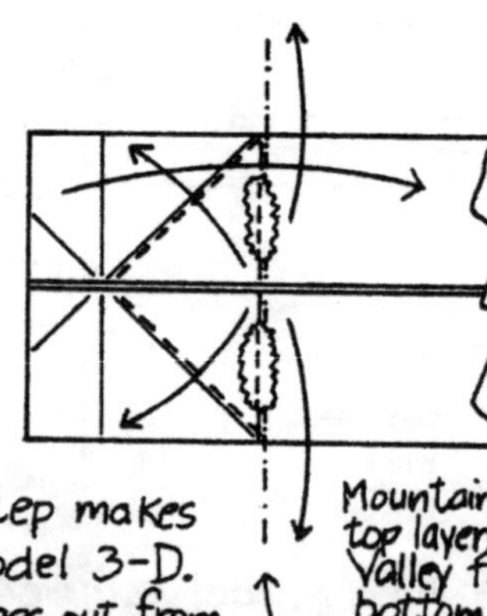

This step makes the model 3-D. Pull edges out from center. Left end stands up vertically.

Mountain fold top layers. Valley fold bottom layer.

(28)

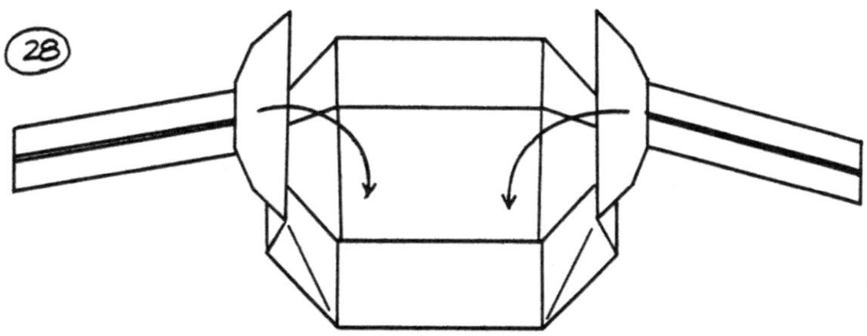

When sides of basket are upright, flip handle assemblies over top edges to lay flat against inside surfaces.

(29)

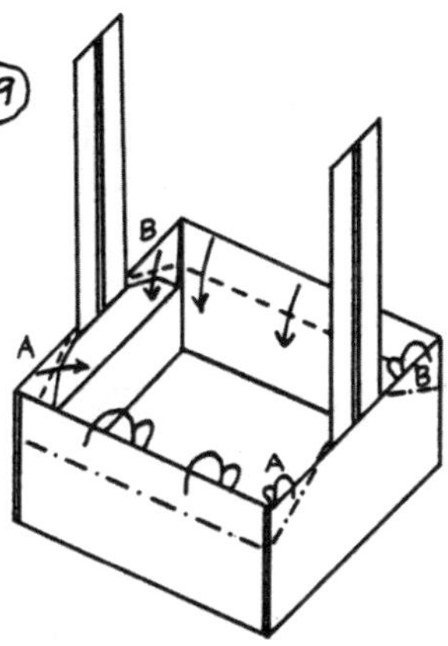

This step forms the basket's final shape while locking handle assemblies to sides of basket. Fold both edges "A" to inside, snugly around edges of handle assemblies. Where the folds meet the corners, mountain fold the long edge to the inside. Repeat sequence with "B". Paper at corners curls around inside of each corner—does not fit flat, so avoid tearing.

JOINING THE HANDLE ENDS:

(30) Curl each handle end inward with numerous bends, close together. Picture not shown.

(31)

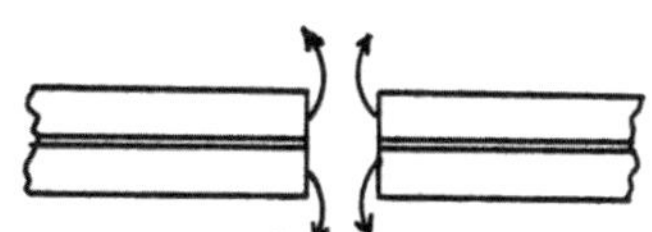

Top view of handle ends nearly meeting. From underneath, partly unfold layers outward.

(32)

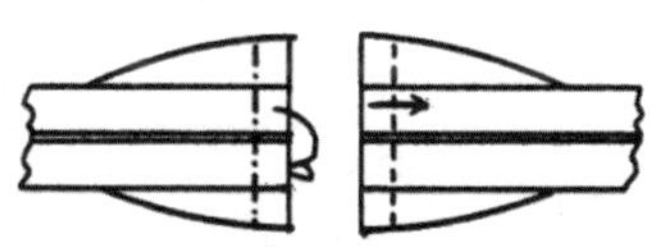

Mountain fold on one handle end and valley fold on the other.

(33)

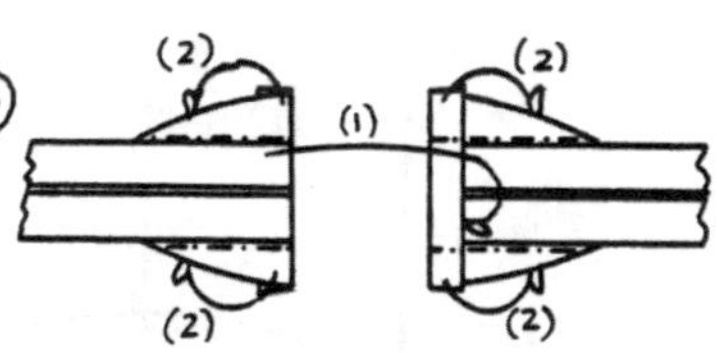

(1) Link tab on left end around tab on right end.
(2) Lock handle ends together by re-folding sides underneath.

(34)

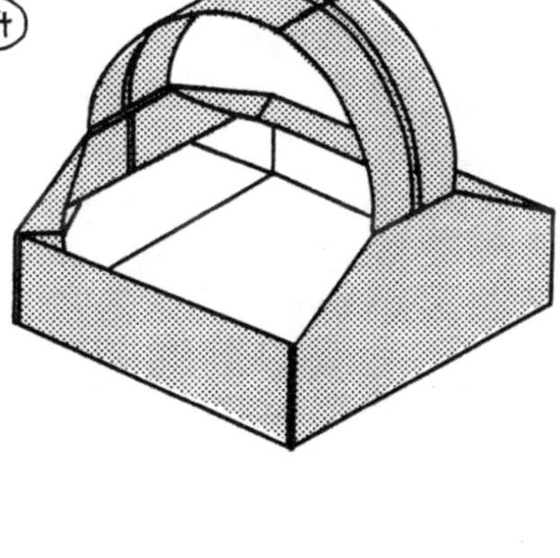

RABBIT

Square paper; begin white side up.

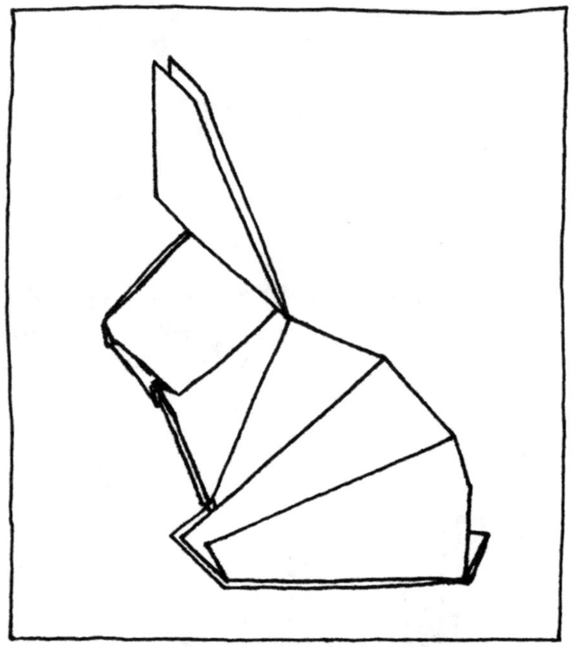

1

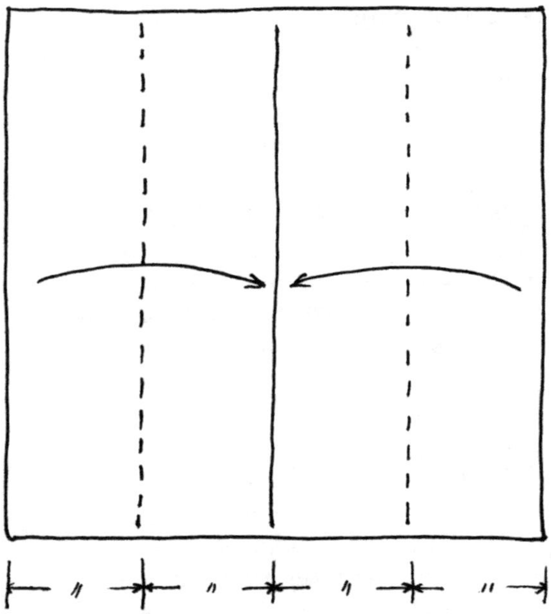

2

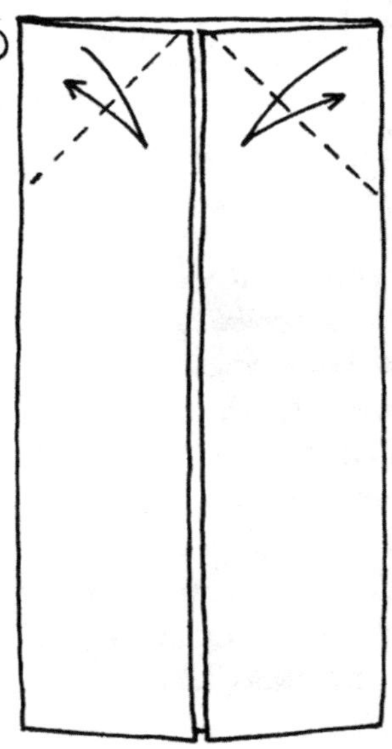

3

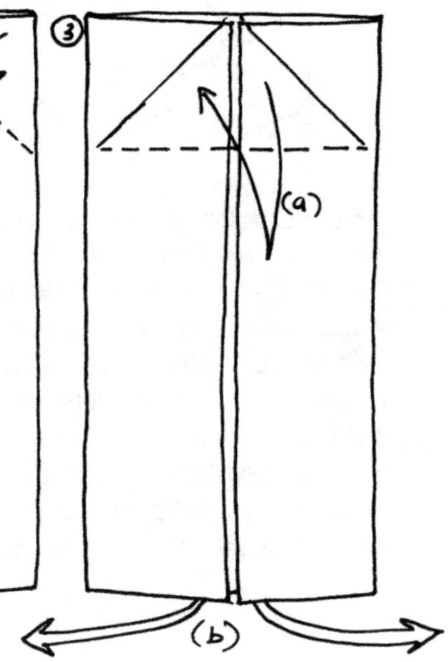

4

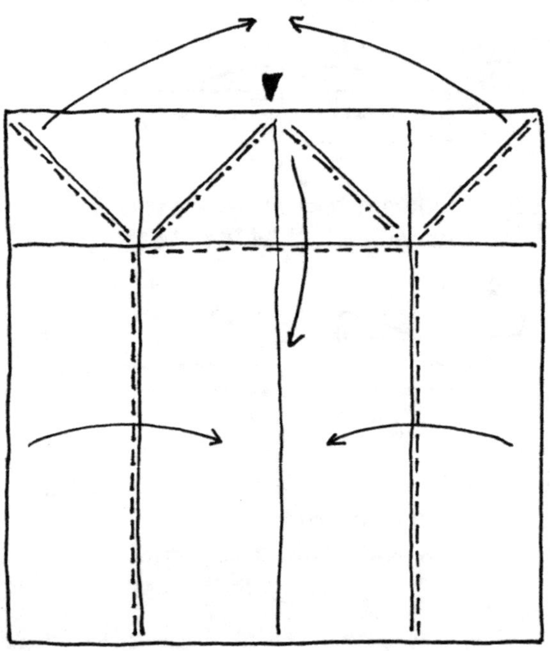

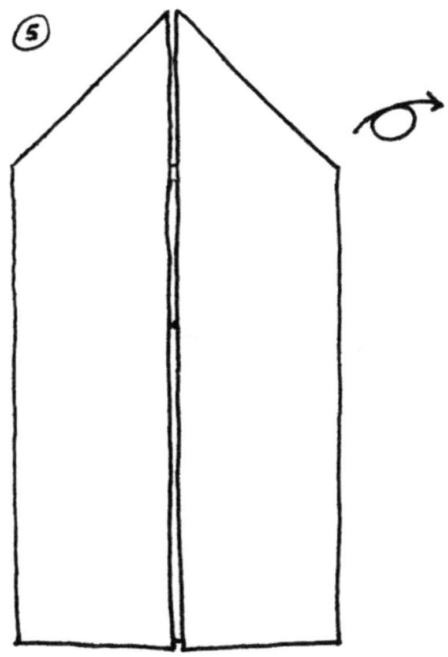

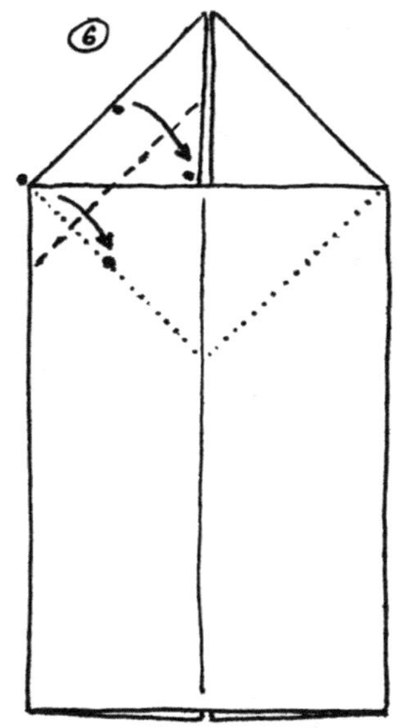

Dotted lines show edges underneath.

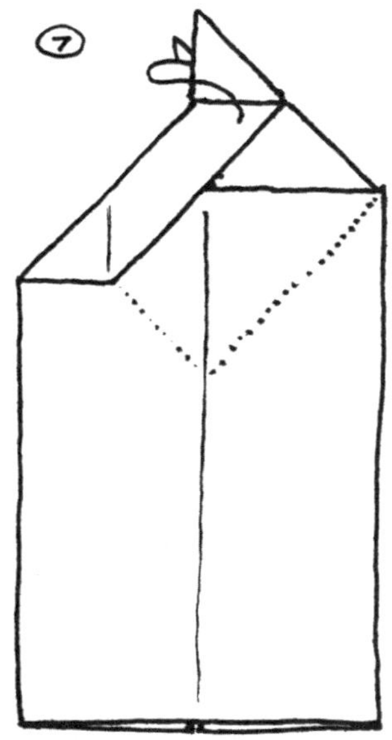

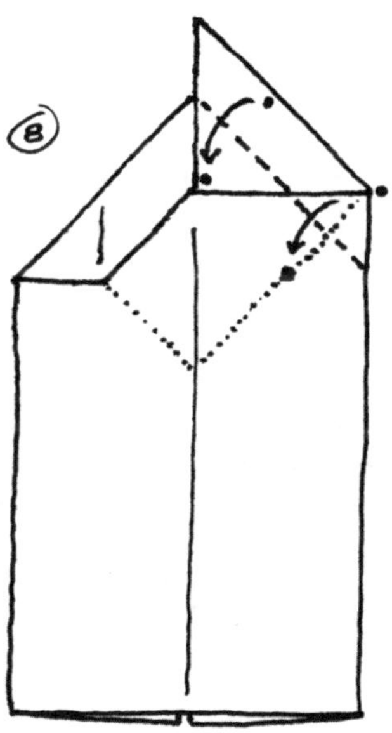

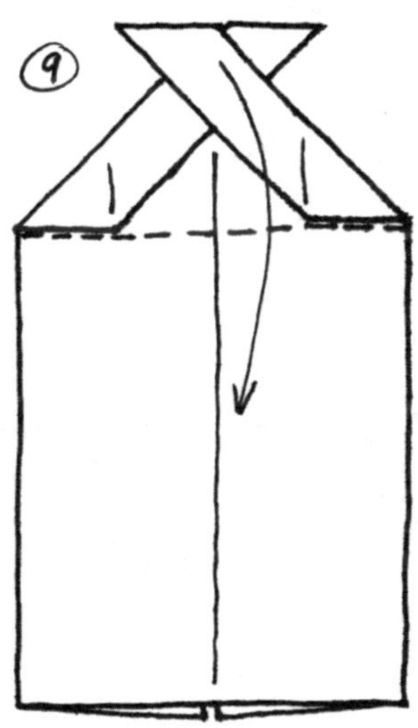

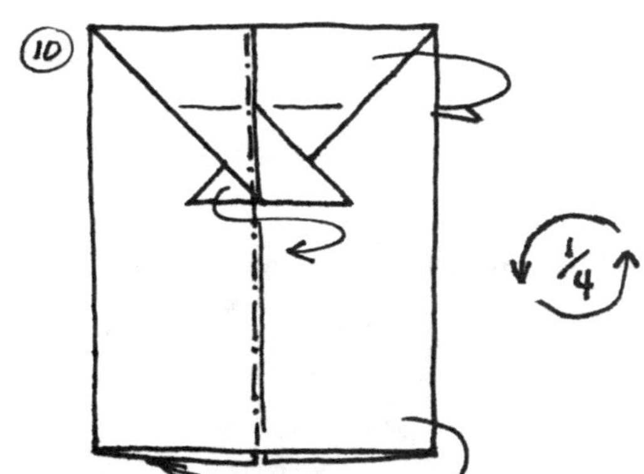

Allow ear flap to swing out from underneath.

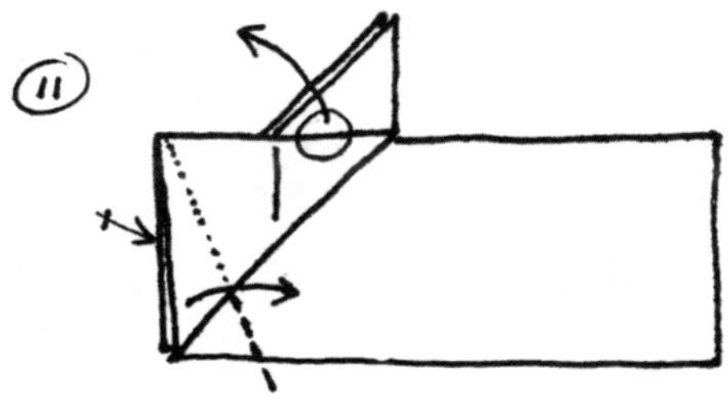

Hold ear flaps, and pull up.

Picture gets larger.

⑫

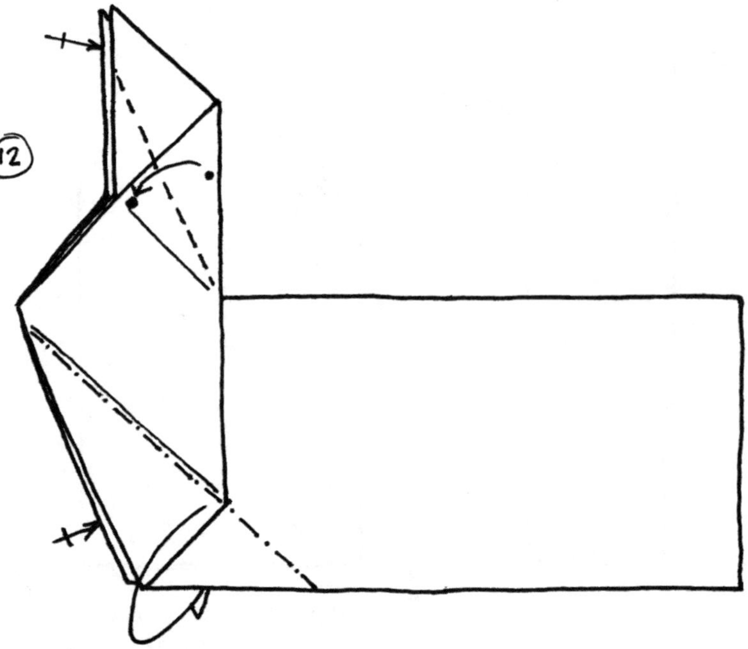

⑬

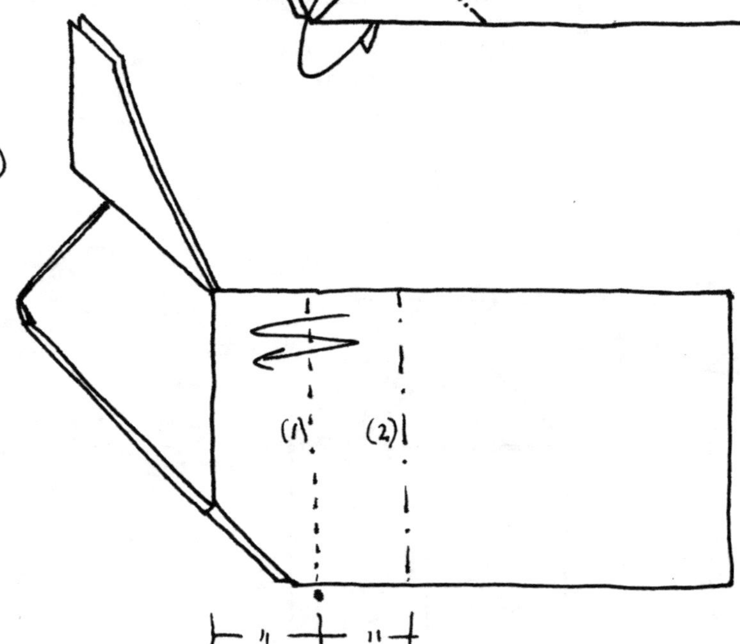

Notice crease (1) is not at corner.

⑭

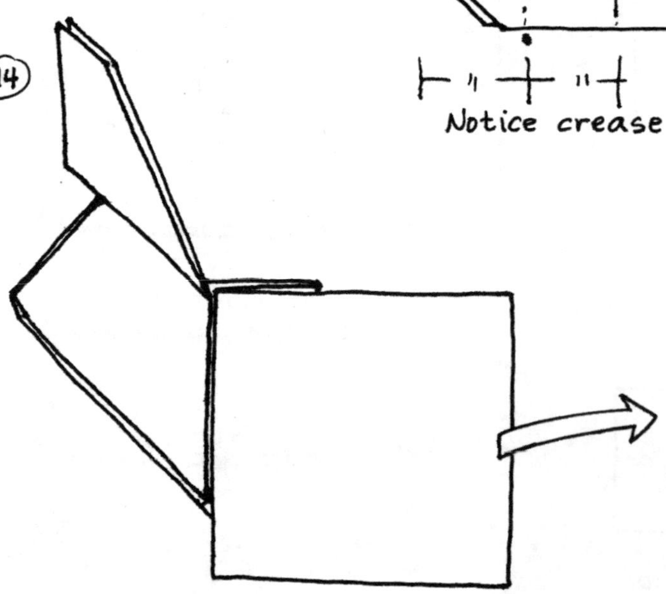

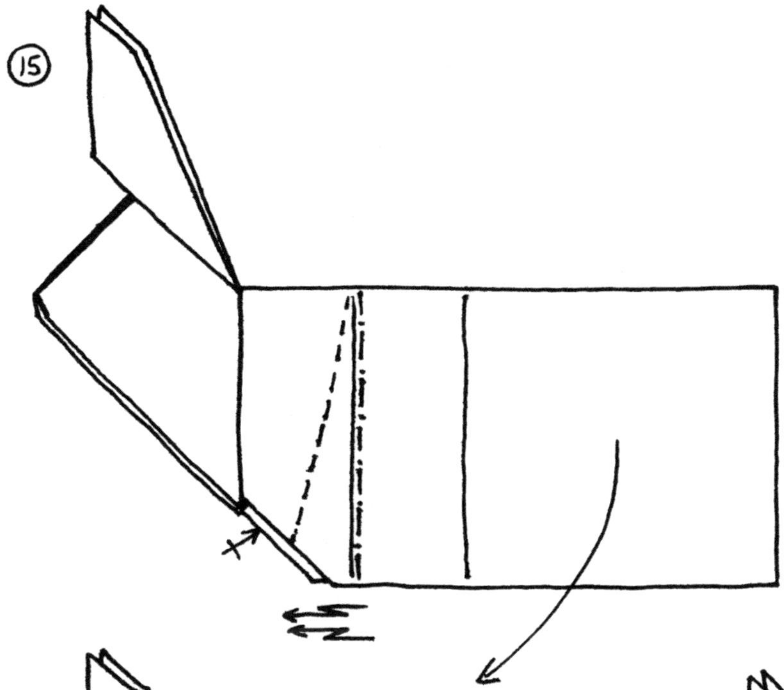

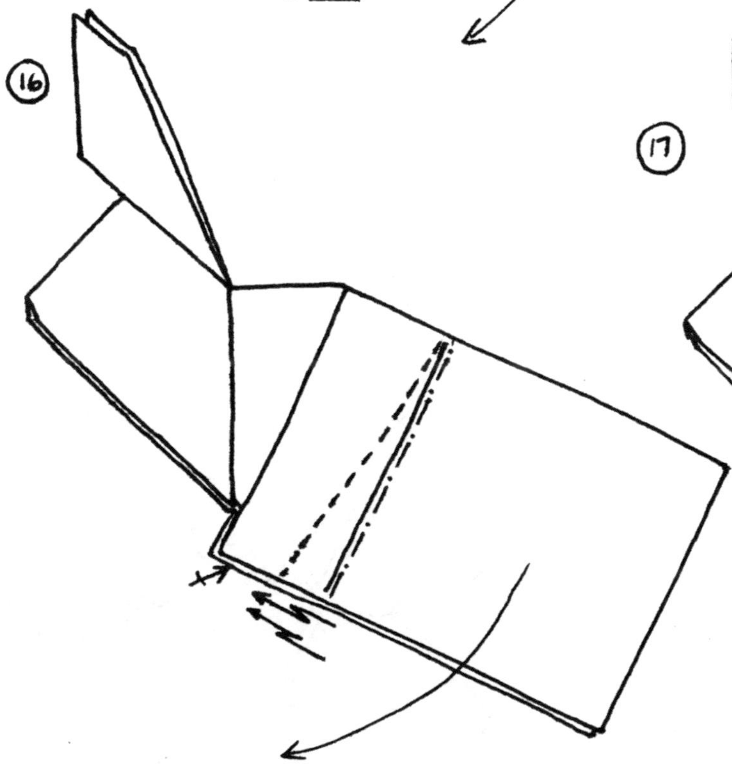

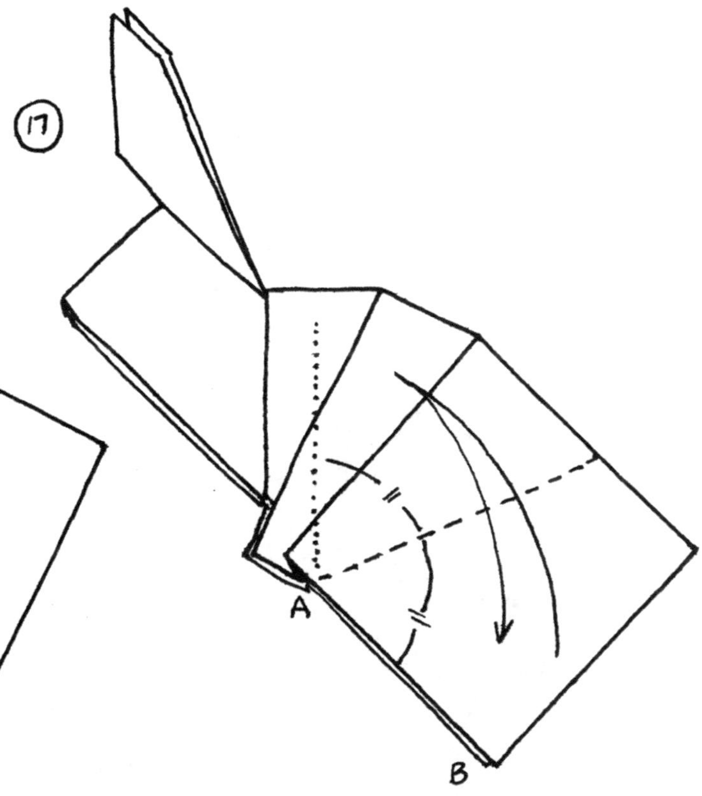

Dotted line is a parallel imaginary line, parallel to folded edge at neck. Place edges AB along this line, fold and unfold.

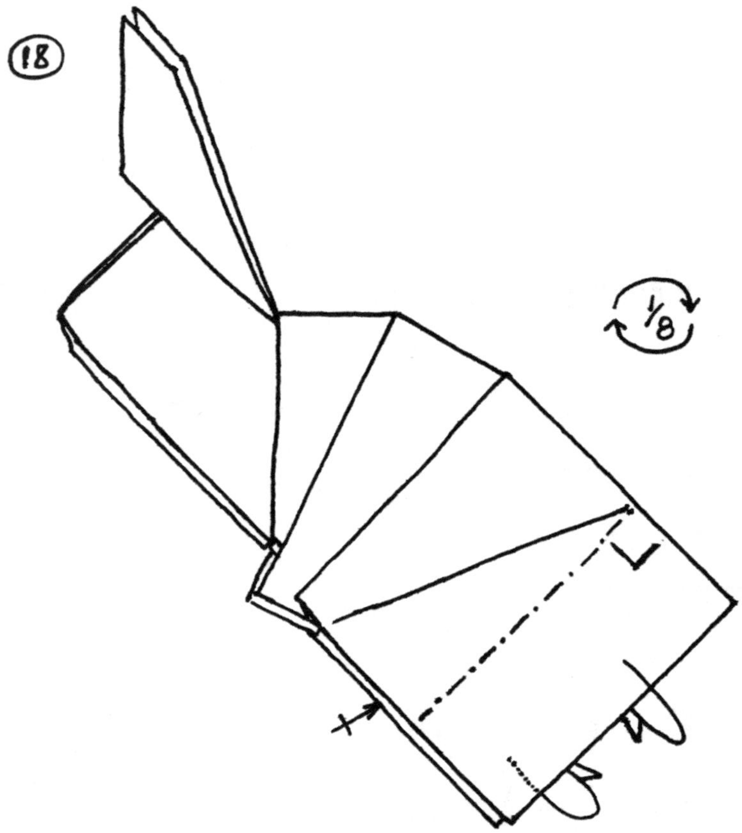

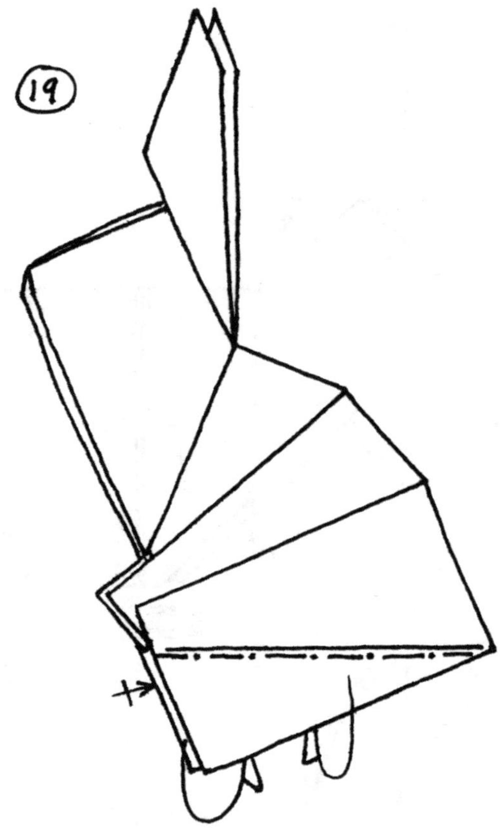

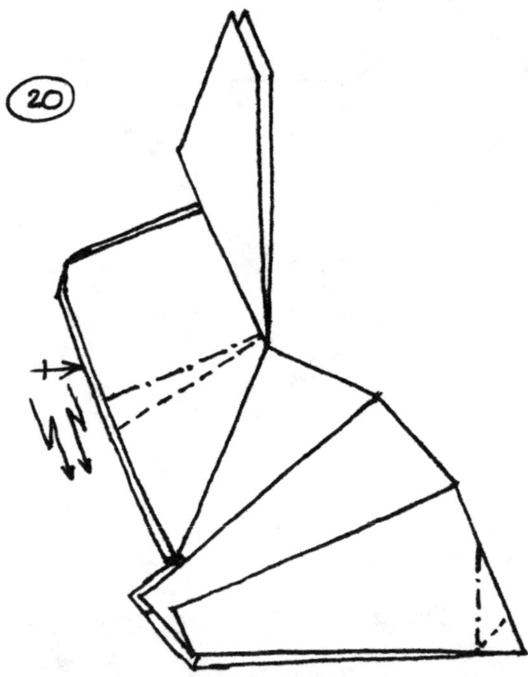

Crimp neck. Double reverse fold to form tail.

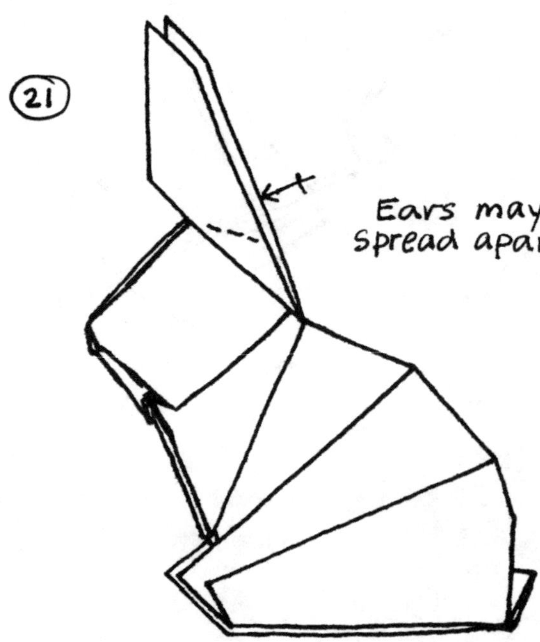

Ears may be spread apart.

EXPANDING BALL

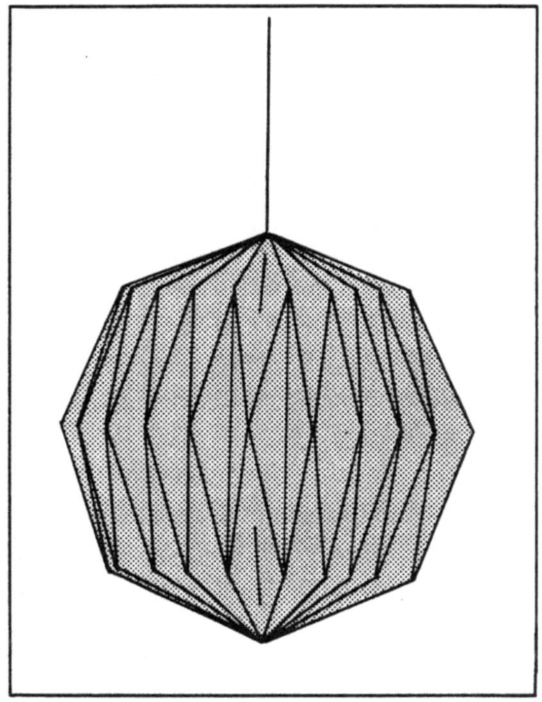

Use 8 squares of foil paper.
Make 8 modules.

The diameter of a finished ornament is about equal to 3/4 the edge length of the square used.

Pre-fold the square in thirds.
Begin color side up.

①

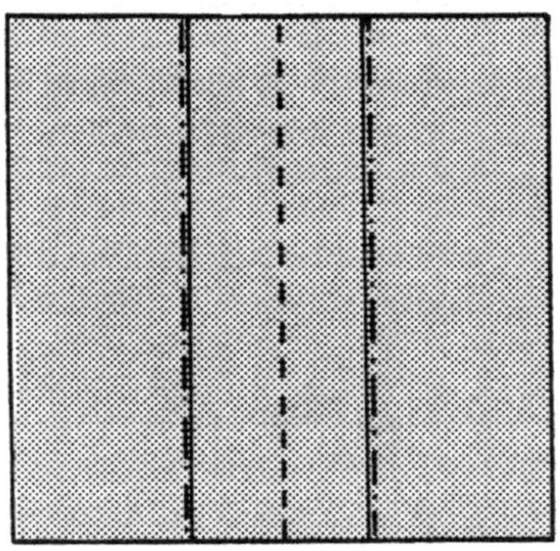

Make 3 folds shown.

②

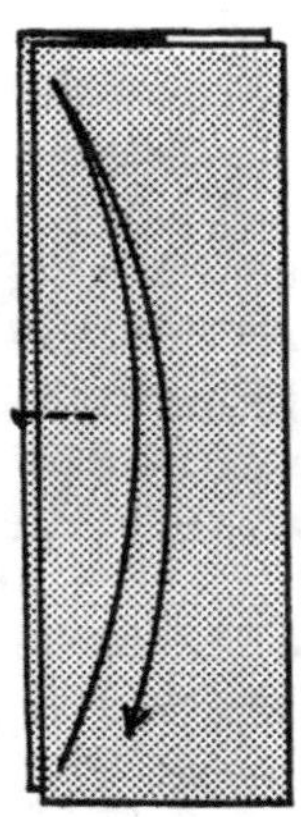

Bring corners together, pinch a landmark, and unfold.

③

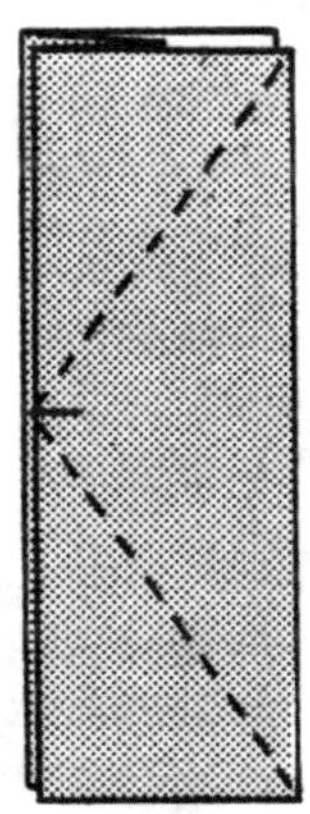

Fold carefully to prevent layers from slipping. Then unfold.

④

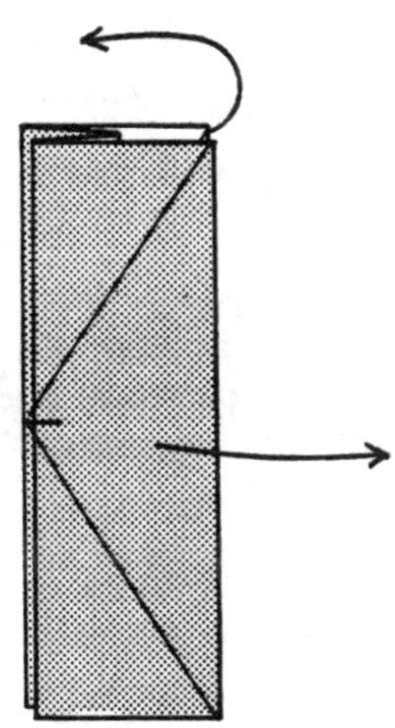

Unfold all.

Color side up.

⑤
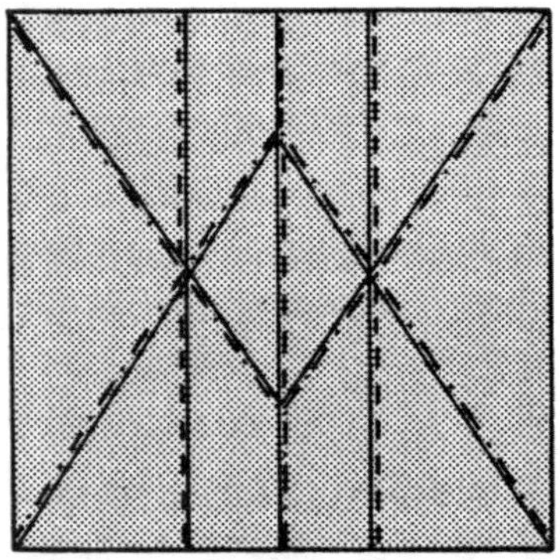

Make all mountain and valley folds shown. Collapse model while sinking central diamond. See step 6.

⑥
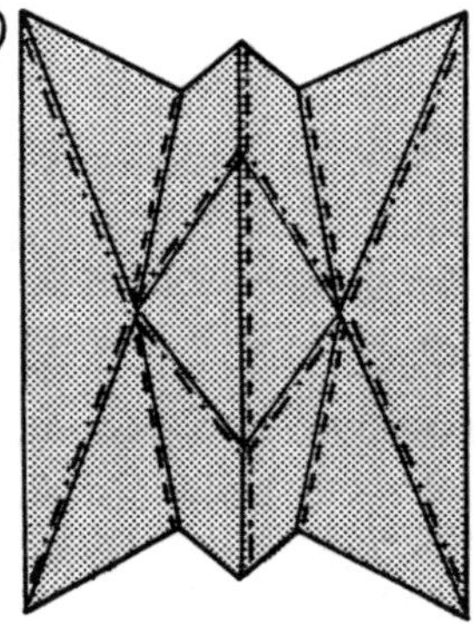

Collapsing...

⑦
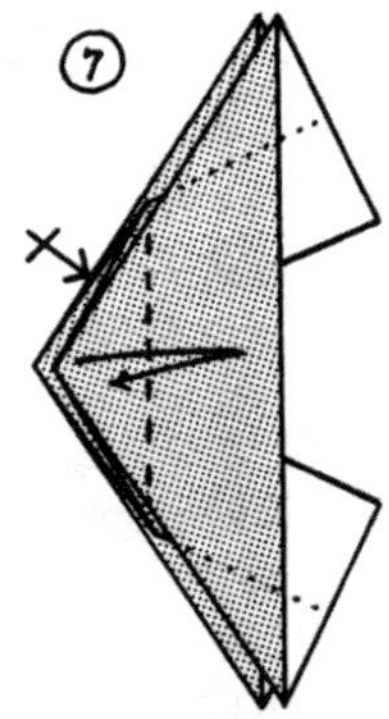

Collapsed and flat. Fold point to right and unfold. Repeat behind. Dotted lines show hidden folded edge.

⑧
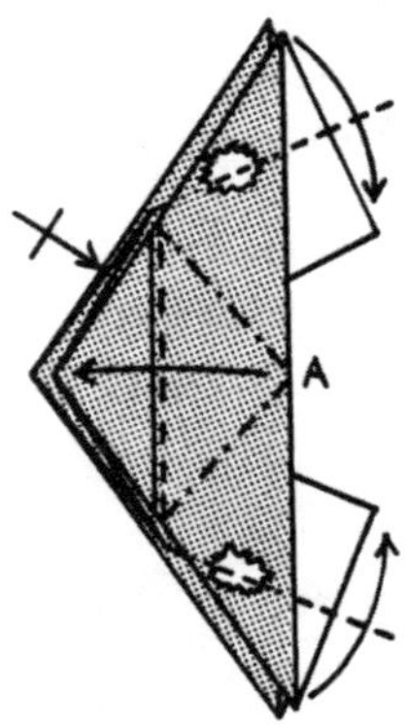

Pull point A to the left, making a sort of petal fold. Repeat behind.

⑨
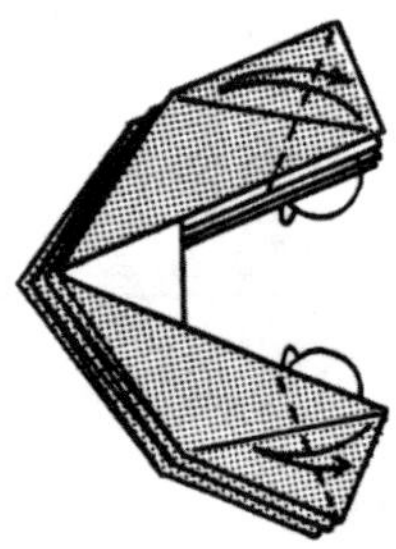

At top, preliminary fold two flaps together, and unfold. Repeat behind with other two flaps. Repeat sequence at bottom.

⑩
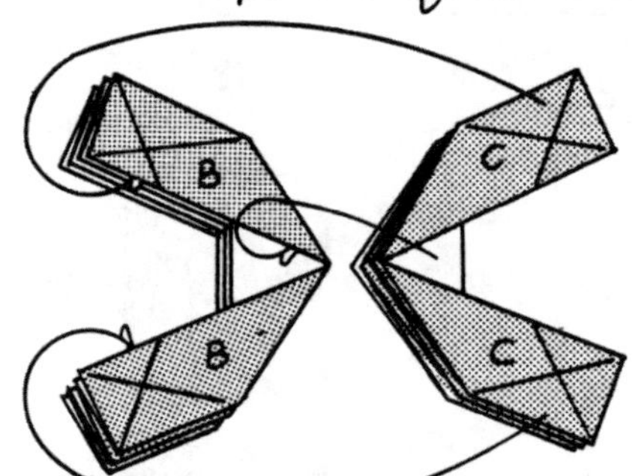

Here are two finished modules. To assemble, begin to place surfaces B and C together, and insert the first outside folded edges of C into first pocket behind B. Allign modules side to side and lock as in steps ⑪ and ⑫.

⑪

This is an enlarged, expanded view of top edges only. The three layers in point D, when braught together flat, are used in next step.

⑫
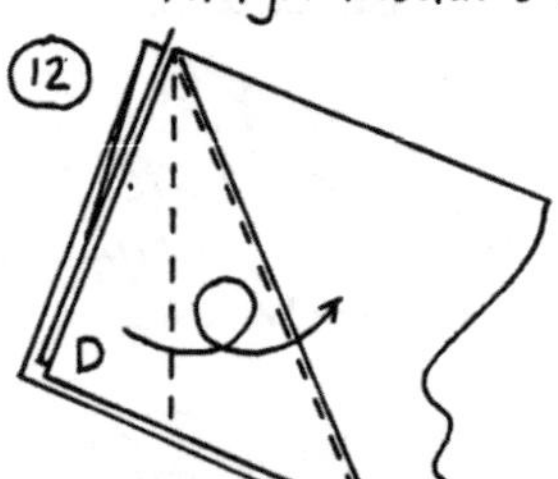

Inside view of point D. Roll twice to lock. Repeat other end. NOW, ADD ALL MODULES AS IN ⑩ THRU ⑫

⑬
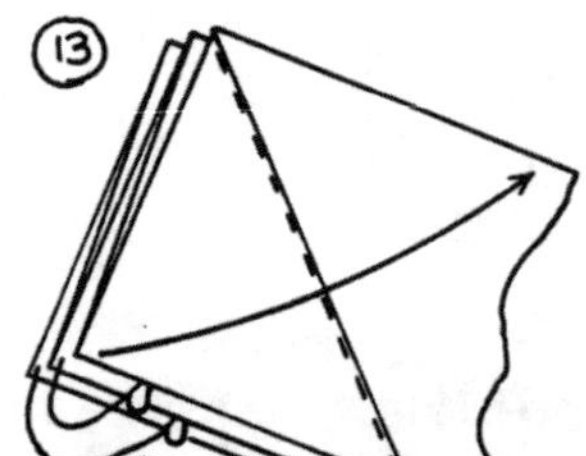

All other flaps, both ends, like this-one at a time.

(14) When Step 12 is completed with all modules, they will be connected side-to-side. Step 13 joins the ends. Opposite sides, when brought together, can expand the model into a ball shape.

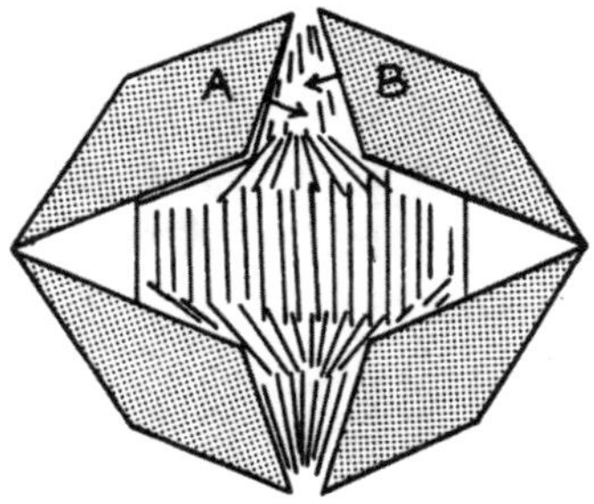

The inner surfaces will appear as above. To join sides A and B, unfold the first flap under surface A, and unfold the corner of surface B.

Then expand model into a ball shape. Just as B is about to meet side A, bring the bottom edge of surface B over and behind surface A to fit into the channel directly behind. Since you are closing just one end, then when all is alligned, use a tweezer to reach in hole where bottom end is not yet joined and do a Step 13-type of fold to lock other end of model.

To close other end, pull out surface of one side and wrap around first outside folded edge of other side.

top view

TRIANGULAR SOLID

The model works best from plain paper such as Kami, rather than foil-backed paper.

A 6 inch (5 7/8 actual) Kami square makes a model with triangle edges 3 inches long, and a height of 7/8 inch. Begin white side up.

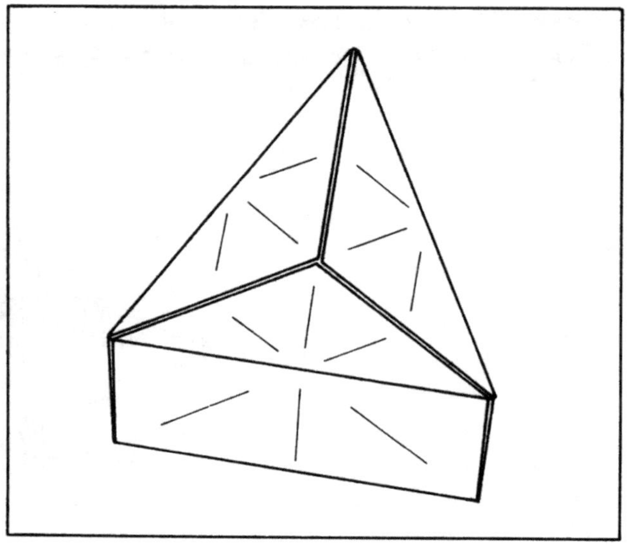

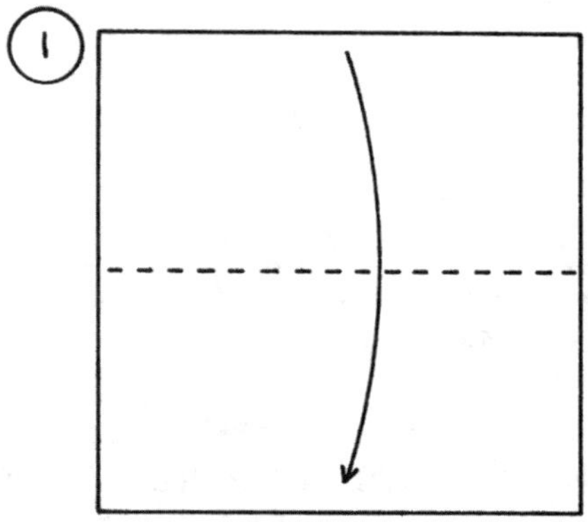

Fold in half, top edge to bottom.

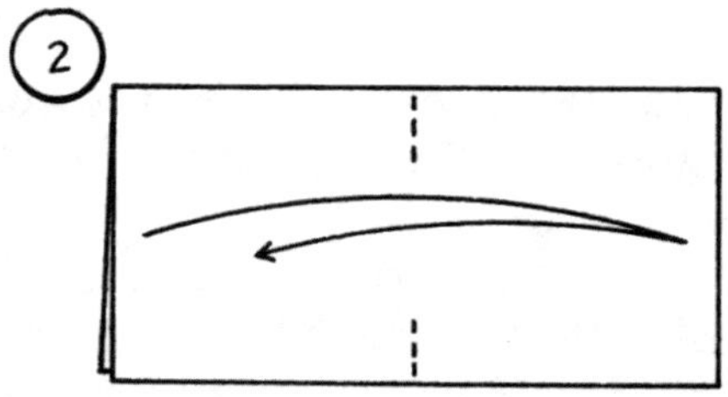

Landmark center at top and bottom.

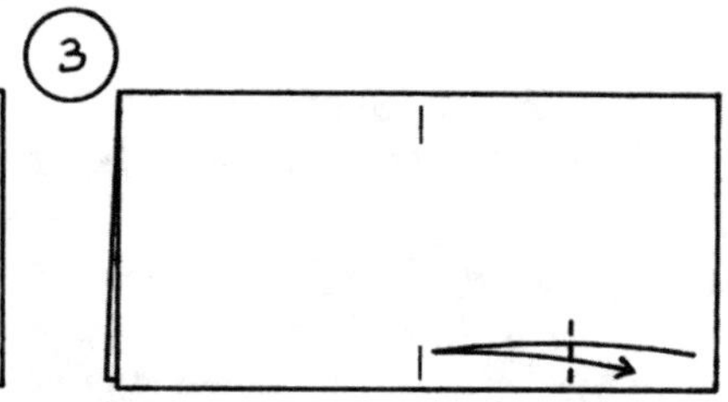

Landmark mid-point.

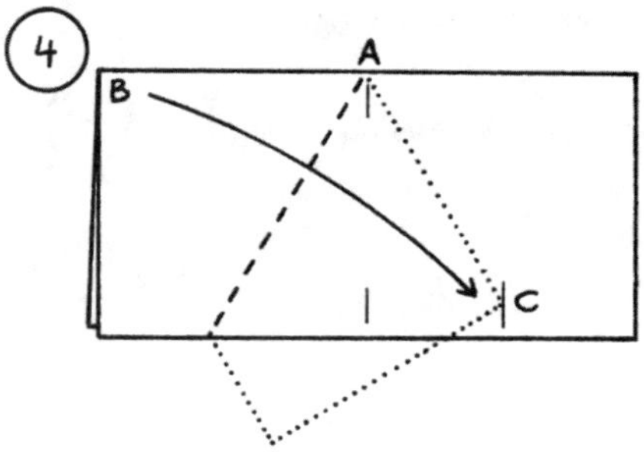

Begin valley fold at landmark A, placing corner B at landmark C.

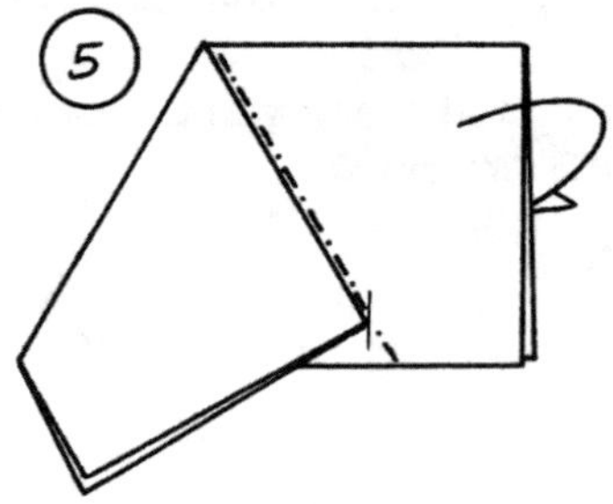

Mountain fold behind. Left and right edge pairs should all allign.

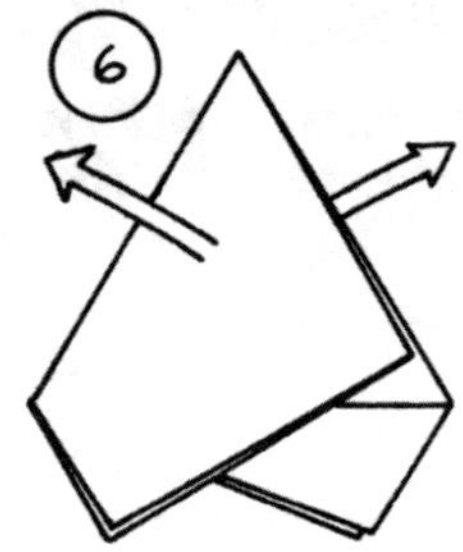

Unfold all the way.

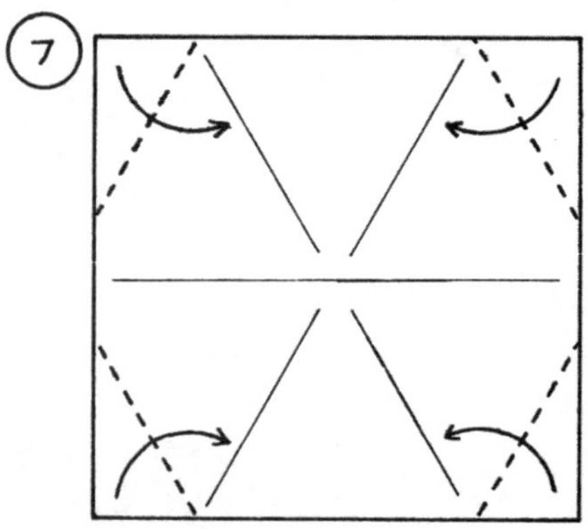

Valley fold corners to creases.

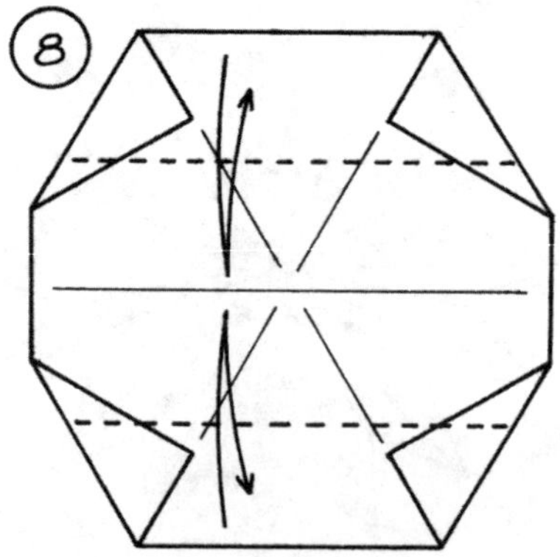

Fold and unfold edges to center. Flaps ommitted in future pictures.

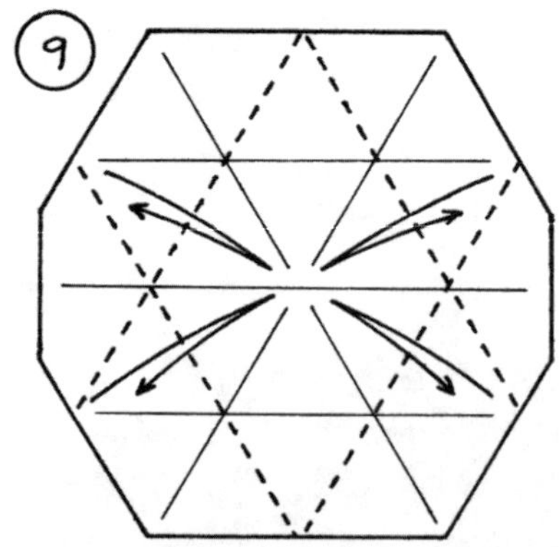

Similar to step 8, fold and unfold four edges to center.

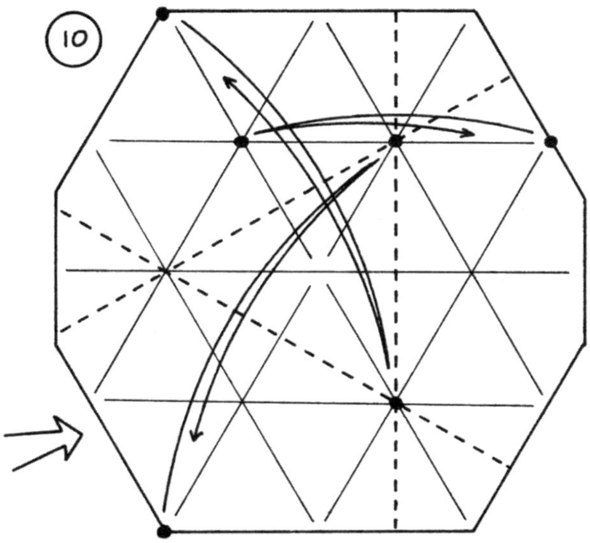

Picture gets larger. Fold and unfold the three valley creases. Locate them by alligning corners or intersections point-to-point.

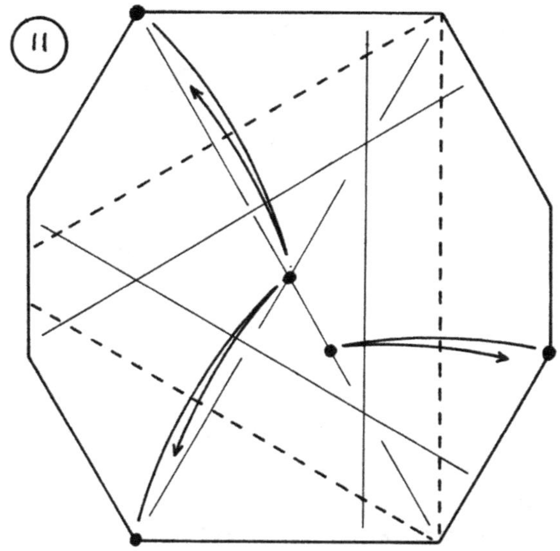

Some creases are ommitted to simplify view. Fold and unfold the three creases. Locate by alligning point-to-point as shown.

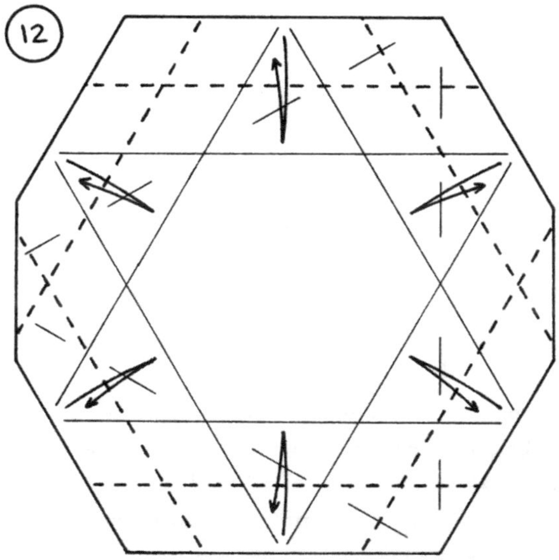

The six existing creases which form shape of Star of David are guidelines for this step. Fold and unfold six valley creases shown.

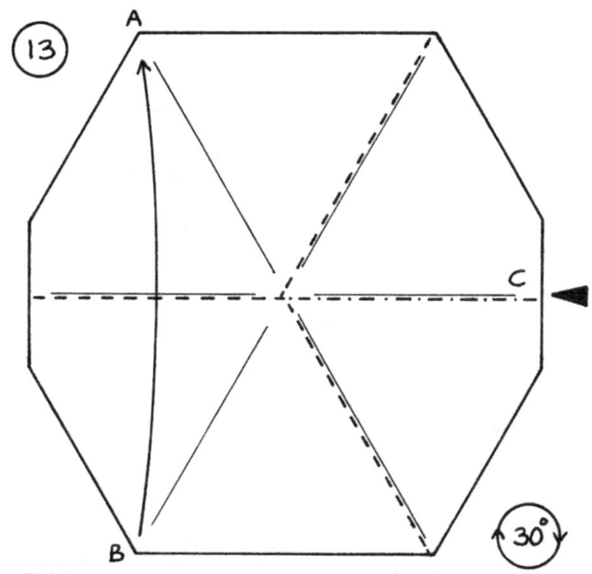

Fold corner B up to A, while reverse folding area C inside the layers. Rotate model 30°.

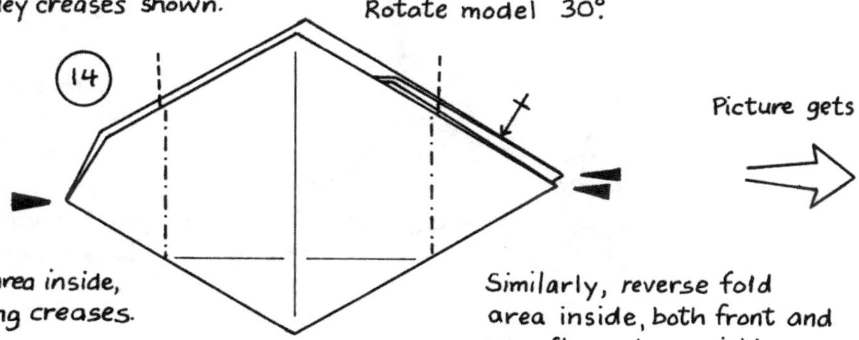

Picture gets larger.

Reverse fold area inside, using existing creases.

Similarly, reverse fold area inside, both front and rear flaps, along existing creases.

15

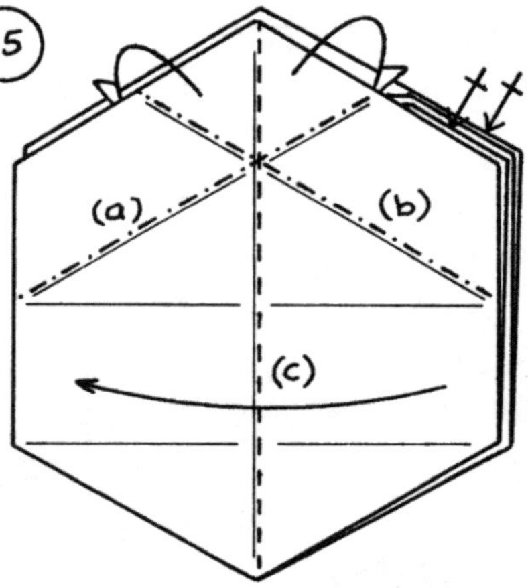

(a) Mountain fold upper left section behind. Then, (b) mountain fold upper right section behind. Next, (c) fold right half to left like a book page. Repeat (a) and (b), turn page, and repeat (a) and (b) again.

16

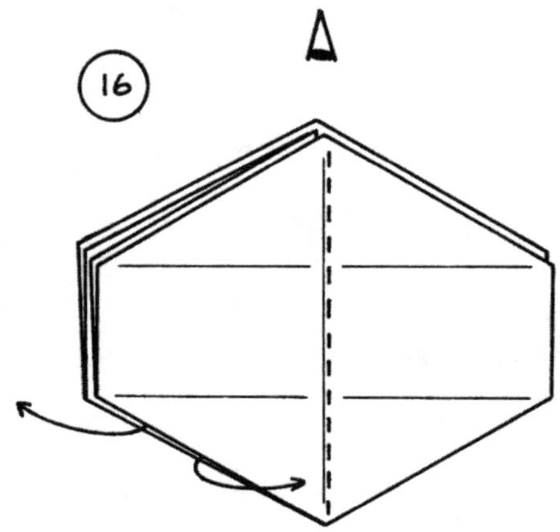

Look from above and position the three flaps at 120° from each other.

17

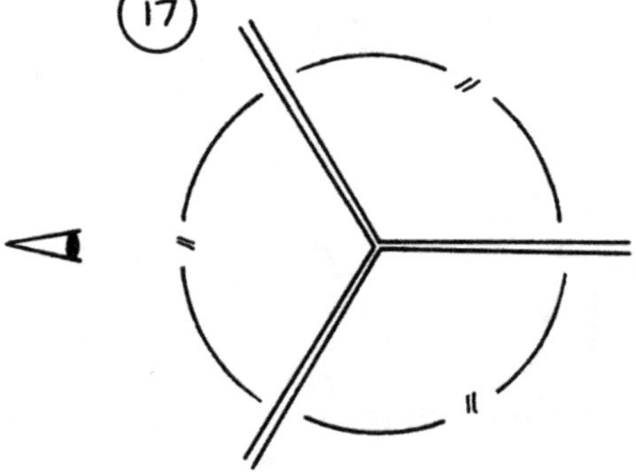

Top view, result of step 16. Return to side view as in picture 16.

18

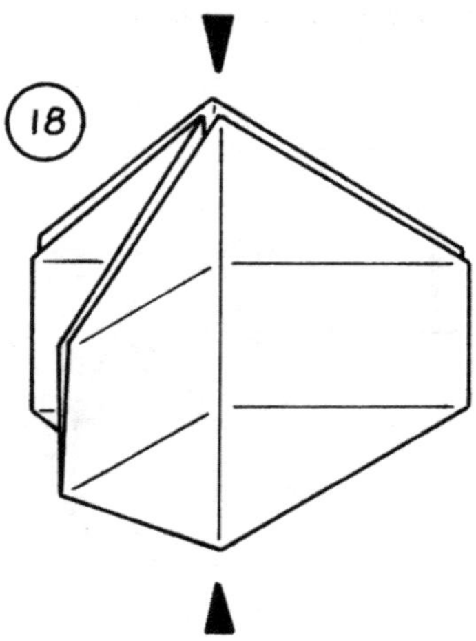

Hold top and bottom tips of model with thumb and forefinger, and with flaps positioned as in step 17.
Push top and bottom... coax it a little... into 3-D shape.

19

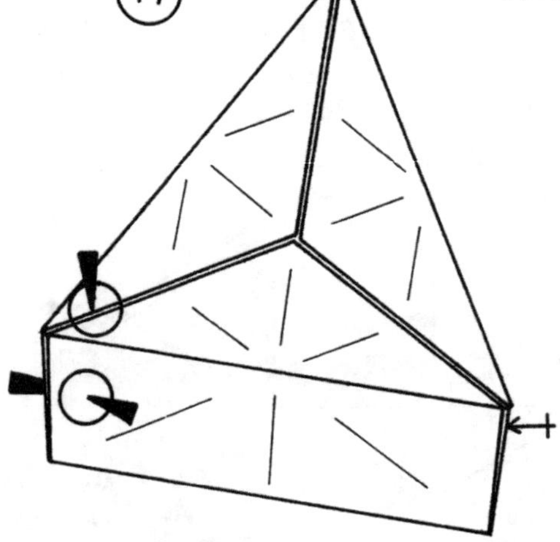

Finish corner by gently pinching the sides and pressing the top. You can feel paper repositioning inside, as you smooth the outer surfaces flat. Repeat at other two corners.

LILY

This model was inspired by a 4-petal flower designed by Bill Peck of Detroit, MI.

Use a thinner, foil-backed paper.

Model begins by folding a square into a hexagon shape. It is not necessary to cut off any paper flaps created in steps 9 and 10.

Begin color side down.

(1)

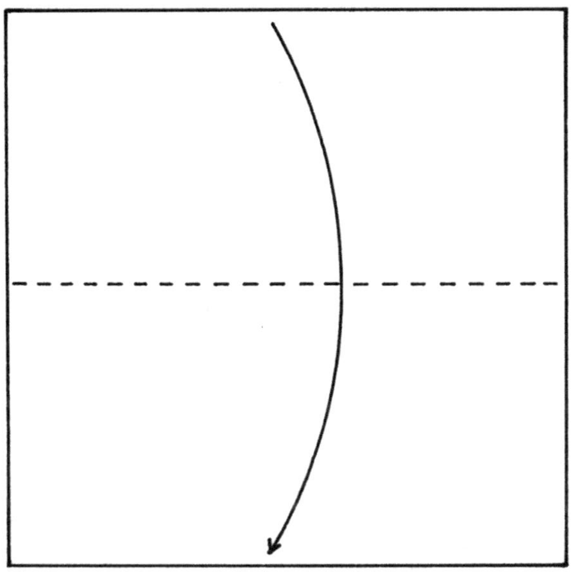

Fold in half, top-to-bottom.

(2)

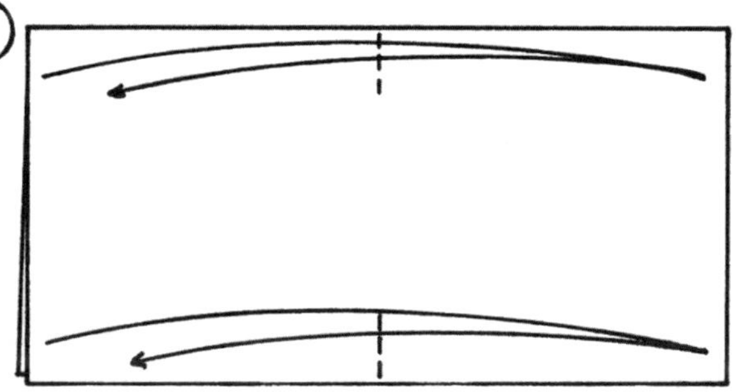

Crease landmarks at mid-points of top and bottom edges.

(3)

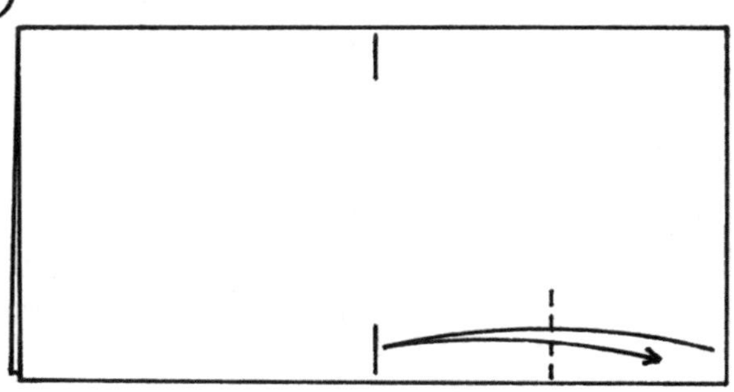

Crease landmark at mid-point between corner and center mark.

(4)

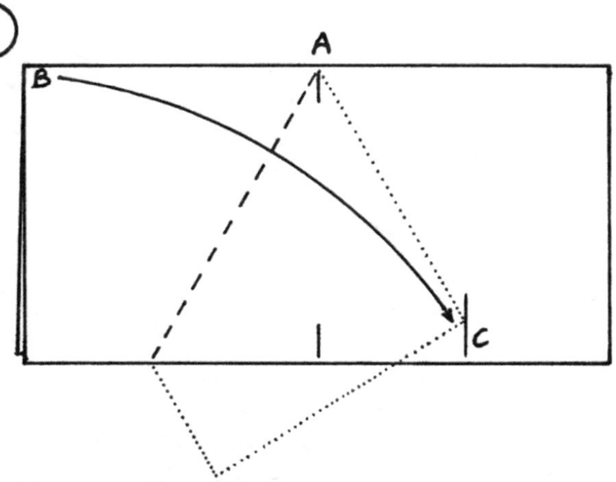

Begin valley fold at point A as you place corner B at landmark C.

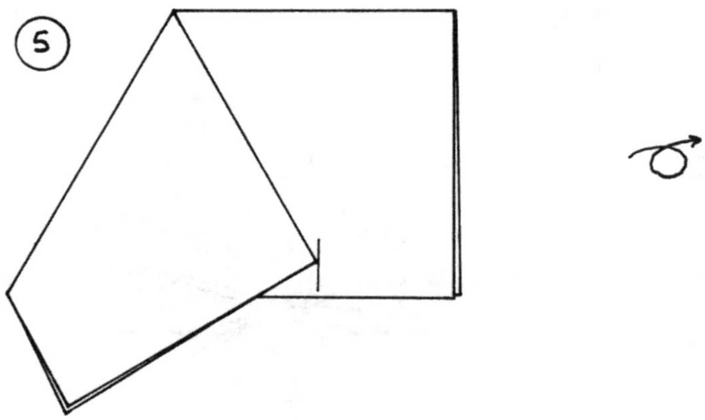

Step 4 finished. Turn model over side-to-side.

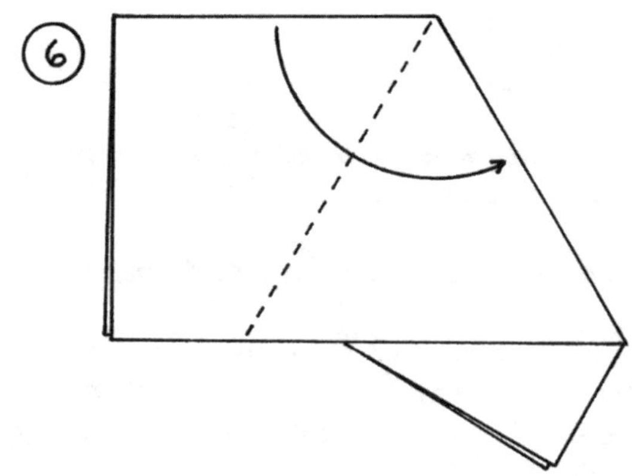

Valley fold top edge over to right edge.

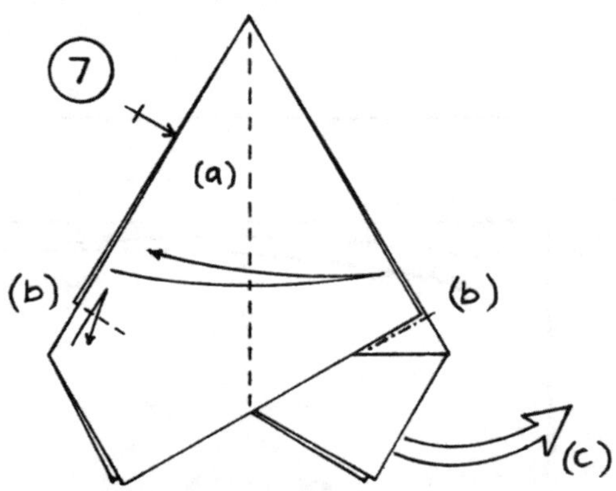

Prevent layers from slipping: (a) Valley fold and unfold top flap. Repeat behind. (b) Make the two landmarks, matching edges shown. (c) Unfold all and position color side down.

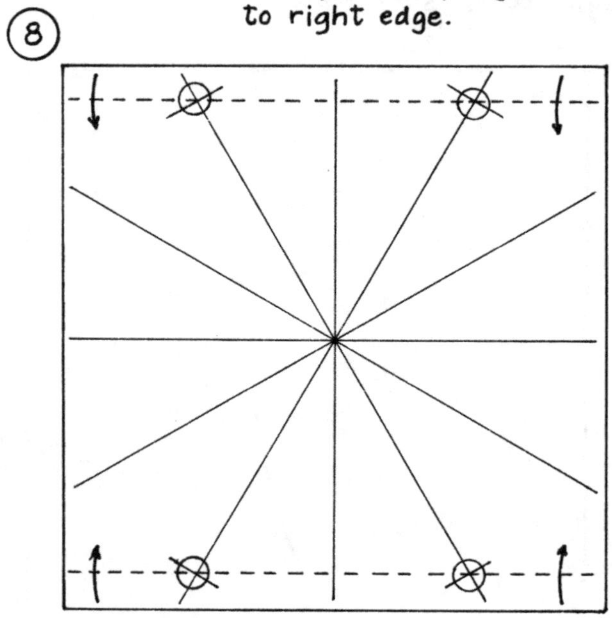

Valley fold through the circled intersections of the radii, and landmarks "b," step 7.

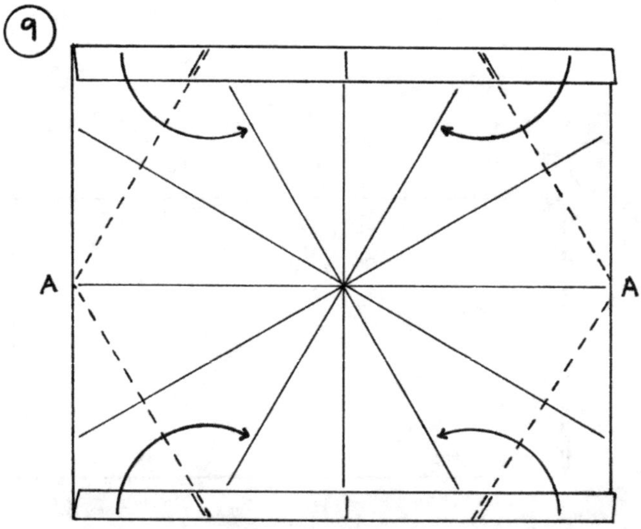

Form hexagon shape by valley folding edge segment to radius. The folds might not intersect point A, but this is OK.

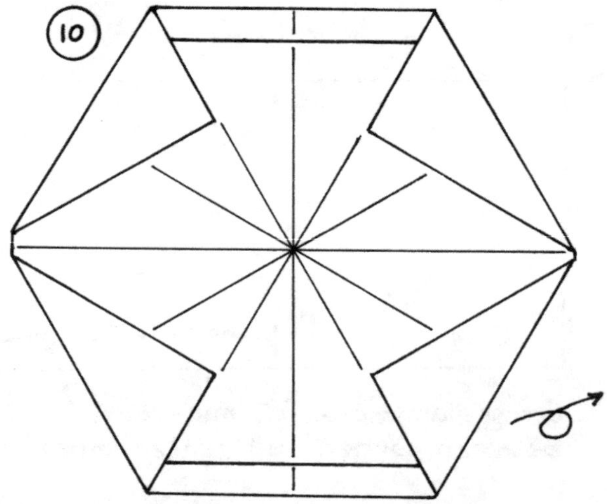

Step 9 finished. Turn model over side-to-side.

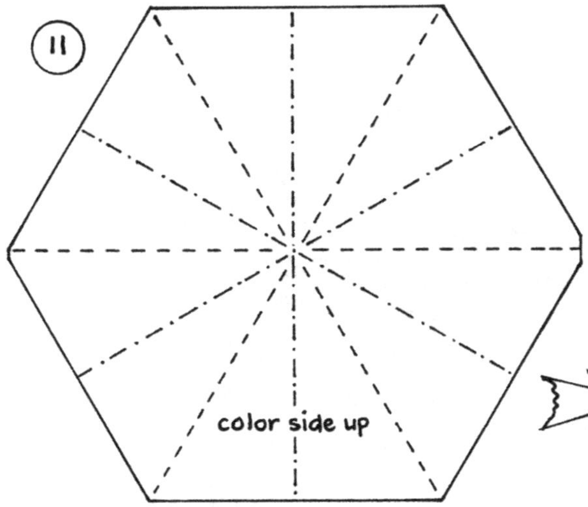

Use existing creases to form mountain and valley folds shown. Use folds to form a 6-flap preliminary base. Picture gets larger.

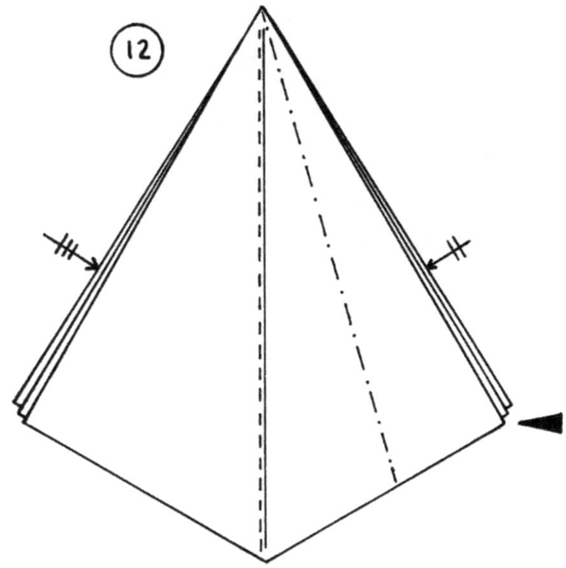

Squash fold top right flap. NOTE: In this step and next several steps, re-arrange flaps as you fold to keep an equal number of flaps on each side of center line. Squash fold the 5 other flaps.

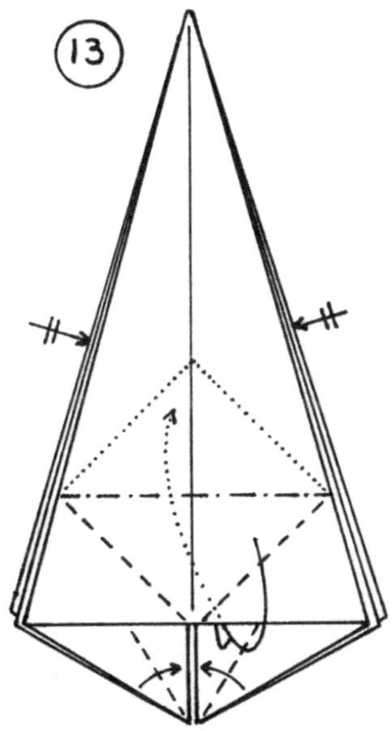

NOTE: There are 6 flaps on each side of center line, steps 13-16. Not all flaps are shown. In this step, raise the horizontal edge and form a petal fold. Then, reverse fold triangular area up inside. See dotted lines. Repeat on back. Re-arrange flaps as needed to show above position, and repeat 4 more times.

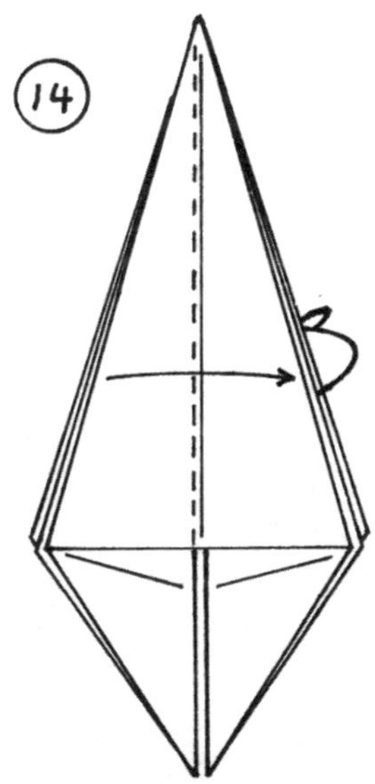

Fold top left layer only, to the right. Fold rear right layer only, to the left.

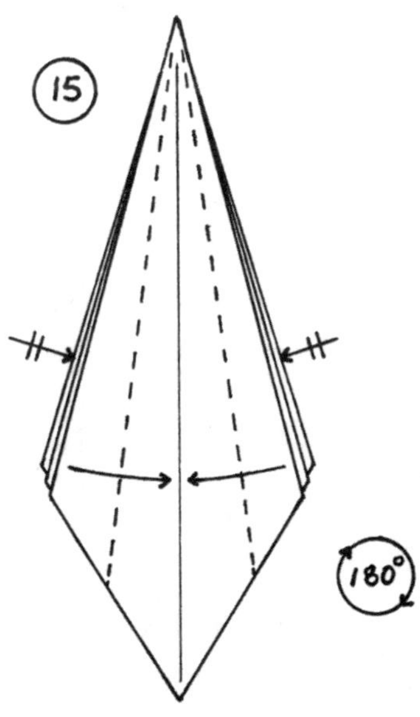

Form valley folds, but leave small space between edges. Repeat behind. Re-arrange flaps and repeat 4 more times. Rotate model 180°.

16

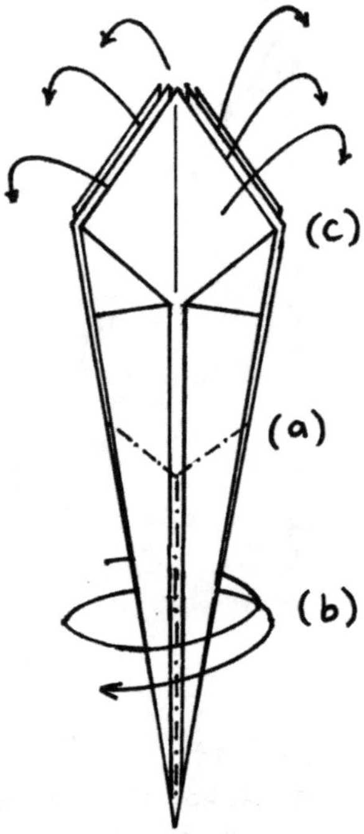

(a) Feel where the greatest, inside thickness ends, then form a rabbit-ear fold to narrow stem.
(b) Twist the stem.
(c) Open out and shape the petals. Curl petals back. Slightly curl and twist a few petals to make them appear more natural.

17

Finished LILY.

120° MODULE SERIES

MAT
SOCCER BALL
DODECAHEDRON
TRUNCATED ICOSAHEDRON

Three modules connect at 120° angles. Using 3" X 2" sheets, a Soccer Ball will have a 3½" diameter. A Dodecahedron will be 2¾" tall and 3¼" wide. The Truncated Icosahedron's diameter is about 7½".

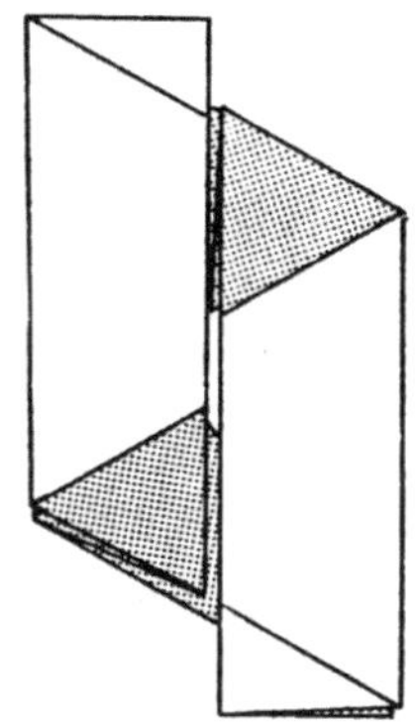

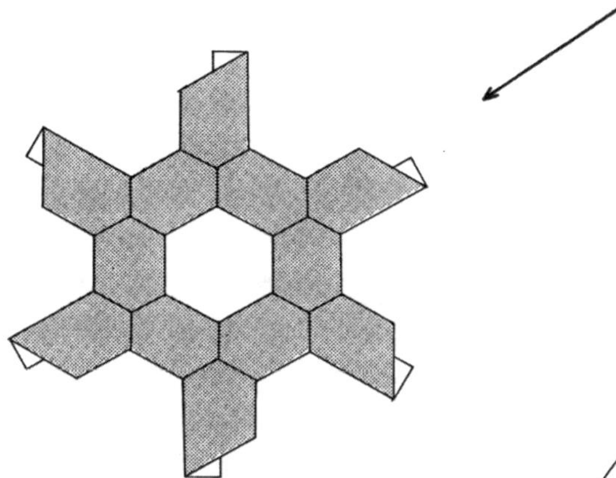

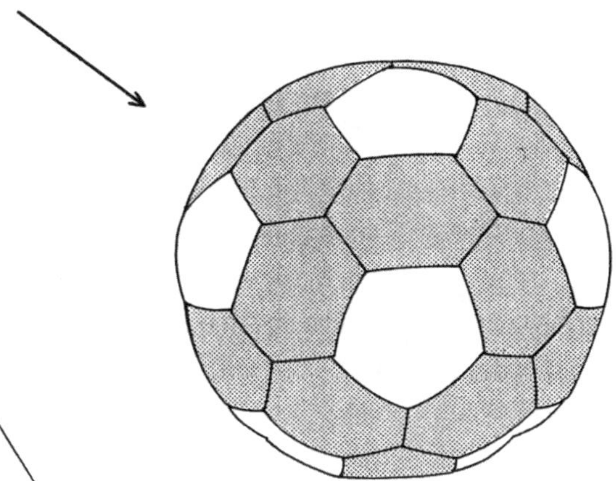

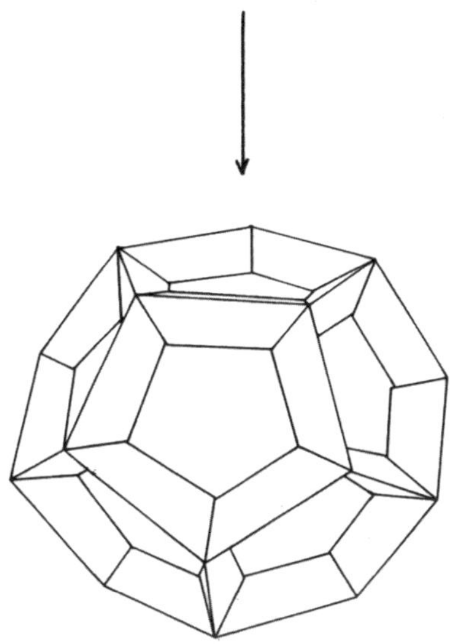

①

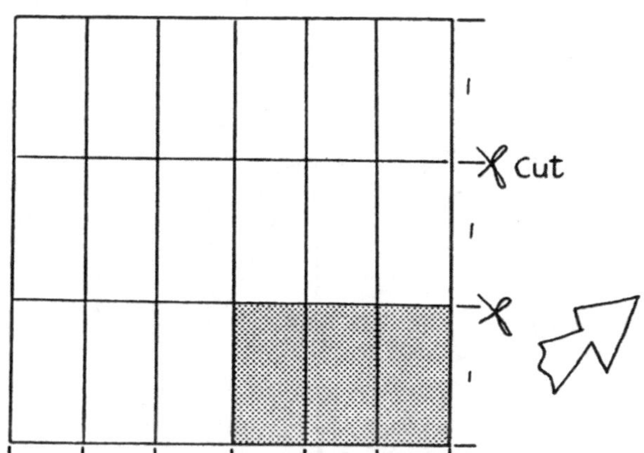

Shaded area is one piece.

②

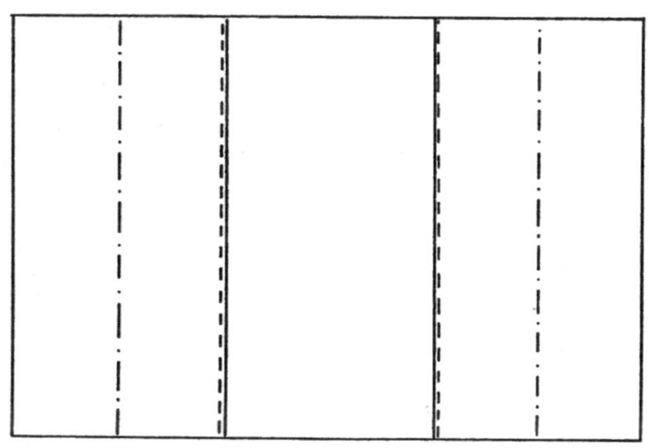

Picture enlarged. Make folds in order shown.

③

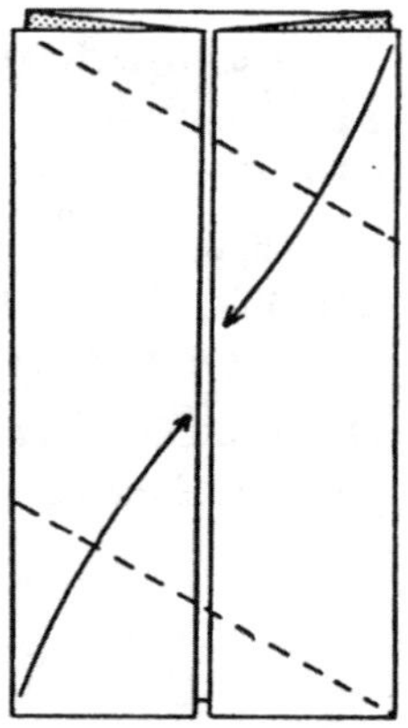

Grip all layers tightly
as you fold to prevent slipping.

④

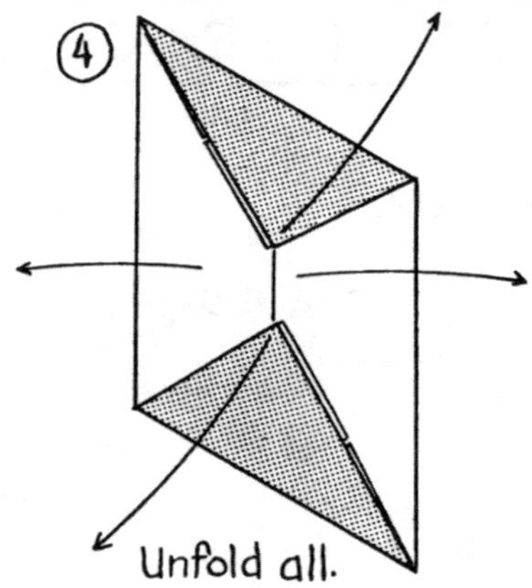

Unfold all.

⑤

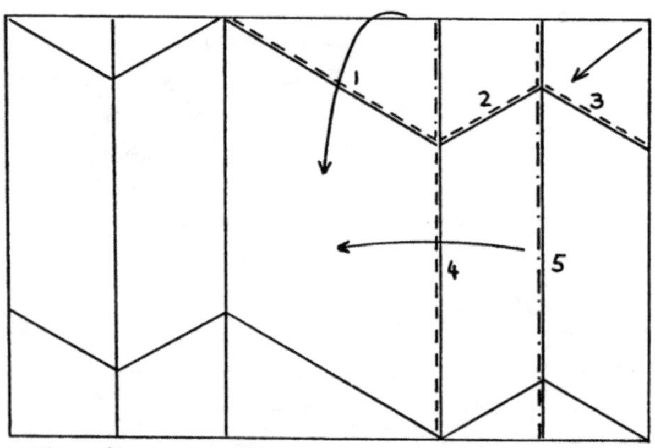

Valley fold along the creases numbered
1, 2, and 3, as you re-pleat the model as in step 2.

⑥

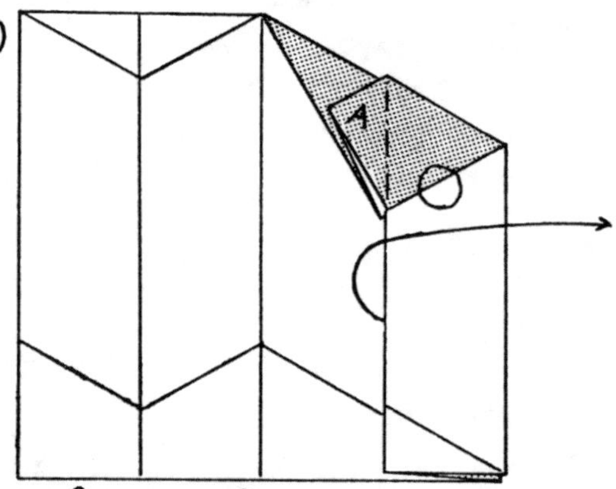

Unfold this flap like a door
while pressing the circled
area. This will cause the
mountain fold to form, as
tab A opens and squashes.

⑦

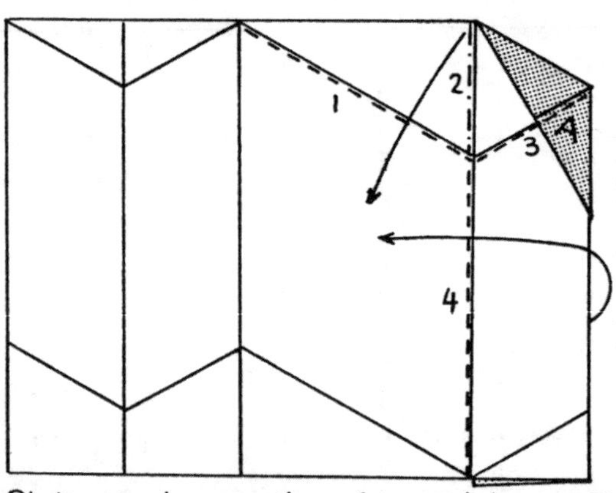

Picture shows step 6 completed with
tab A squashed across corner.
Make next folds in order shown.

⑧

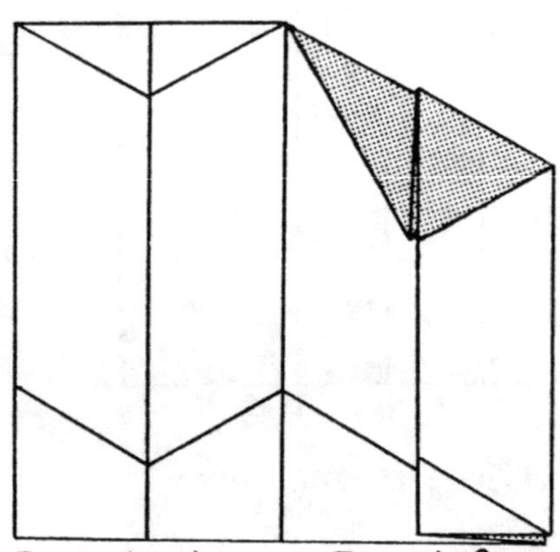

Repeat steps 5-7 on left end.

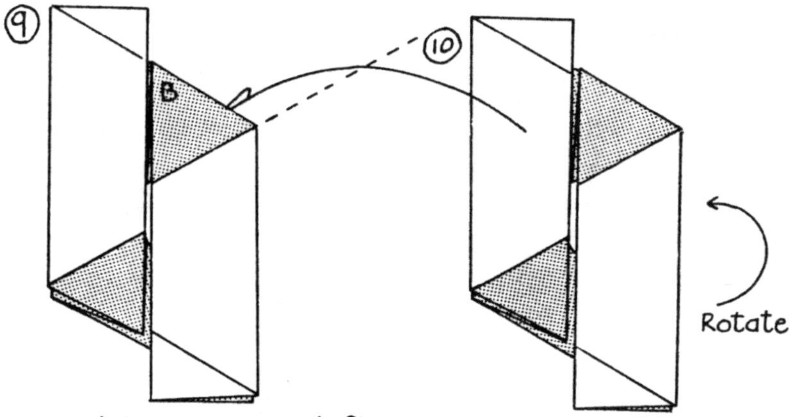

Module completed. Lift point B to notice valley fold behind the triangle. Also notice pocket on left edge of triangle.

Make two more modules.

Here is a second module held parallel to the first in step 9. Rotate the second piece, sliding its left edge underneath the triangle in the first piece to rest on the valley fold inside.

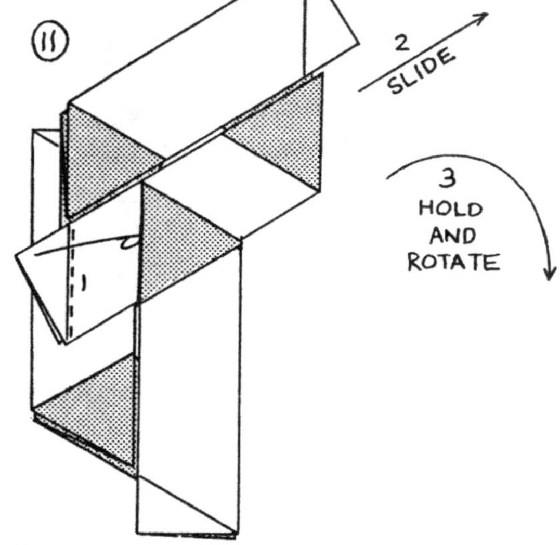

1.) Valley fold tab, and 2.) slide the module in the direction shown, and insert tab into pocket on left edge of triangle.

Hold tightly where joined and rotate to position shown in next step.

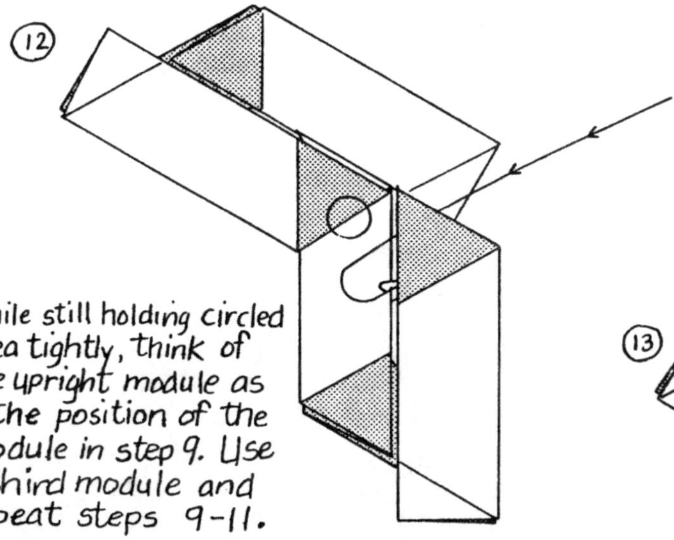

While still holding circled area tightly, think of the upright module as in the position of the module in step 9. Use a third module and repeat steps 9-11.

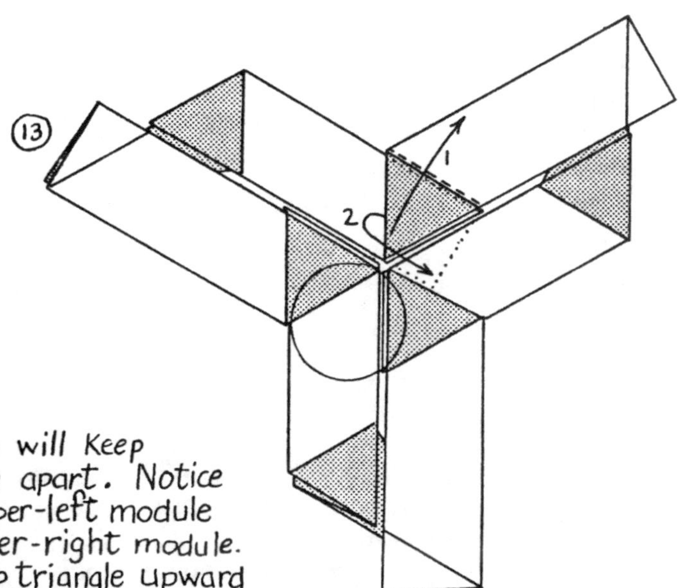

Holding circled area will keep modules from coming apart. Notice right end of the upper-left module is under the upper-right module. 1.) Valley fold the top triangle upward toward the right; then, 2.) re-arrange the right end of the upper-left module to be above the upper-left module.

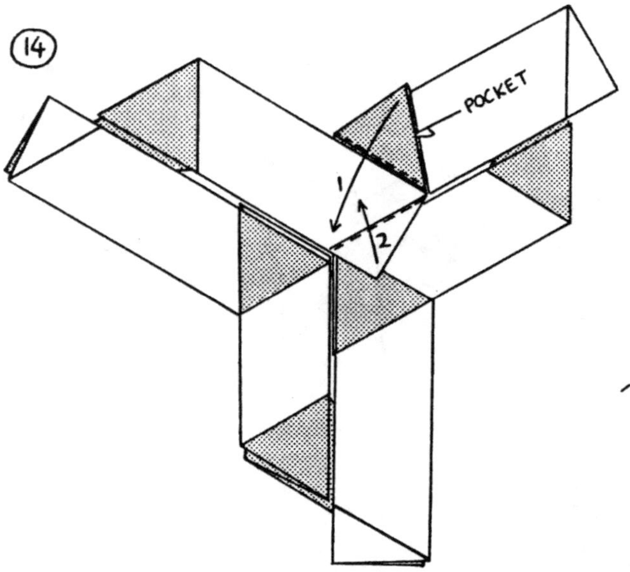

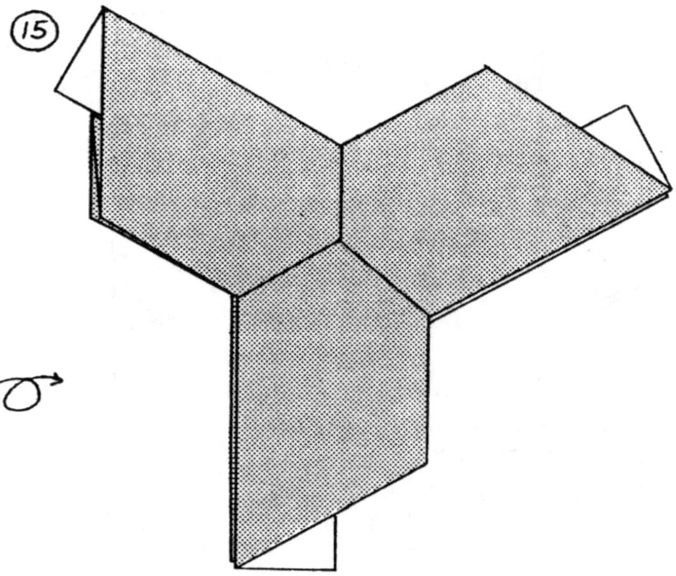

1.) Valley fold upper triangle back down to its previous position; then 2.) insert tab in pocket, as with other connections. Result not shown. Turn model over.

Reverse (good) side.
One connection completed.

VARIATIONS: The 120° Module can be used to make a variety of constructions. All employ connections of three modules, joined according to the diagrams, followed by joining additional modules to the free ends, etc. Modular design also permits use of interesting color patterns.

MATS AND SCREENS: When a pattern is made by six connections joined around a hole, a flat construction is made.

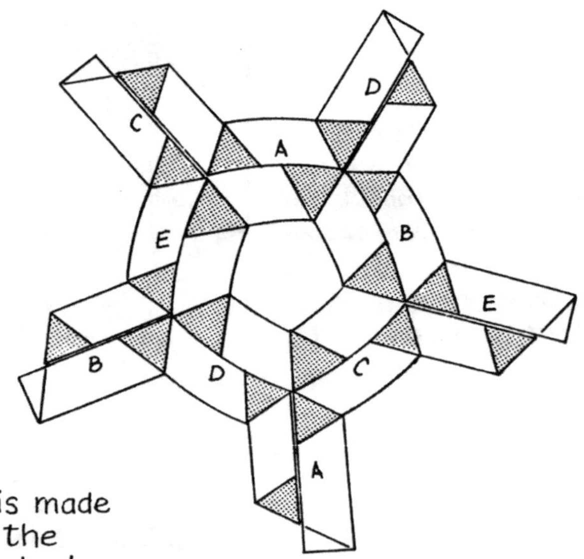

SOCCER BALL: 30 modules. When a pattern is made of just five connections around each hole, the construction will curl into a 3-dimensional shape. I like to prepare 5 foil squares, each a different color, according to the instructions in step 1. Then, in order to construct a soccer ball so that no two pieces the same color are connected, follow letter pattern shown. The order of colors around each hole varies from hole to hole.

DODECAHEDRON, or Inverted Soccer Ball: 30 modules. Made the same as the Soccer Ball except: 1.) Each module, when completed to step 9, must then be valley folded carefully, lengthwise, before assembly; and 2.) during assembly, this fold is used to invert the material partly into each hole, rather than permitting a rounded shape as in the Soccer Ball. This results in a dodecahedron with pentagon-shaped faces.

TRUNCATED ICOSAHEDRON: 90 modules, prepared as for Dodecahedron. It has 12 pentagon faces, with material inverted into the holes as in Dodecahedron, and 20 hexagon faces.

When constructing, use a pattern in which a pentagon shaped hole (with sunken material) is constructed, followed by only hexagon shaped holes at the next concentric level. The hexagon faces are smooth and level to the surface, not inverted. Complete the model, always shaping the globe with pentagon holes, and surrounding these only with hexagon faces. Hexagon faces can touch each other; pentagon faces do not.

This geometric structure is the same as in Robert Neale's modular piece called "No More After This," although the modules are quite different.

FLYING CRANE ON A STAND

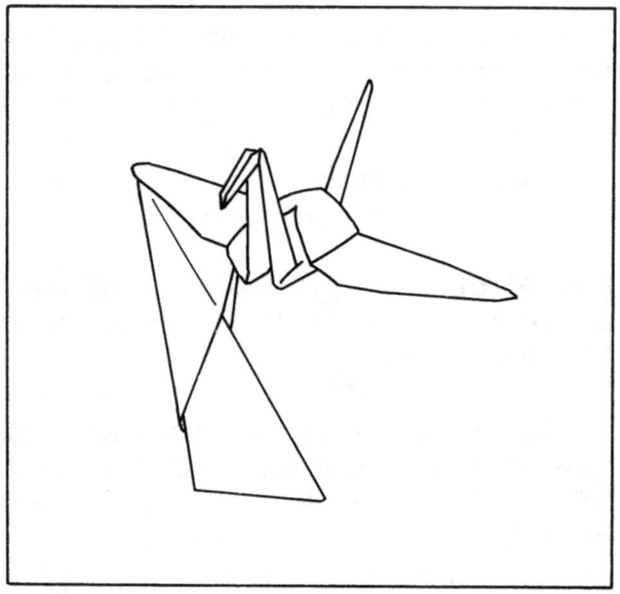

This model may be folded from a dollar bill, and it also looks nice folded from a duo-paper rectangle with proportions similar to a dollar, i.e., 3 x 7. Duo-paper with a foil layer helps the model hold its shape.

Steps 1-5 show how to make two dollar-shaped sheets from a square. A dollar shape made from a 10" square produces a model with height of crane from surface of 2½" to 3" and a wing span of 3¼." From a dollar bill, height is 1½" to 2." Wingspan is 2 ⅛."

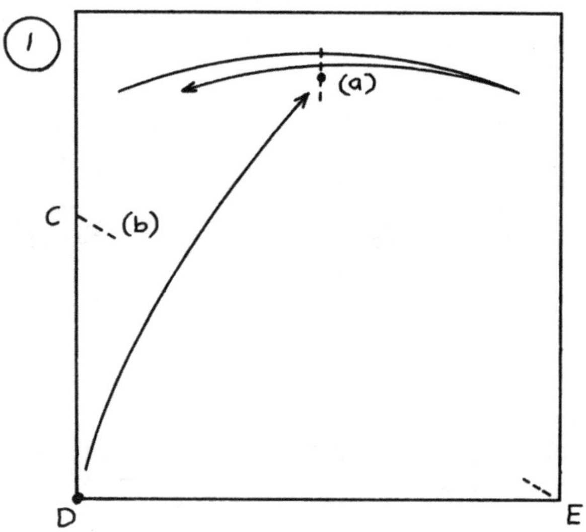

(a) Crease landmark "a" by folding in half and unfolding.
(b) Landmark at corner E while simultaneously placing corner D on landmark "a." Then, crease landmark "C" along left edge.

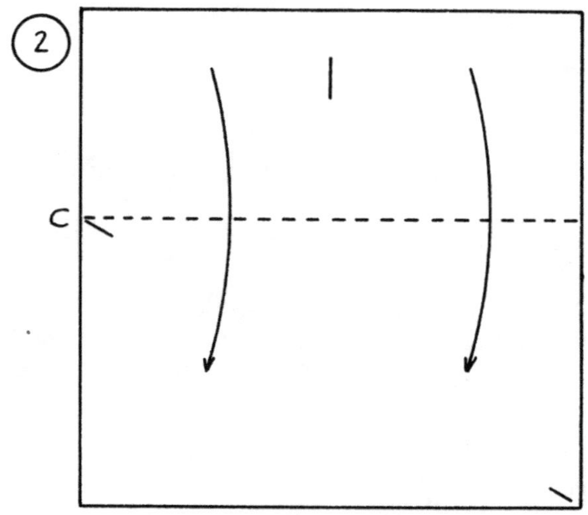

Valley fold horizontally at landmark "C."

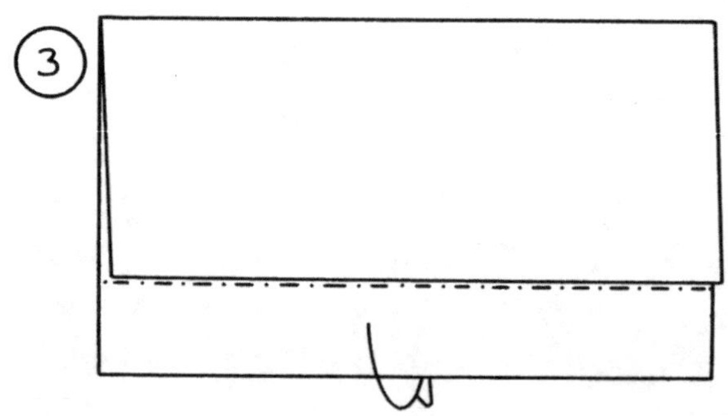

Mountain fold the back layer to match edge of front layer.

4

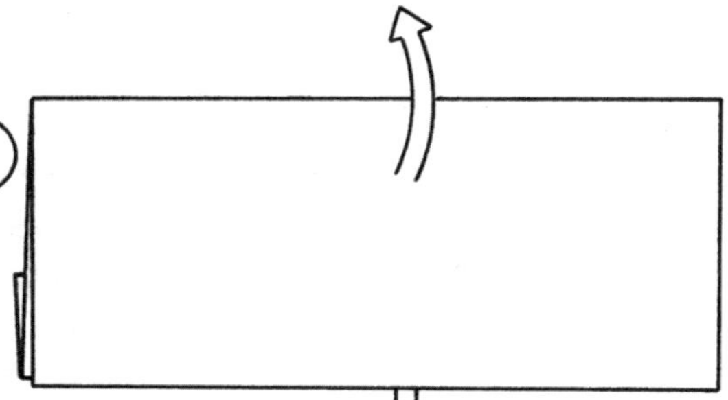

Unfold all.

5

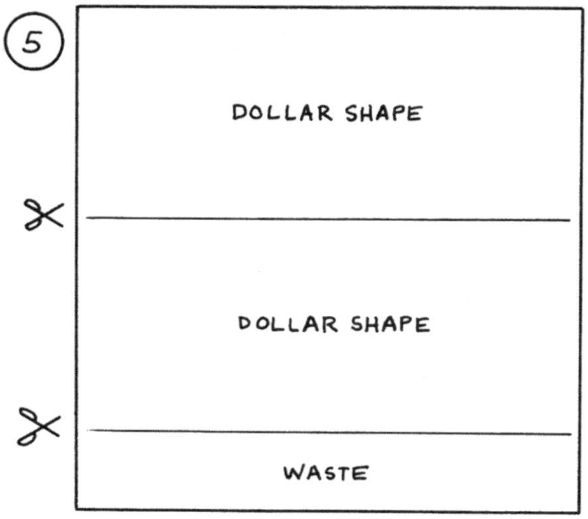

Begin Folding The Model. If using duo-paper, begin colored side chosen for the crane placed down.

Cut along creases.

6

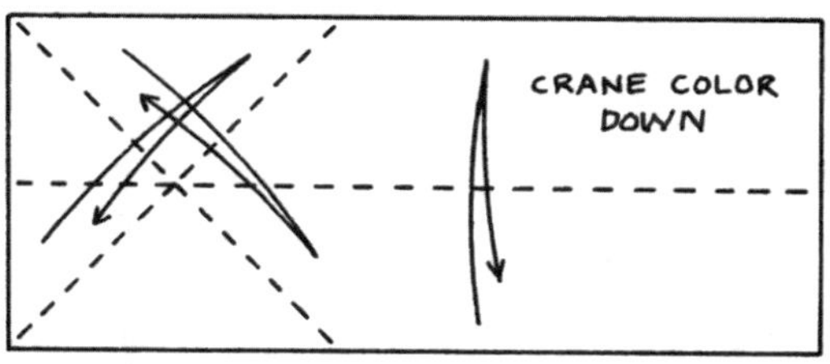

Valley fold in half lengthwise, and unfold. Then, on the left end, valley fold and unfold both diagonals.

7

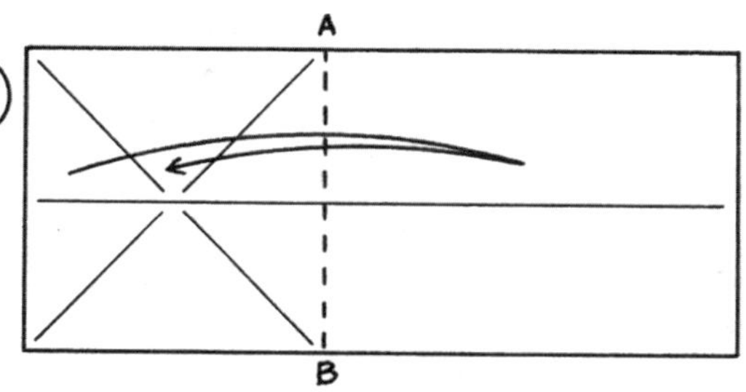

Valley fold and unfold between points A and B.

8

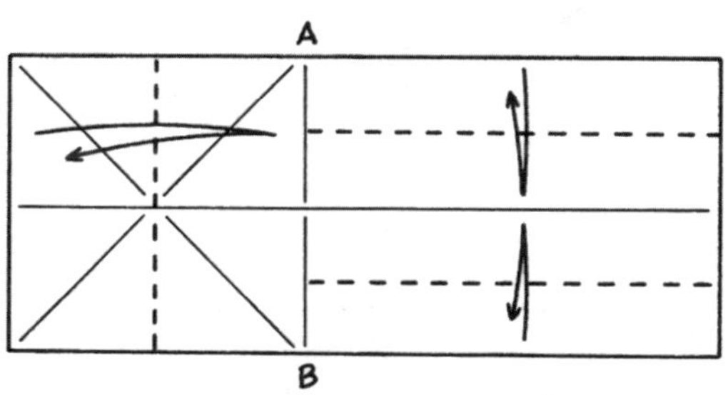

Valley fold and unfold left edge to crease AB. Then, cupboard fold and unfold between crease AB and the right edge.

9

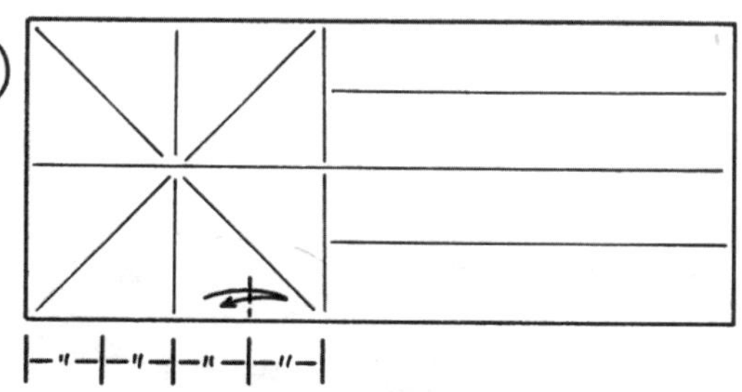

Fold a landmark on edge of the square area, 3/4 the distance from left edge.

10

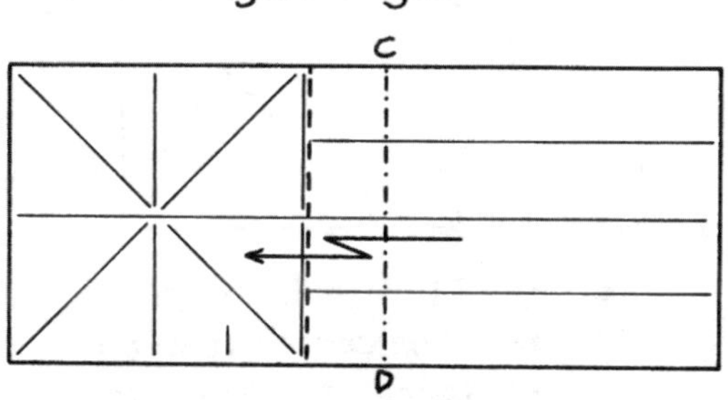

Pleat fold. Crease CD is located by placing it at landmark made in step 9.

11

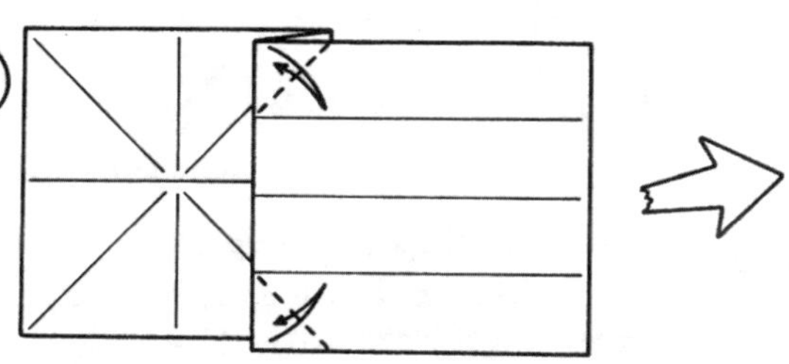

Fold and unfold the two diagonals. Picture gets larger.

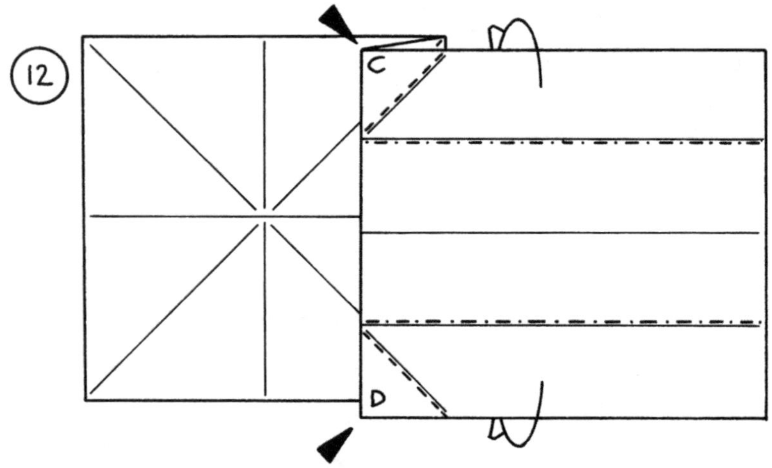

Mountain fold along existing creases, bringing top and bottom edges to the center line on the underside. Corners C and D will flatten and relocate underneath.

(a) Make a rabbit-ear fold on the flap, then position the flap downward.
(b) Rotate the model ¼ turn counter-clockwise.

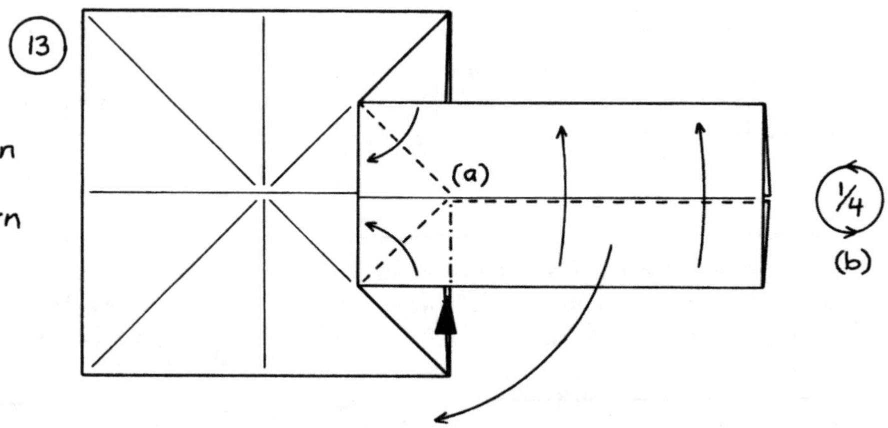

View of step 13 completed. The next several steps are pictured with the Stand Flap removed.

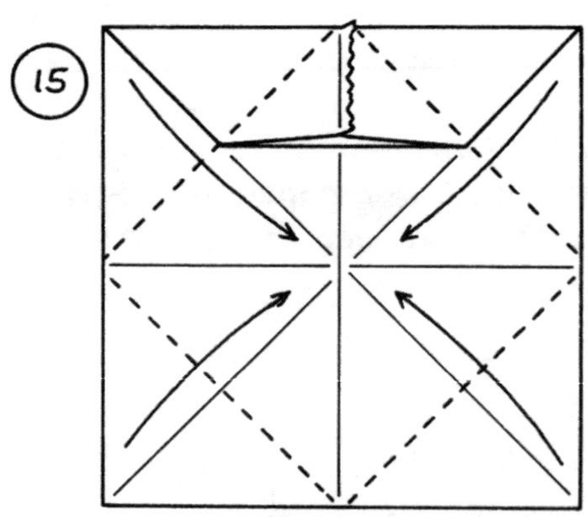

Valley fold all 4 corners toward the center, leaving a small space so edges do not touch. Swing the flap out of the way as needed.

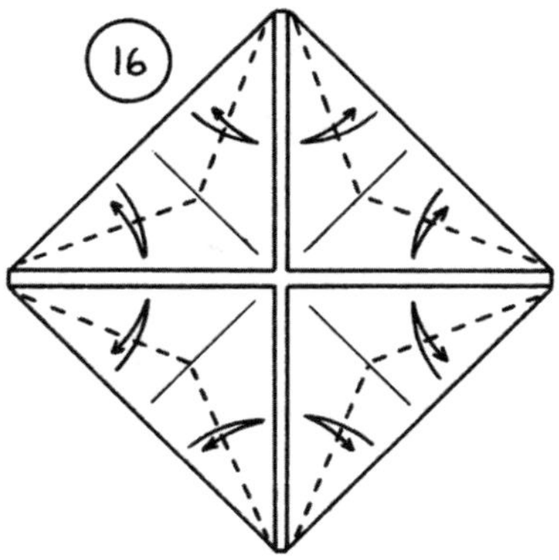

Square shape is now the crane's color on both sides, and the Stand Flap is the opposite color. Valley fold and unfold 8 creases needed to form a bird base, again, leaving a small space.

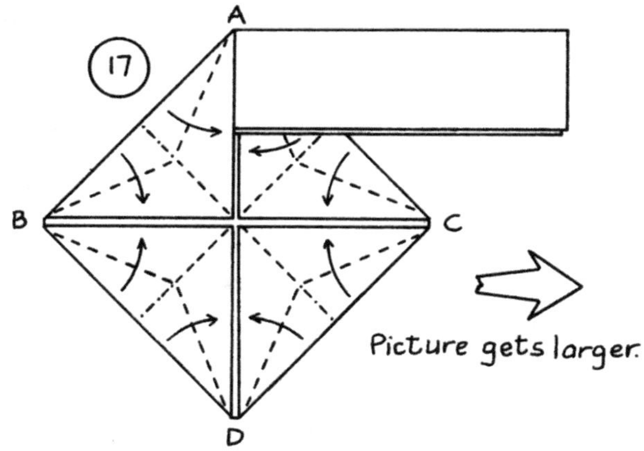

Some details not shown. Form a bird base into the familiar kite-shaped position (A, B and C meet at D). Stand Flap re-positions at bottom.

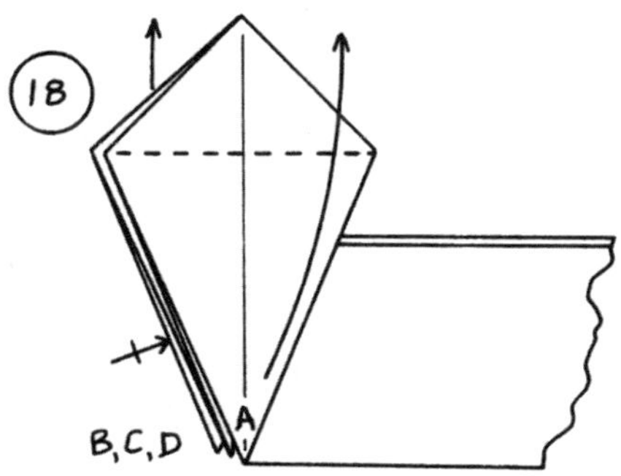

Valley fold front flap up; Stand Flap follows along. Repeat on rear flap.

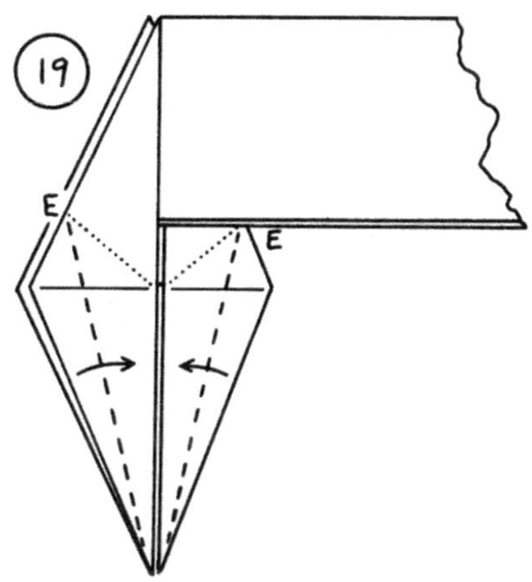

Dotted lines show location of hidden edges meeting the model edges at points "E." Valley fold on front layer from E to bottom tip. Repeat behind by matching rear folds to the front surface folds.

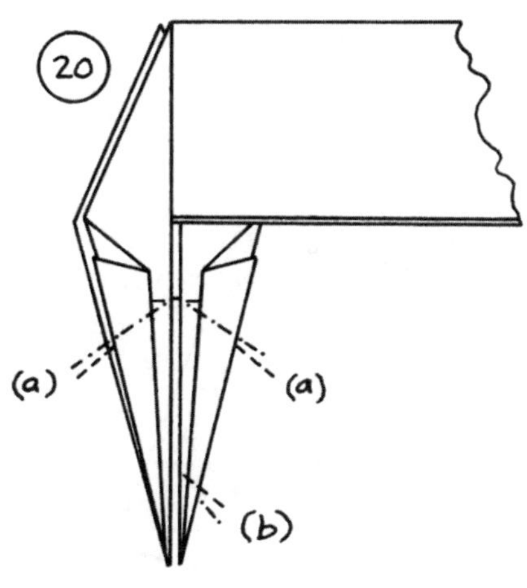

(a) Inside reverse fold neck and tail flap upward.
(b) Inside reverse fold to form head.

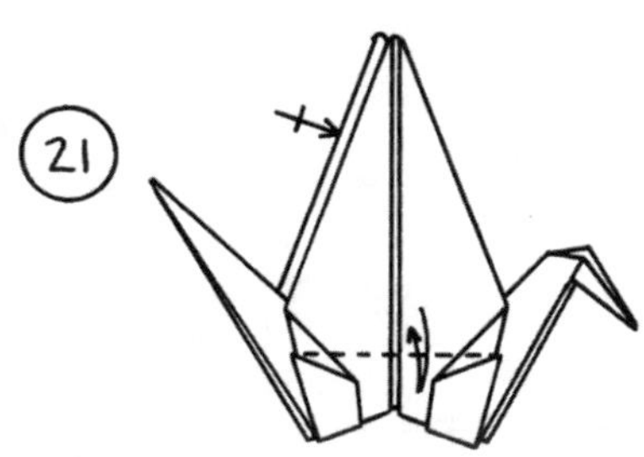

View of finished crane in flat position, with Stand Flap not showing. Valley fold and unfold the wing. Repeat behind.

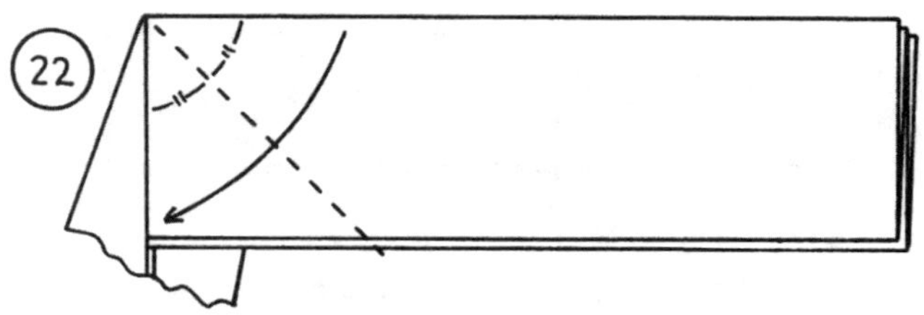

Folding the Stand. Crane not shown, except attachment to wing. Valley fold all layers to center line.

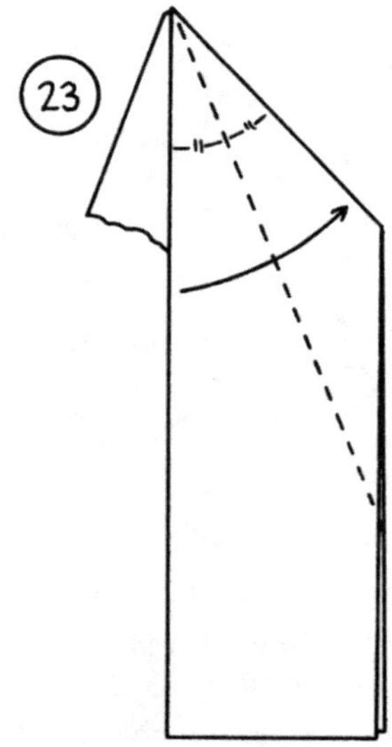

Using all layers, valley fold the left edge to the slanted right edge.

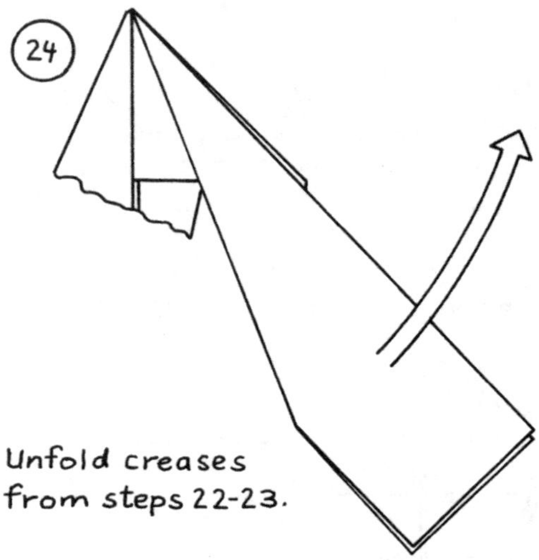

Unfold creases from steps 22-23.

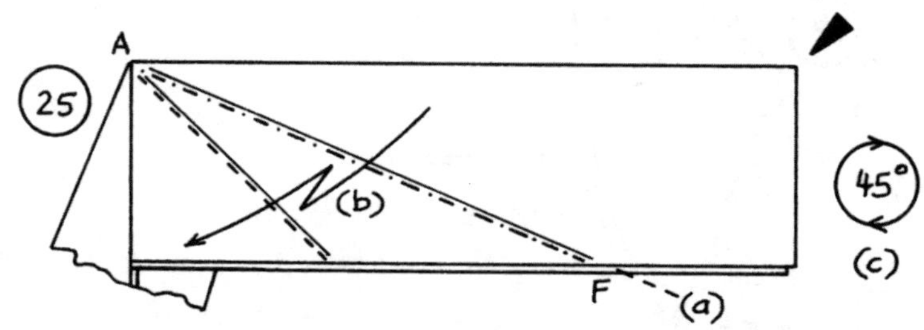

See crease AF; all 4 layers are mountain-folded. (a) Change the back 2 layers to valley folds as viewed from the front. (b) Pleat front 2 layers to the left, forming a squash fold. (c) Rotate 45° clockwise.

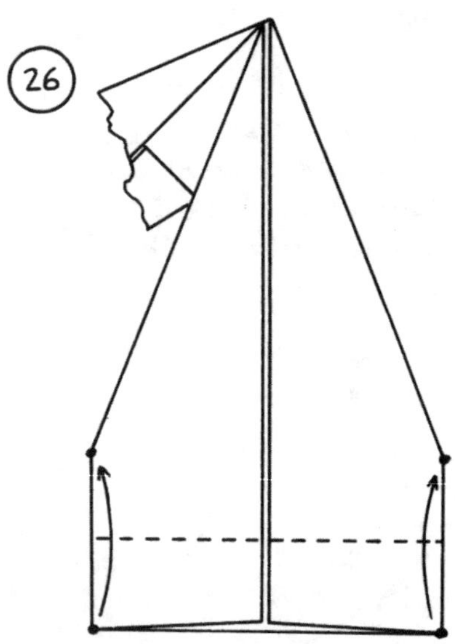

Valley fold bottom corners to side corners.

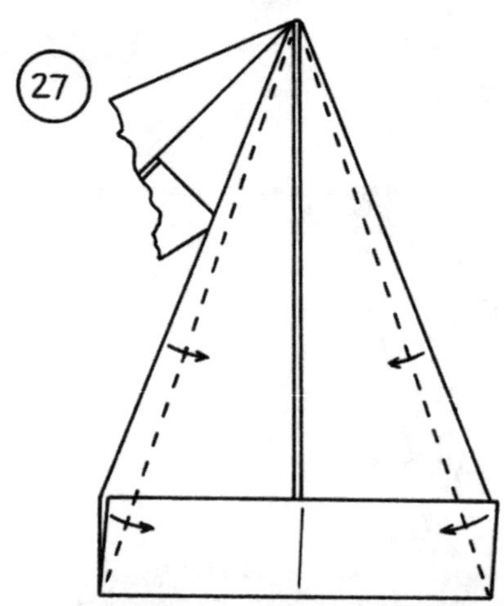

Prevent layers from slipping, and make two valley folds from top point to bottom corners.

28

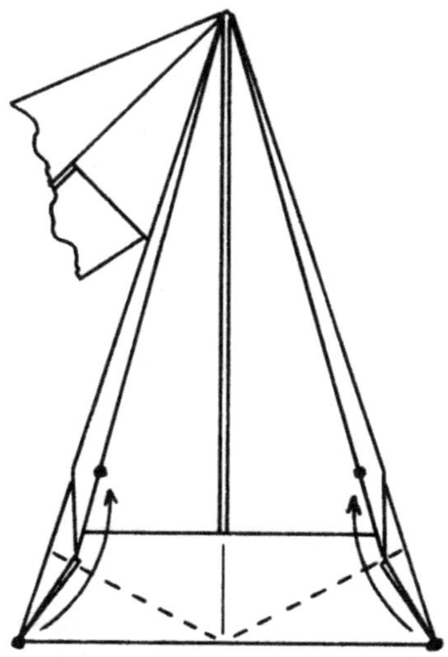

Make two valley folds, beginning at center of bottom edge and located by placing bottom corners on folded edges where marked.

29

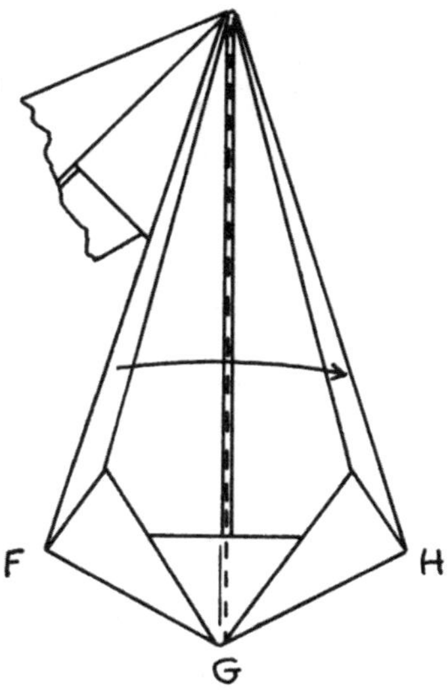

Valley fold in half, left to right. The stand is now finished. Edges FG and GH are the base to place on a surface for display, spread apart as two sides of a triangle.

3-D the Model and Stand It Up.

(1) See step 21. Use the wing creases made in that step to position wings outward at a 90° angle from body.

(2) Gently pull/wiggle wings outward to 3-D the body.

(3) If needed, use a thin tool inserted up through hole underneath to shape the body. I use a paper clip wire with end bent around with pliers. Avoid puncturing paper.

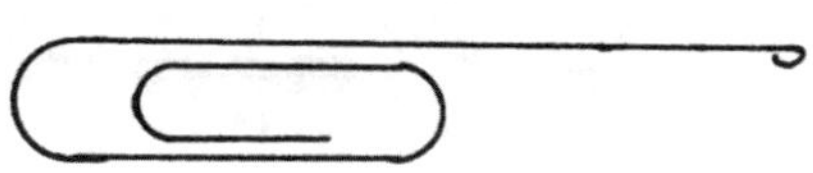

30

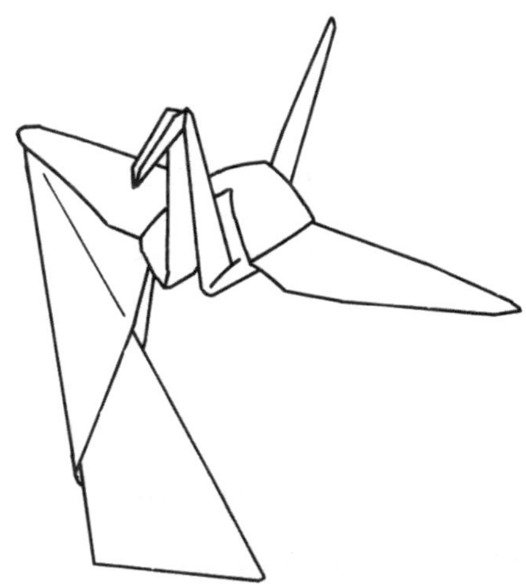

CANDLESTICK

3 x 1 Rectangle. Foil paper.
Precrease in thirds.
Begin white side up.

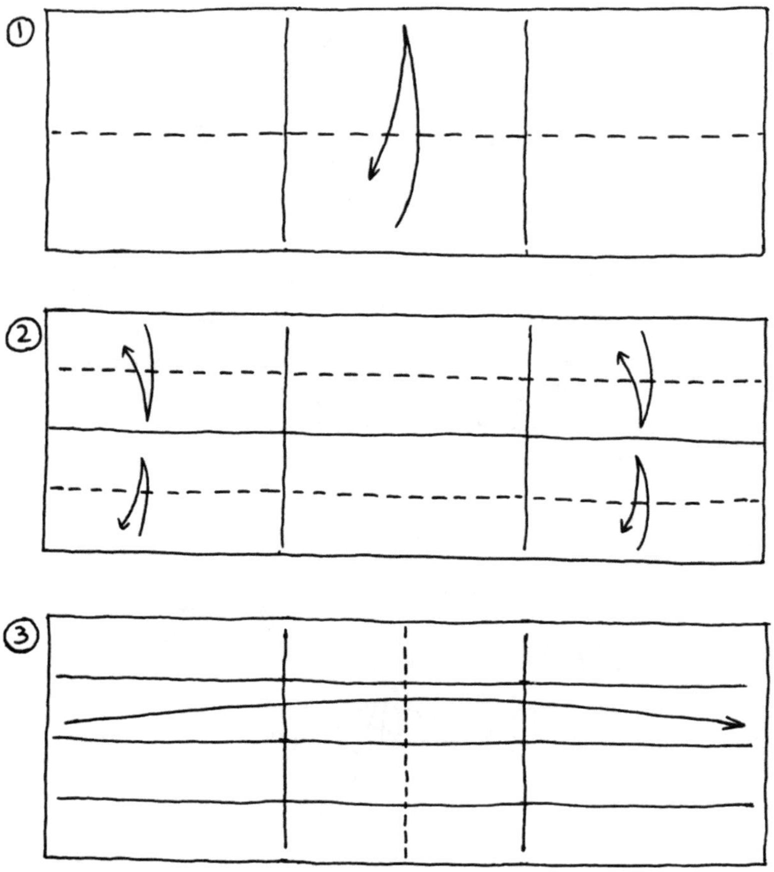

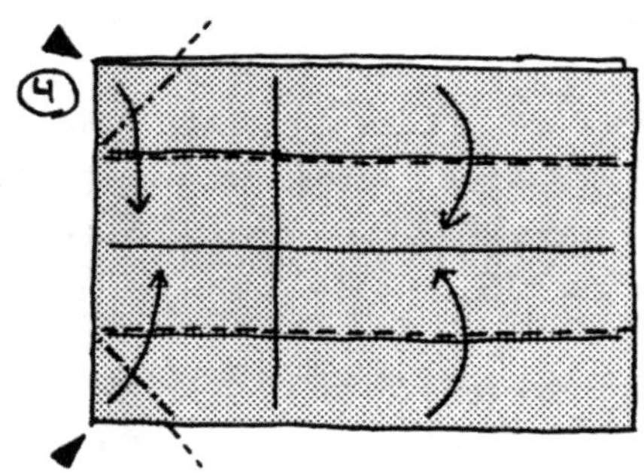

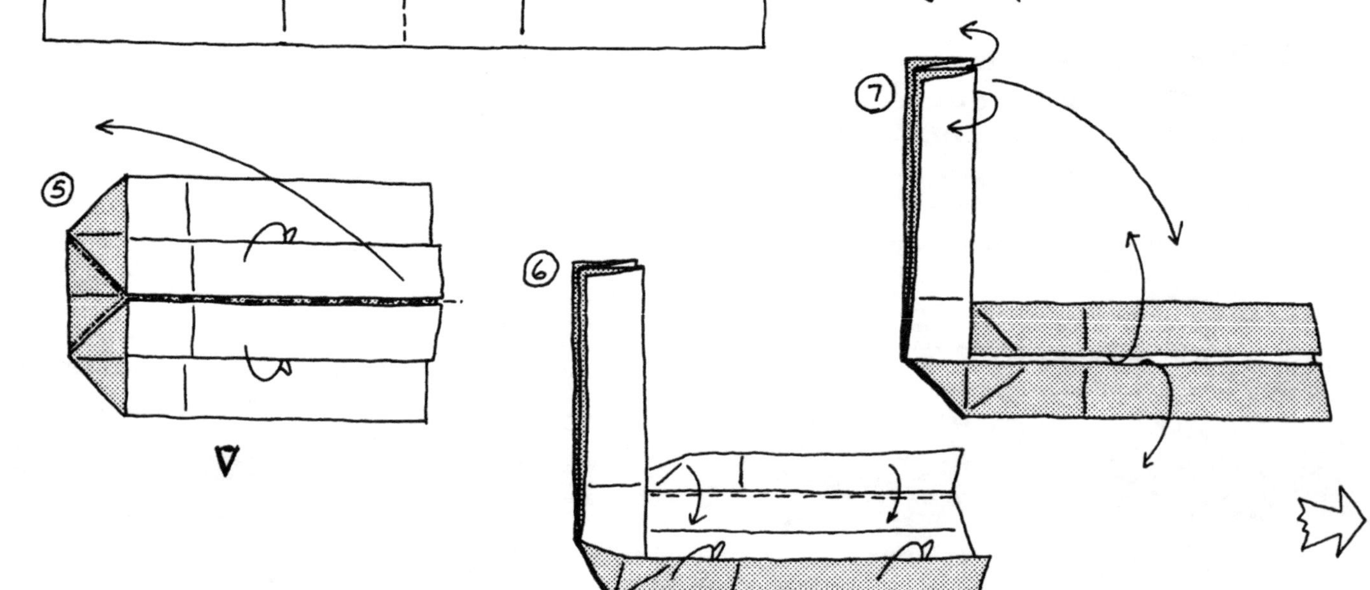

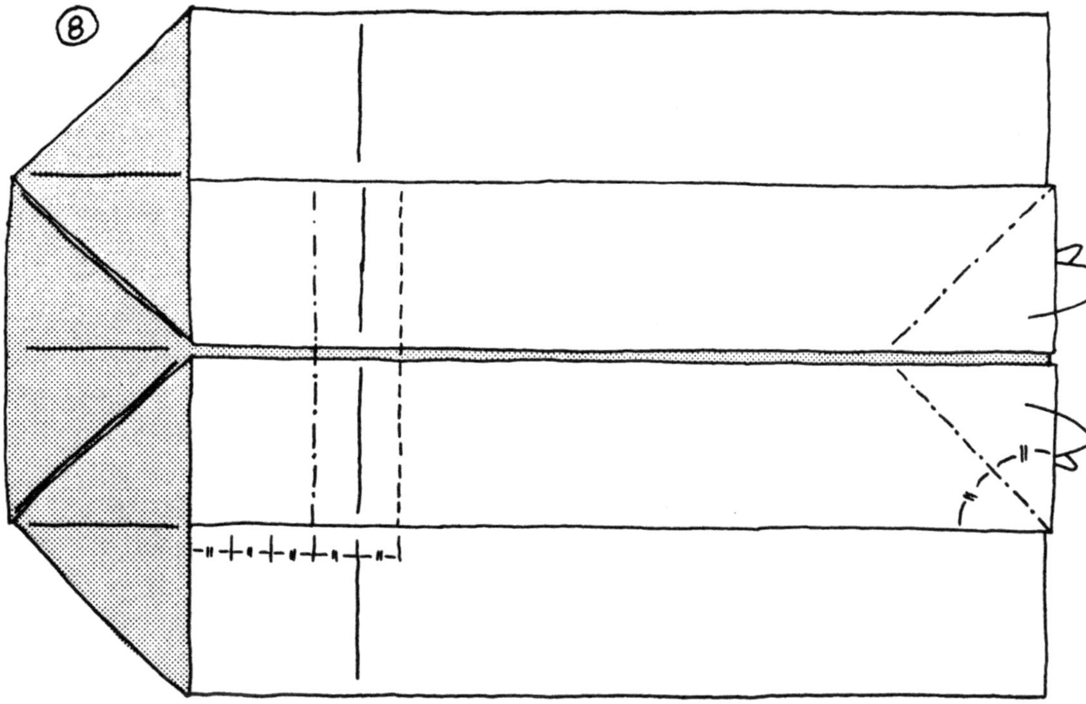

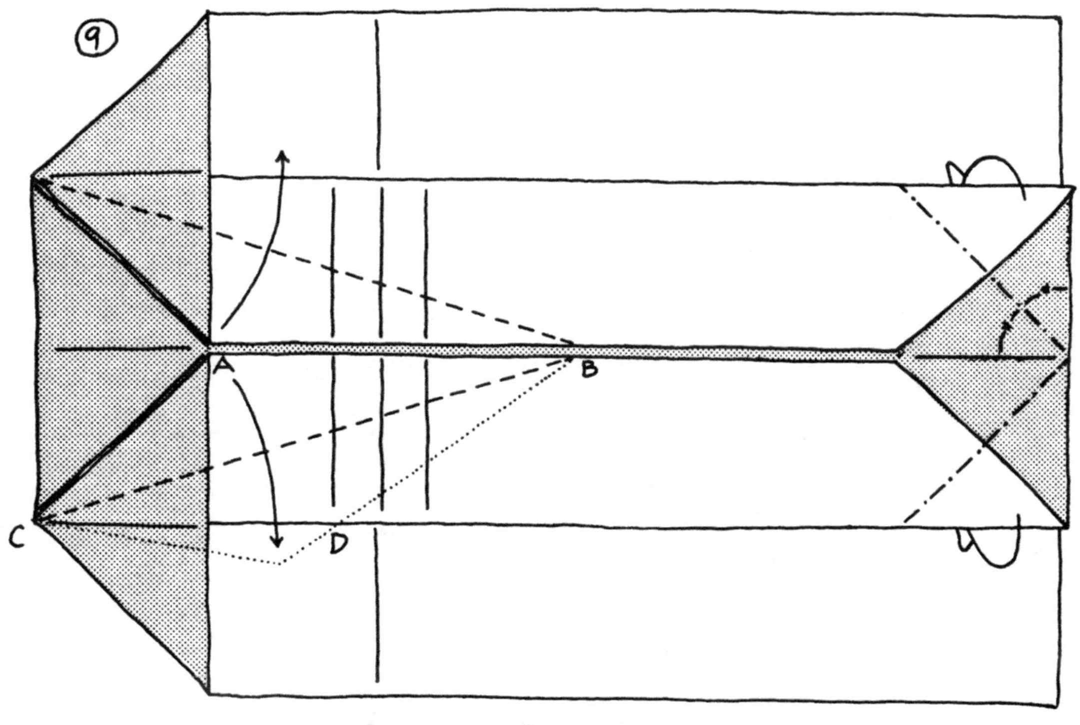

Begin valley fold at C. Position edge AB so that it intersects point D. Dotted line shows resulting position.

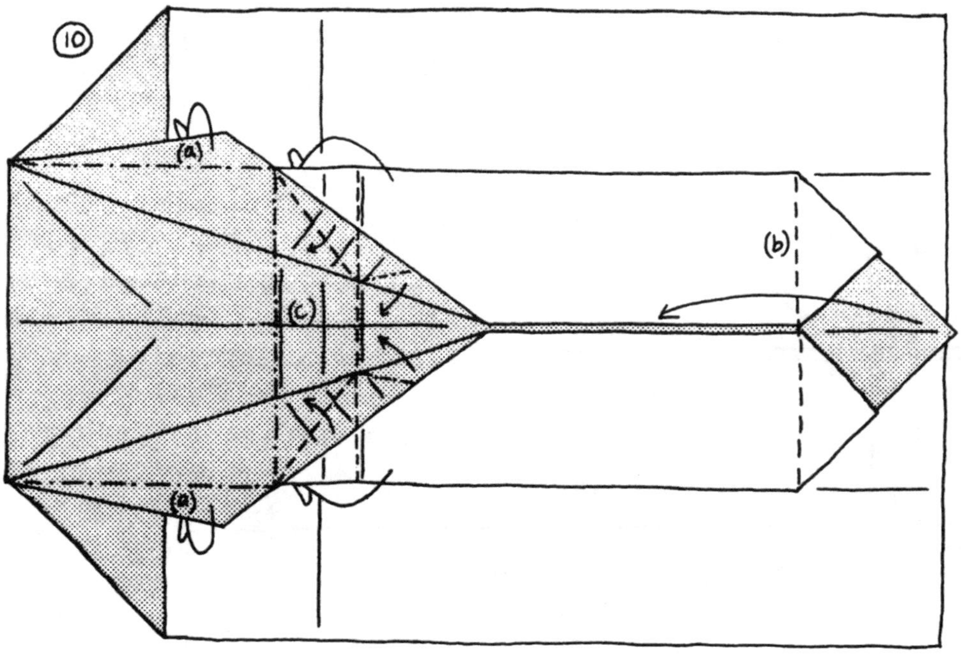

(a) Mountain fold the flaps behind. (b) Valley fold. (c) Use vertical mountain and valley folds to pleat in direction of left end. As you pleat, make the small folds shown inside the pleat.

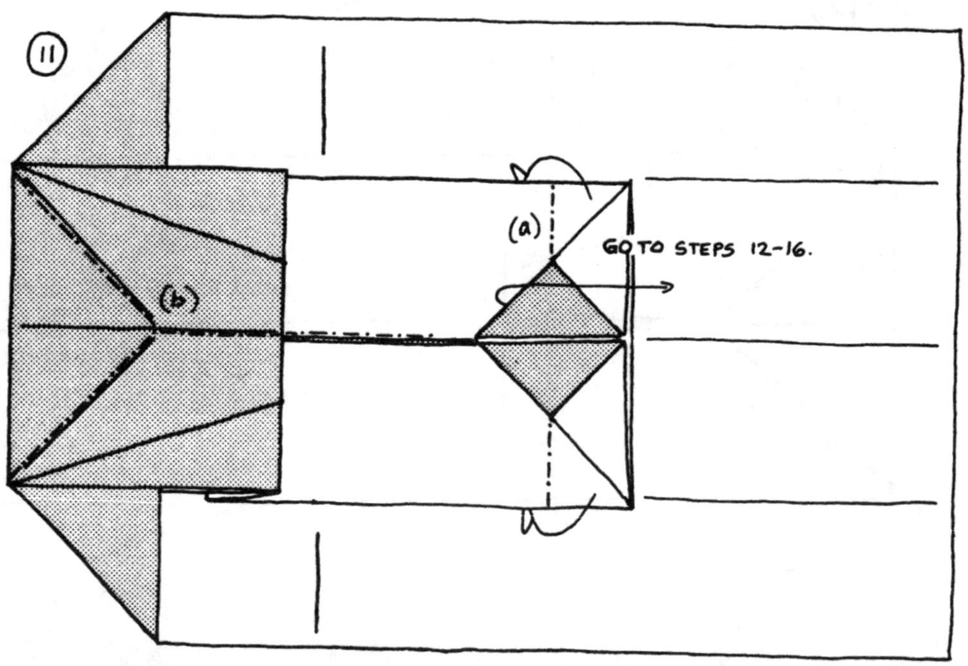

11a: This is the candle flame. Complete steps 12-16 and return to this diagram.

11b: Raise and mountain fold the central flap - same action as step 5.

12

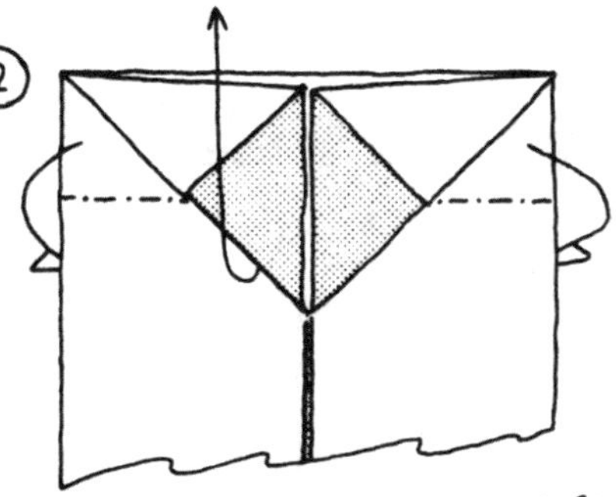

This is the end of the central flap in step 11, rotated 90°.

13

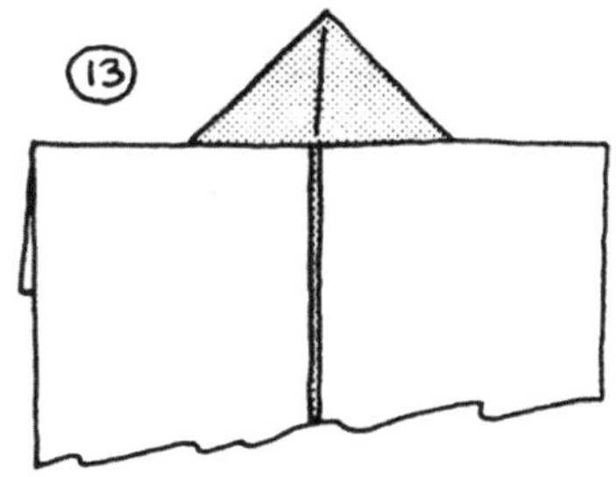

14

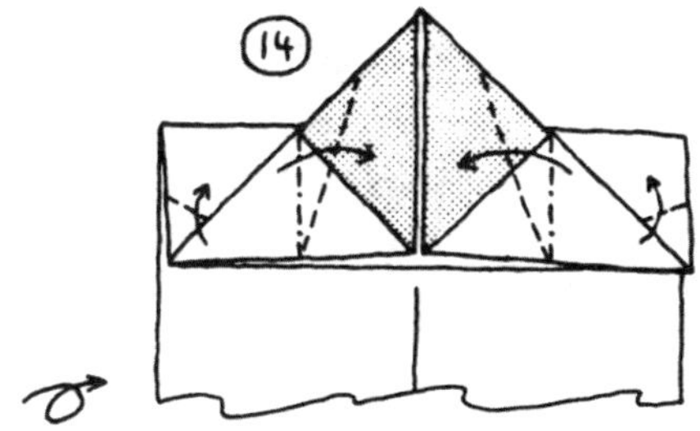

15

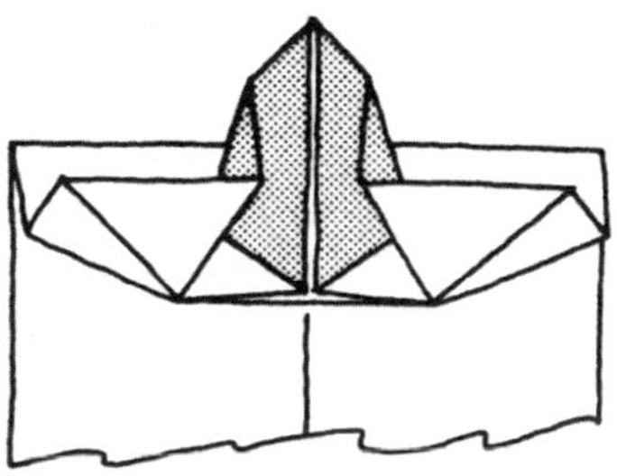

16

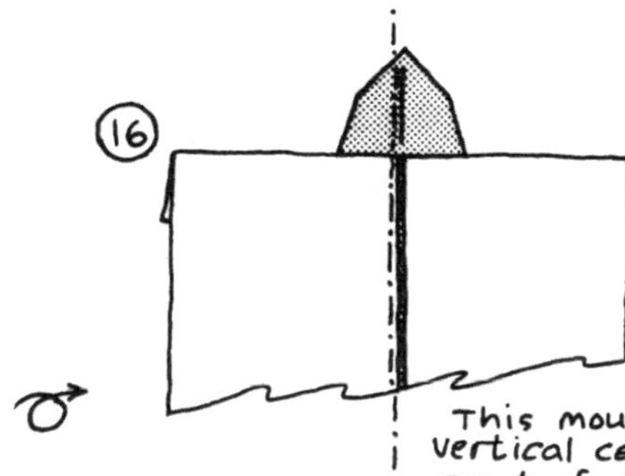

This mountain fold is along vertical center crease and is part of step 11b.

17

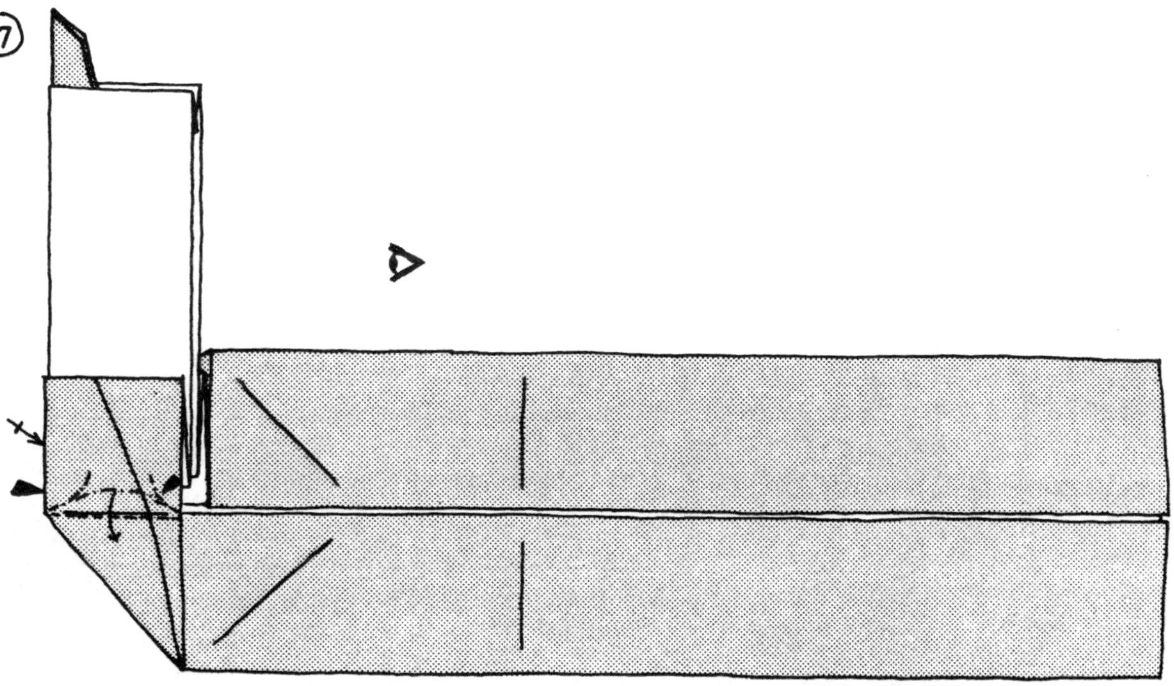

This is steps 11-16 completed.

Next, hollow and curve vertically the front and back flaps of the candle and candle holder into a tube shape.

At the base, form partial squash folds as the tube shape is made as close to the base as possible.

(18)

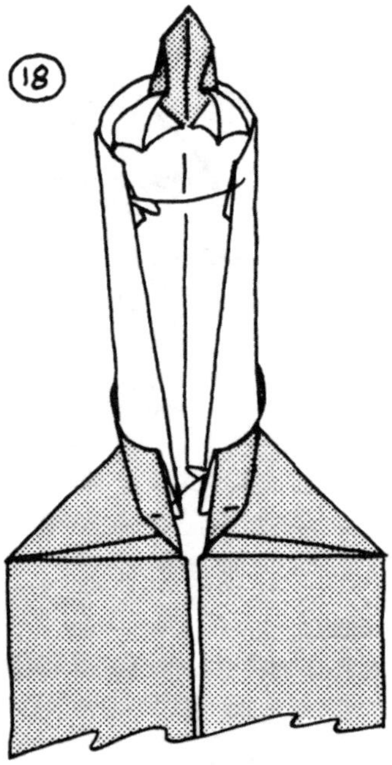

Use pleats at top and bottom to join the left and right sides by inserting the edges as far into the pleats as possible.

(19)

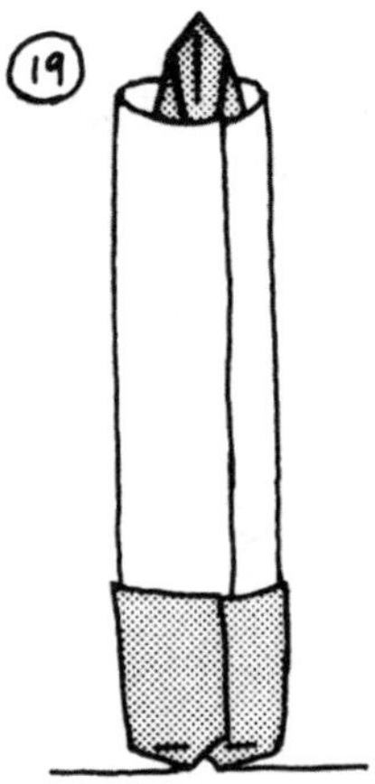

Shows the tube formed. Next use a thin strong stick or rod to insert inside the tube and shape the candle nicely round.

Be sure that the overlapped pleats at both top and bottom are well-rounded to make the tube stay closed.

Pull the flame away from the side of the tube, and twist.

(20)

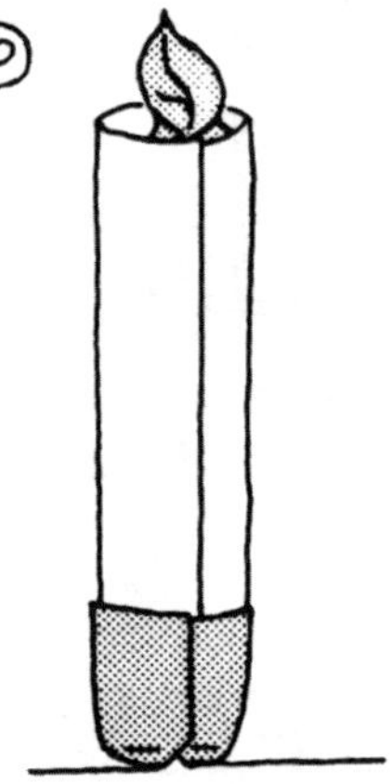

Shaping the flame:

While performing this, you may have distorted the candle shape and will need to restore it.

(21)

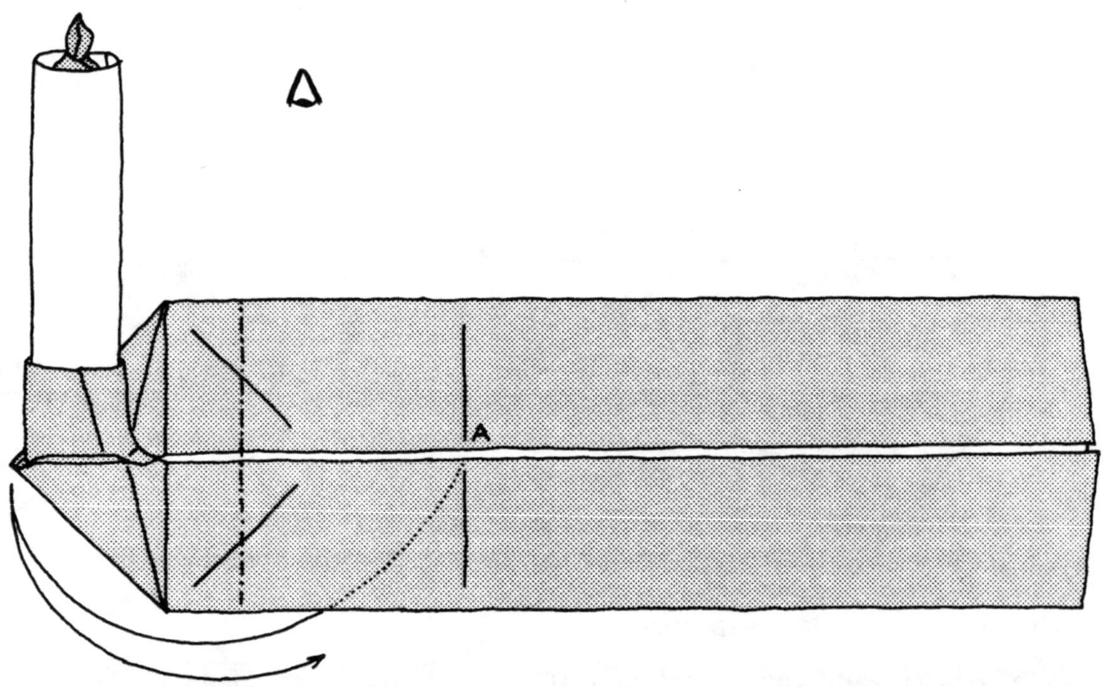

Locate and crease the mountain fold by swinging the long flap underneath candle and placing intersection A at point B.
Then unfold back to this position.

(22)

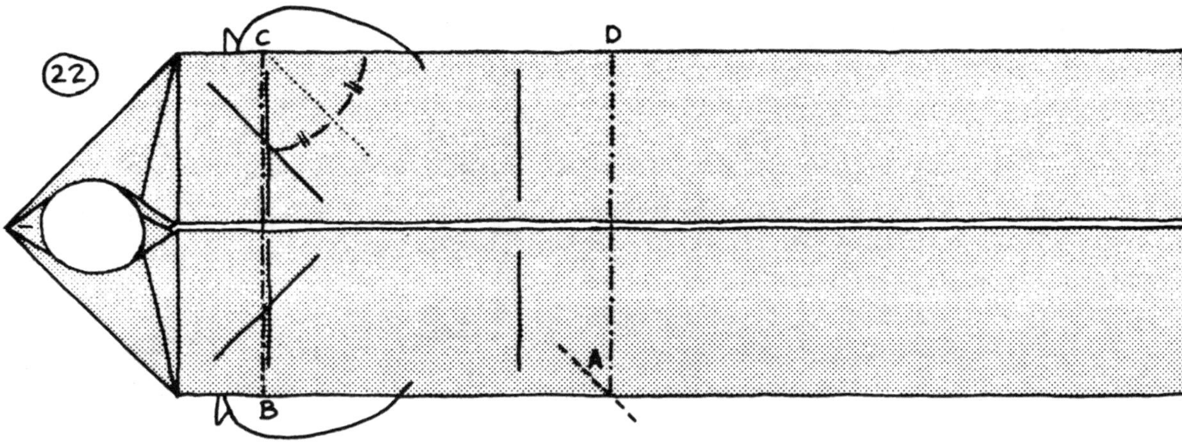

Bisect angle BCD, but do not fold except at A to landmark bottom edge.

Then, mountain fold AD. This step completes a square area ABCD which will be used for the candle base.

Lastly, mountain fold BC and AD together, swinging long flap underneath the candle.

(23)

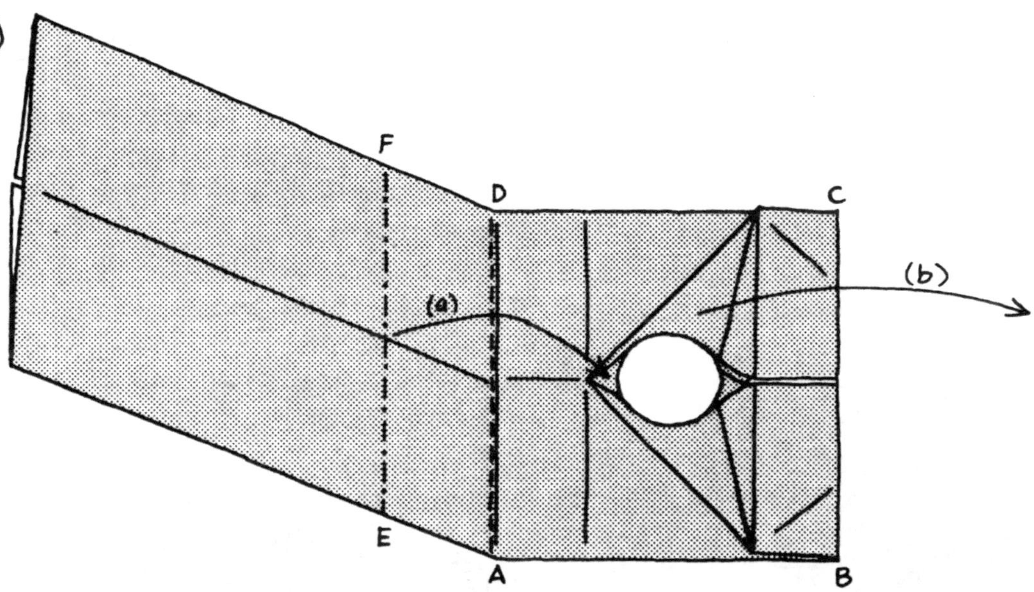

(a) Pleat the long flap by first valley folding existing crease AD and then mountain folding EF. Position EF so that it covers the small squash fold at the base of the candle.

(b) Allow flap with candle to unfold loosely to right so it is not in the way of next sequence. Later, the flap is returned to this position so that crease EF holds the candle in place.

24

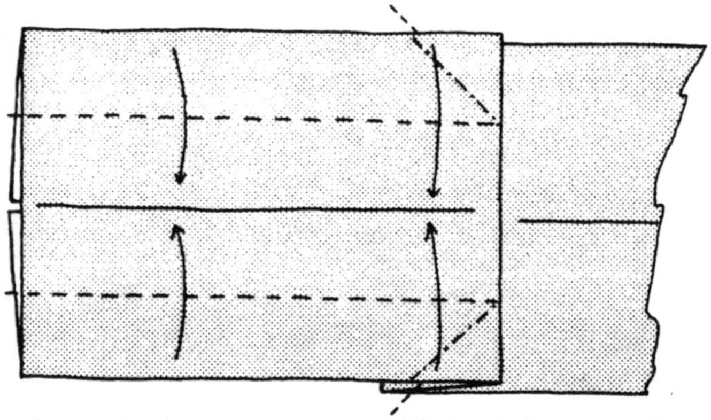

25

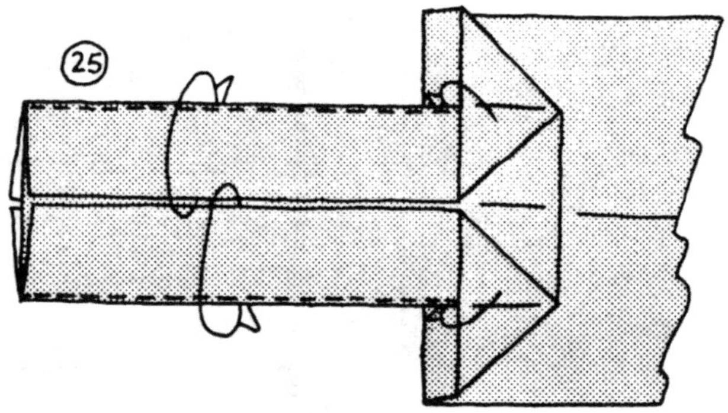

26

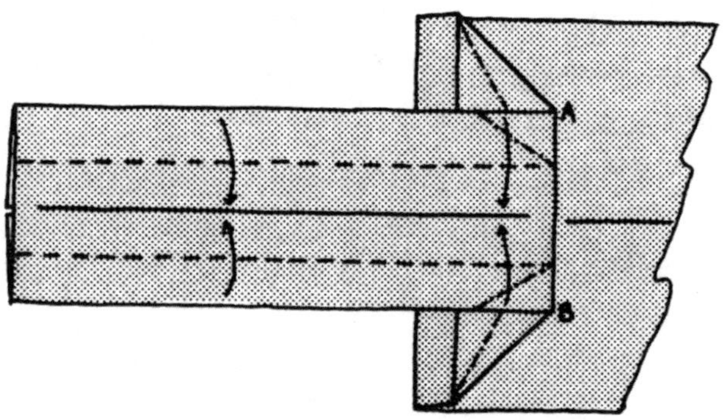

Narrow long flap again. Spread-squash corners A and B.

27

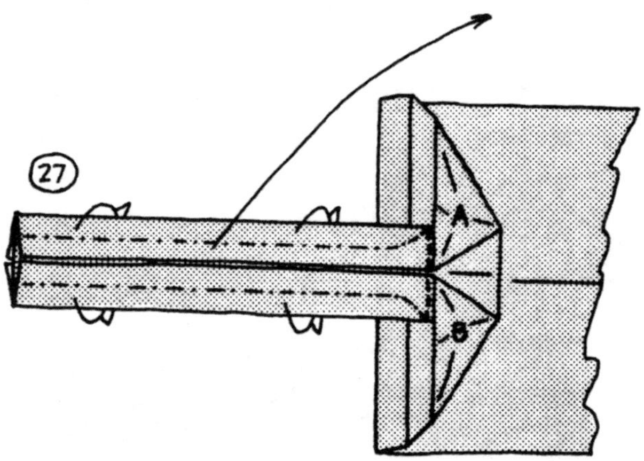

28

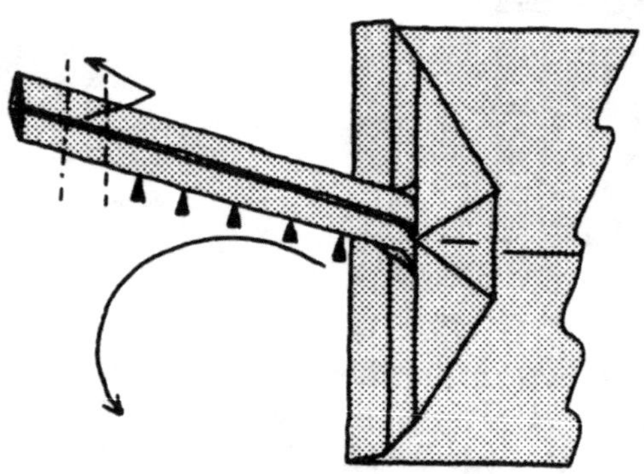

Curl the handle flap with numerous small bends. Pleat the end.

29

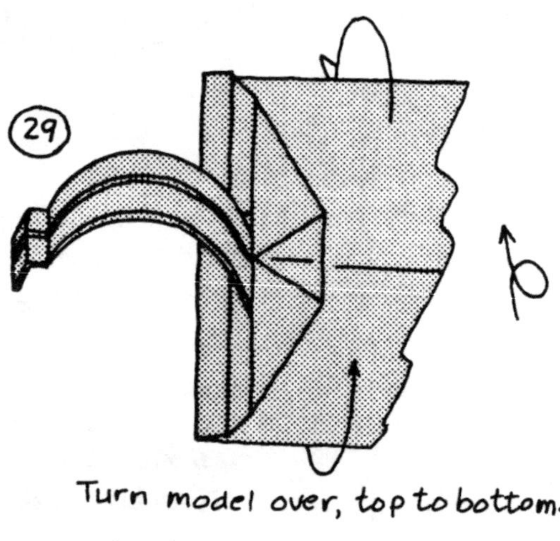

Turn model over, top to bottom.

30

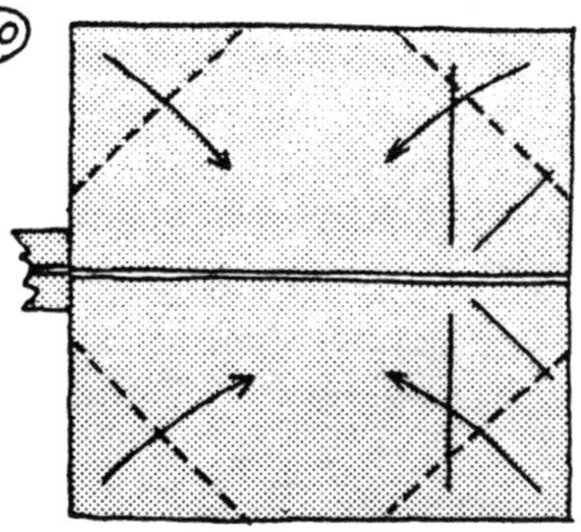

31

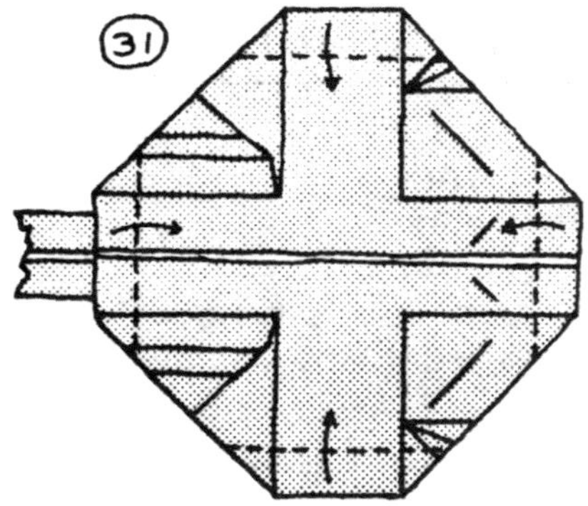

32

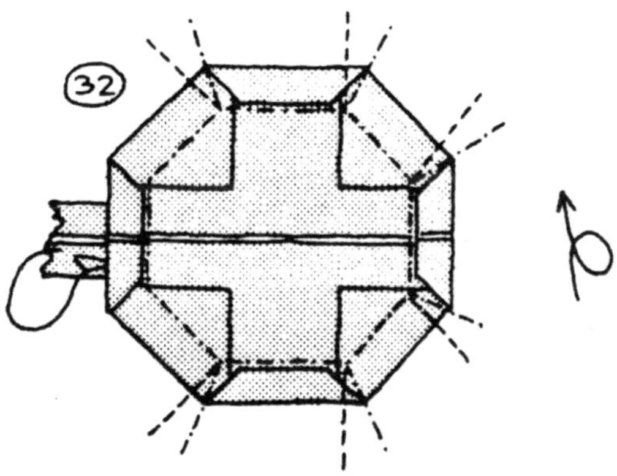

Some edges not shown.

First, mountain fold around the octagon shown.

Then, make six crimp folds at corners. It is easier to perform the crimps from top surface.

Hold each crimp in place and roll and press the crimp on a tabletop.

Lastly, insert "L"-shaped end of handle flap in pocket. Shape the model: rounded base, straight candle.

33

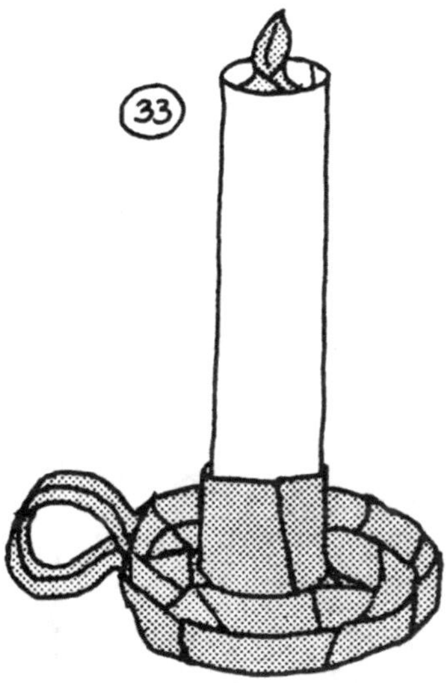

CLAW HAMMER

3 X 1 Rectangle.
Use foil paper.
Begin white side up.
Pre-crease at 1/3 from left
and in half lengthwise.

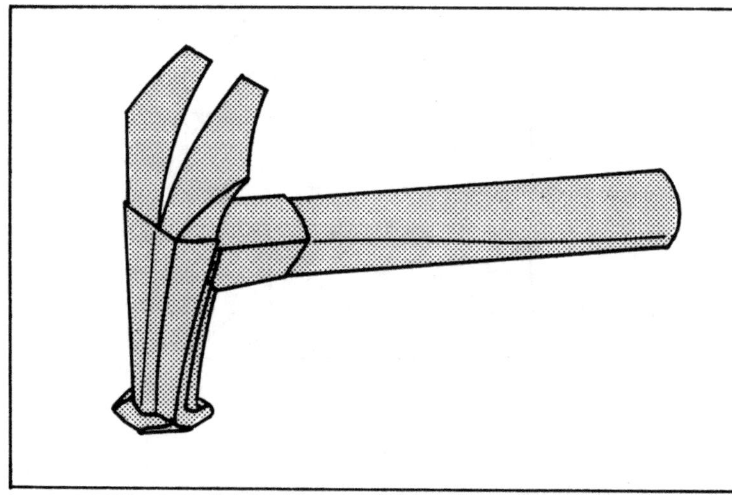

1

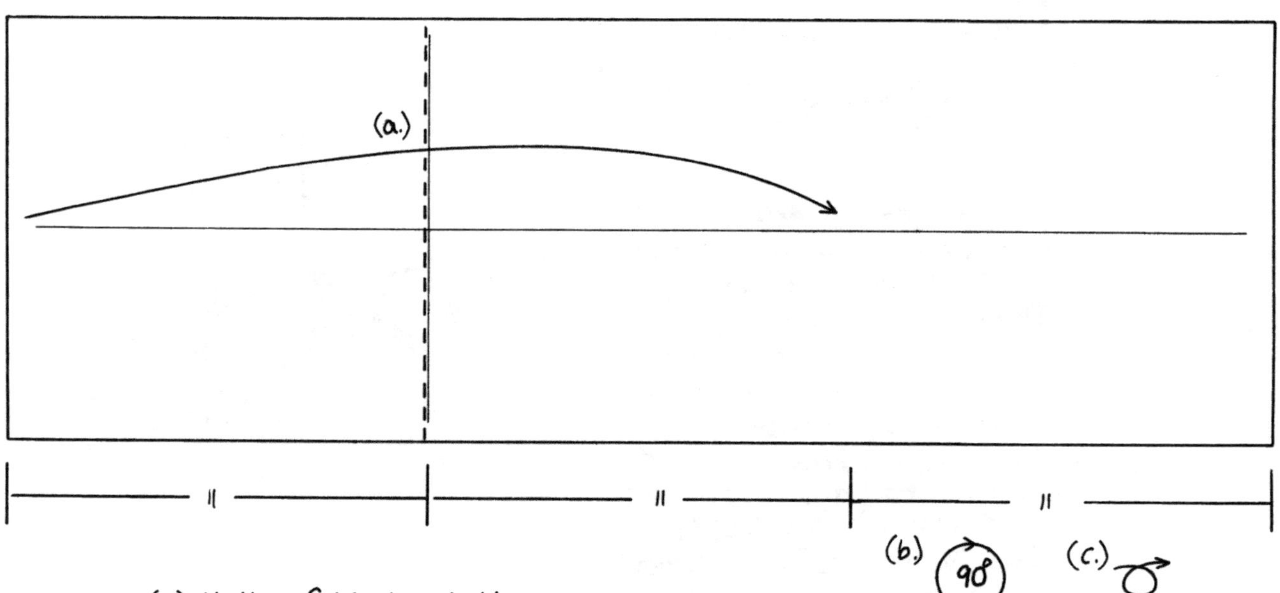

(a.) Valley fold at existing crease.
(b.) Rotate clockwise 90°.
(c.) Turn model over side-to-side.

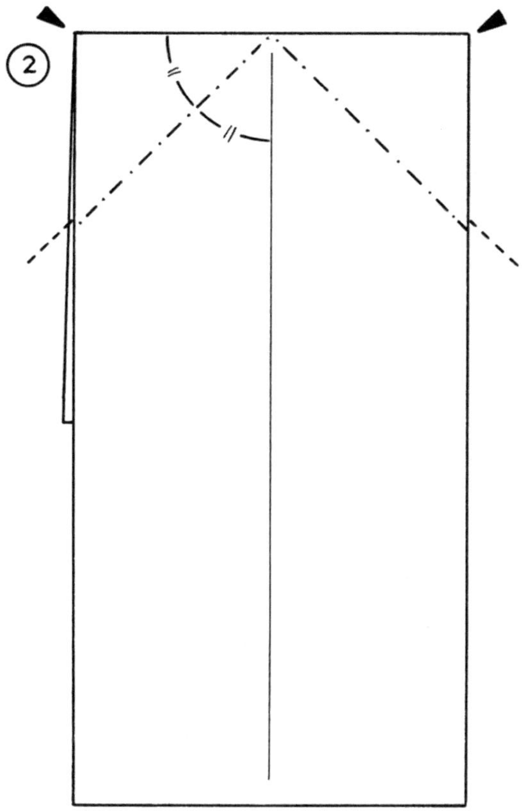

Reverse folds

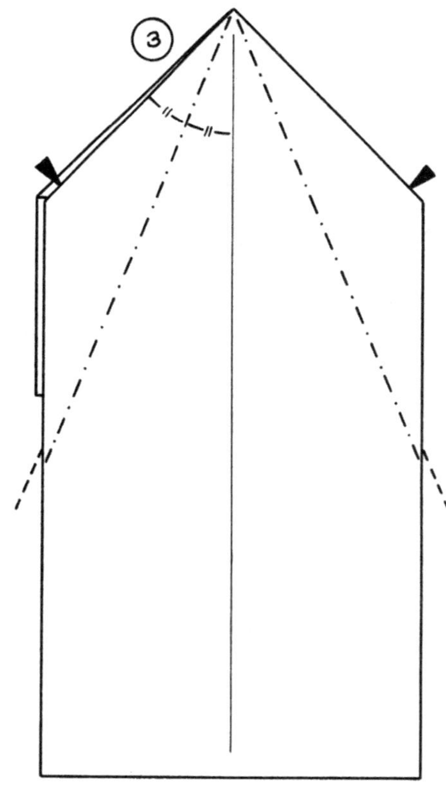

Reverse fold front left and right flaps only.

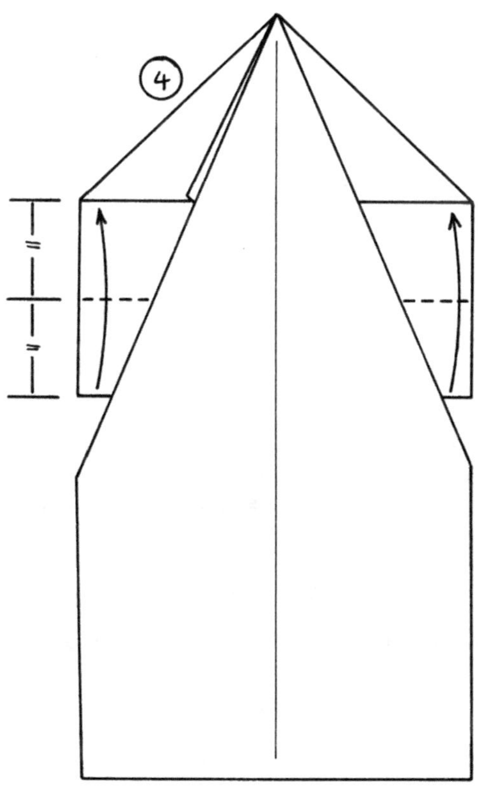

Valley fold rear flap.

Turn over

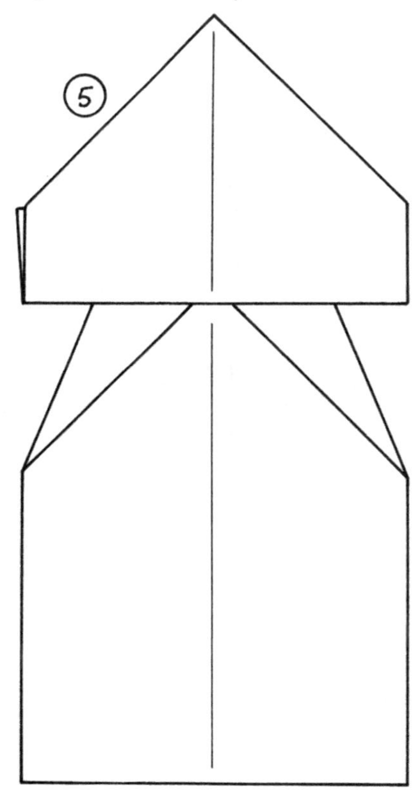

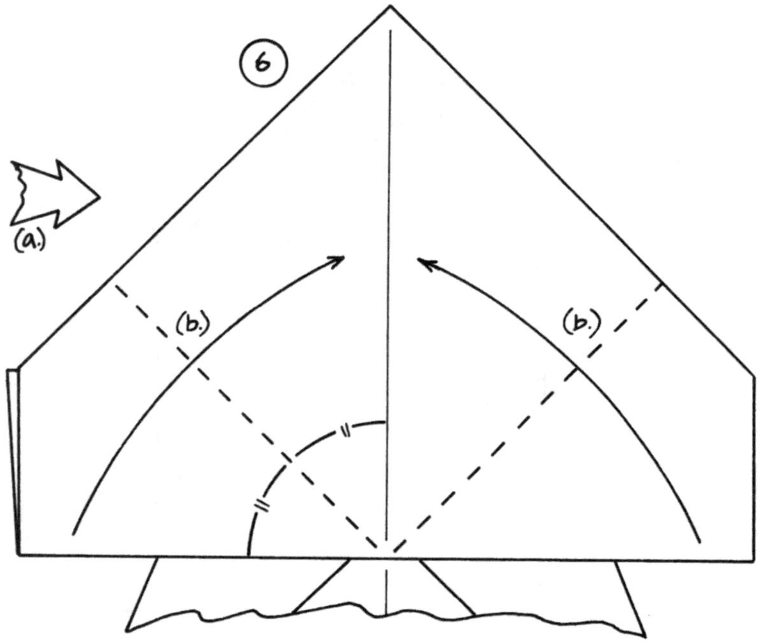

(a.) Picture gets larger.
(b.) Valley folds.

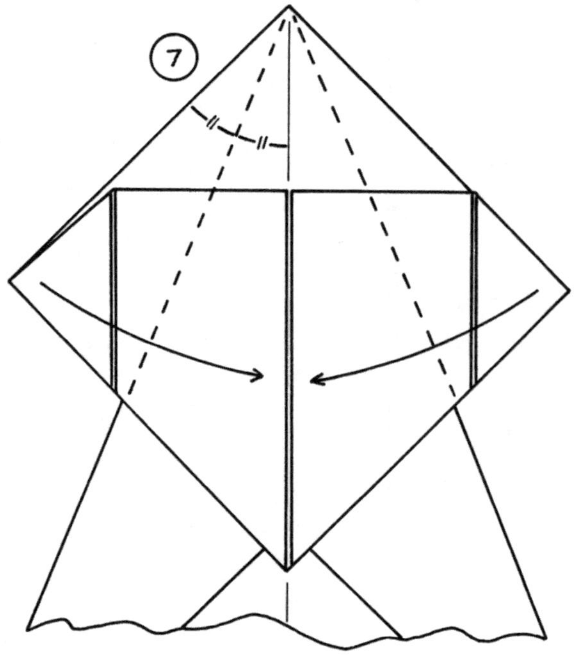

Valley folds.

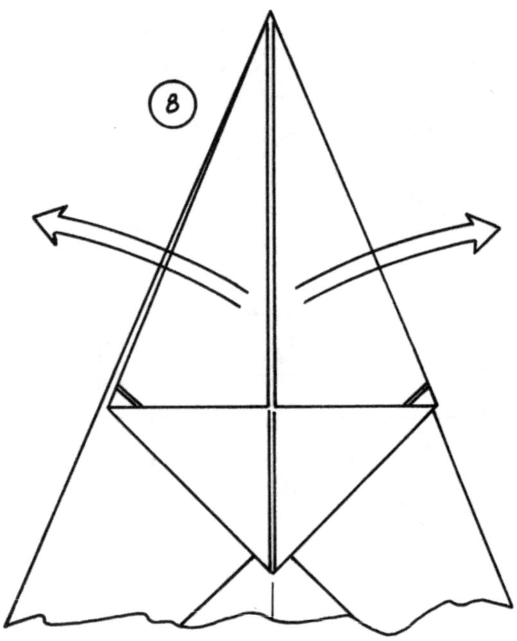

Unfold flaps back to position in step 6.

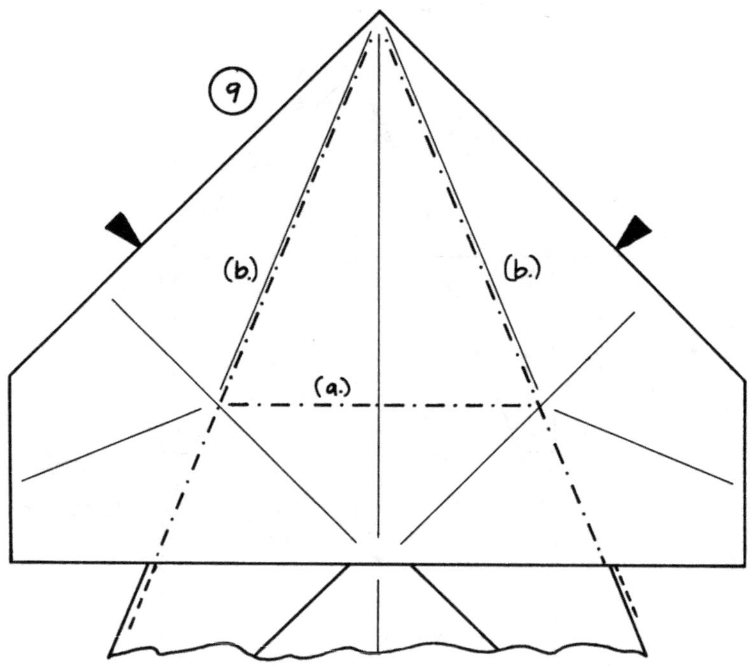

(a.) Mountain fold and unfold between corners of upside-down kite shape.
(b.) Reverse fold side flaps.

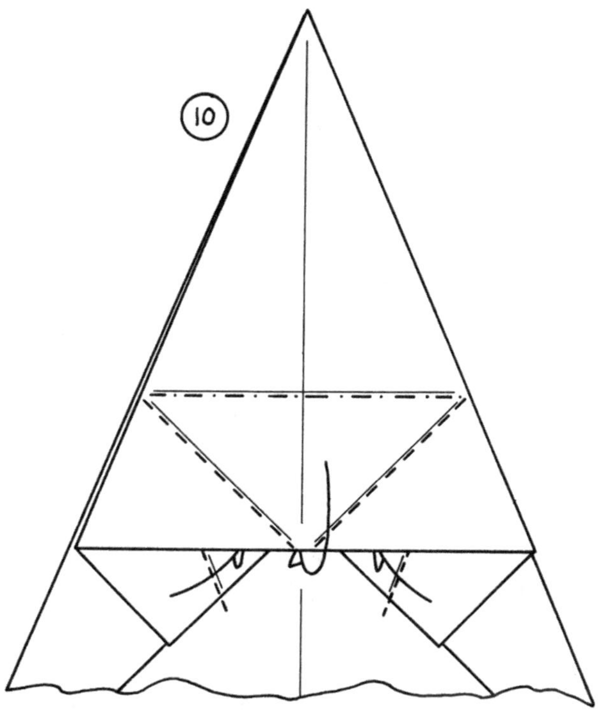

Use existing creases to reverse fold triangular area up inside model.

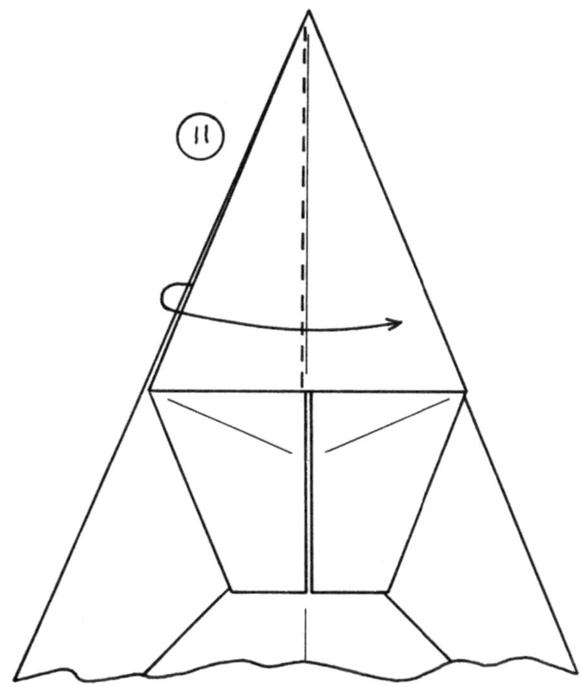

There are four flaps on each side of center line. Fold top two flaps on left to the right.

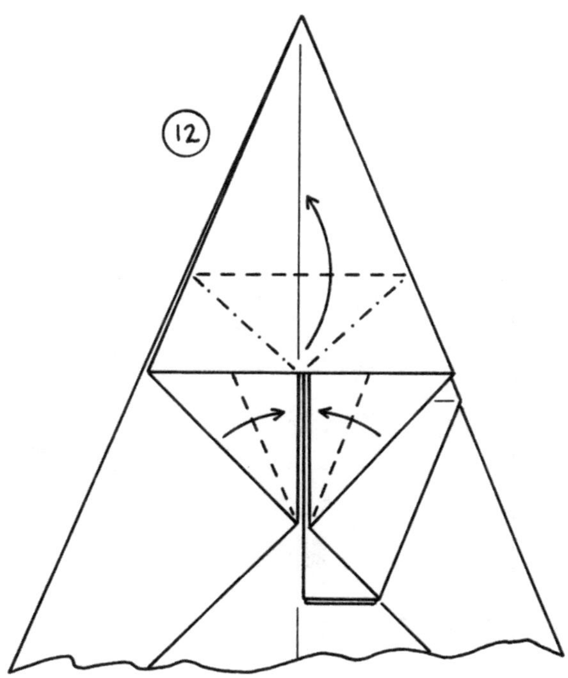

Petal fold.

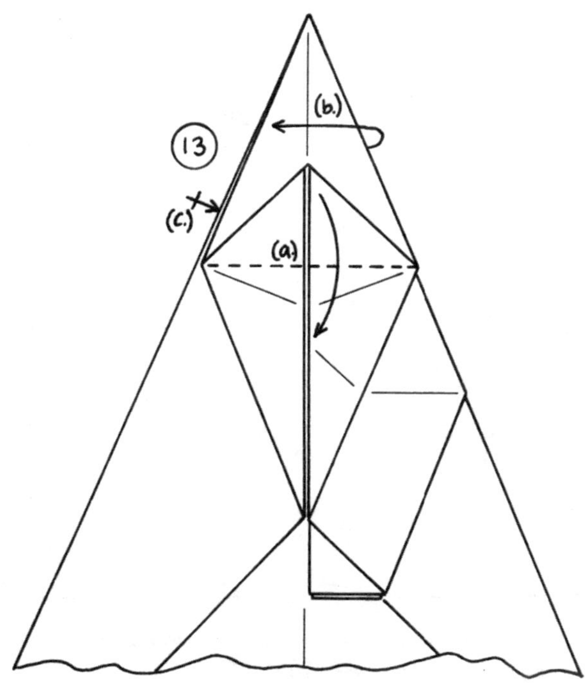

(a.) Valley fold the triangular flap down.
(b.) Fold four flaps from right to left.
(c.) Repeat steps 12 and 13; then return flaps to position of step 11.

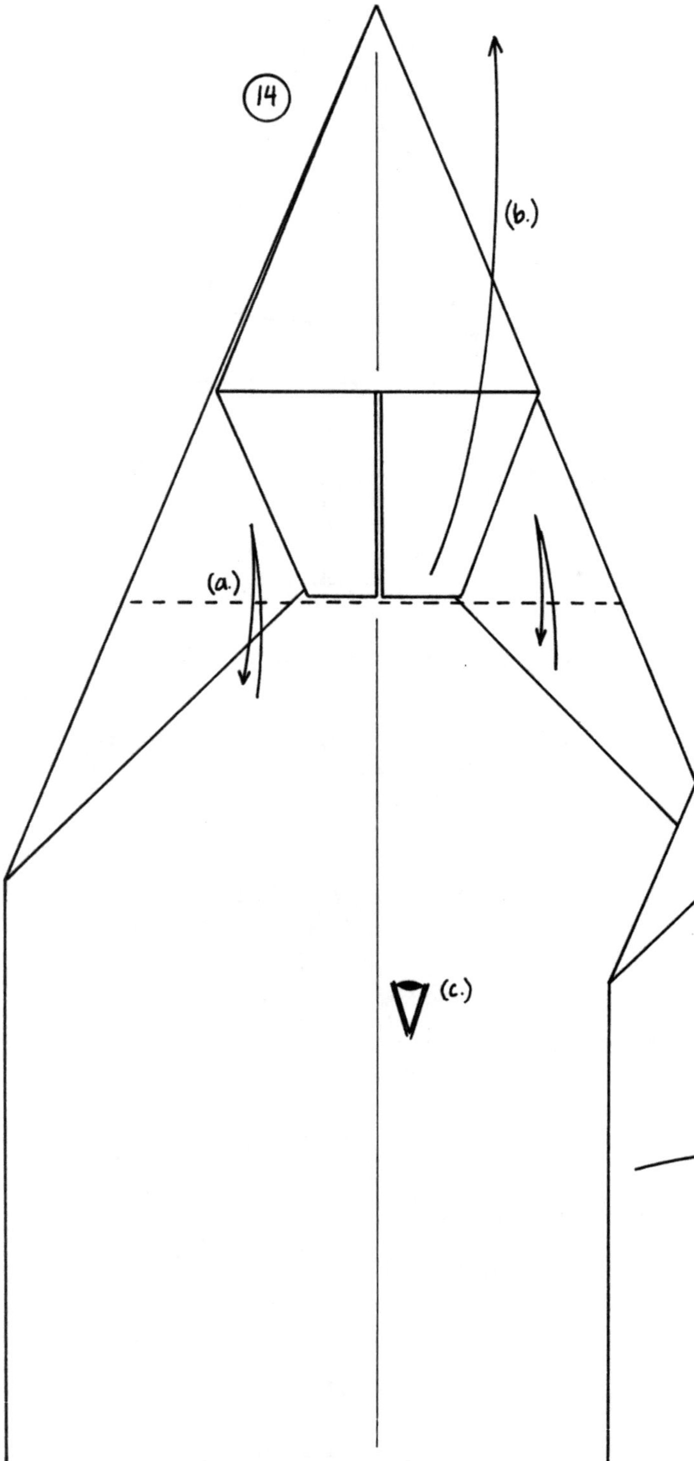

(a.) Fold and unfold along a line matching bottom edge of front flap.
(b.) Lift, but do not fold, and...
(c.) Look underneath.

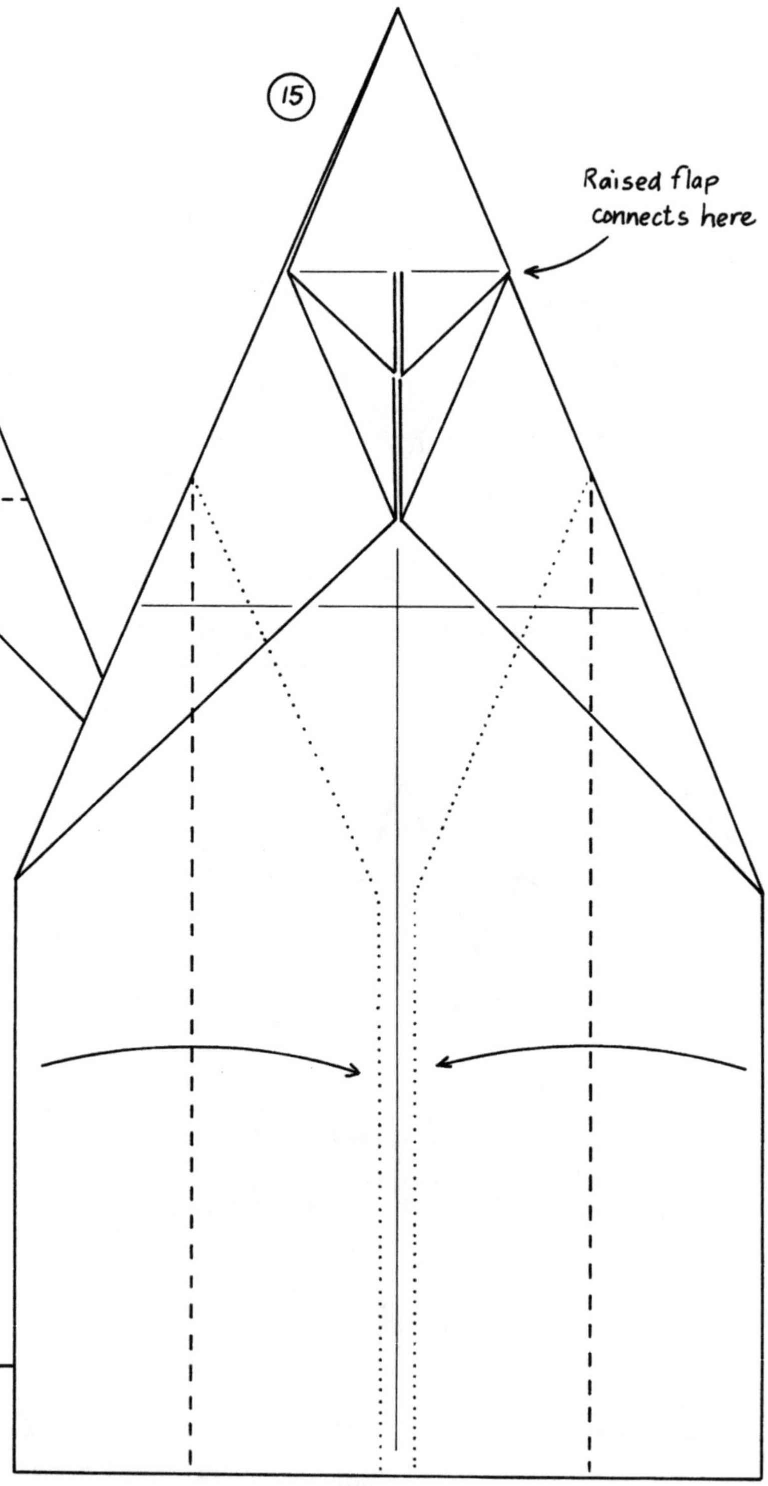

Flap lifted in step 14 is not shown.
Valley fold side edges almost to center line.
Dotted lines show positions of folded flaps.

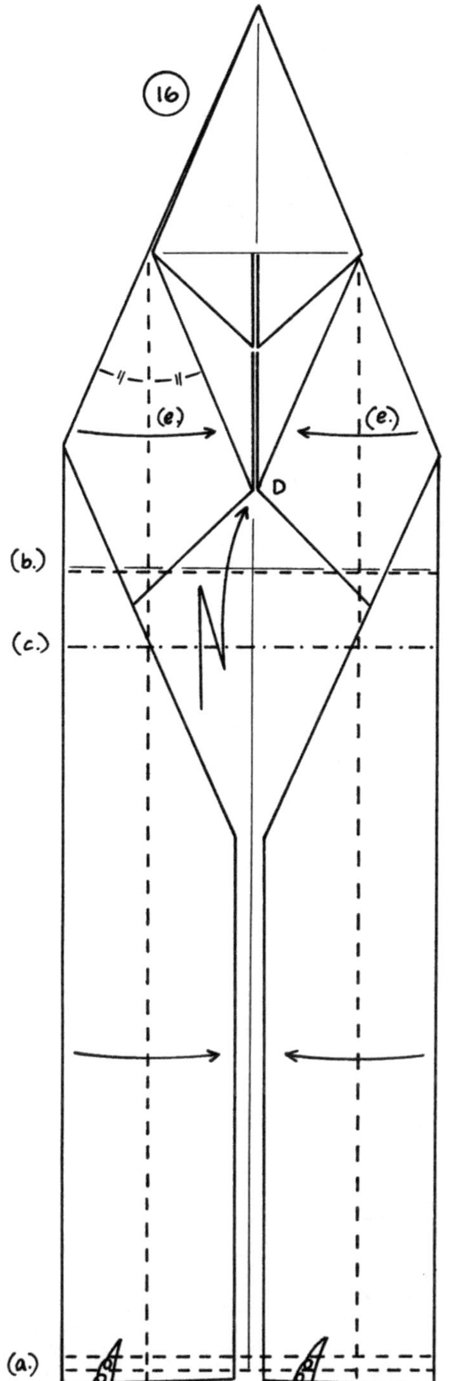

(a.) At bottom, roll over twice a thin hem, and unfold.
(b.) Valley fold using existing crease made in step 14, then pleat...
(c.) locating mountain fold "c" at point "D."
(e) Narrow handle flap again, locating the creases by bisecting the angles at top.

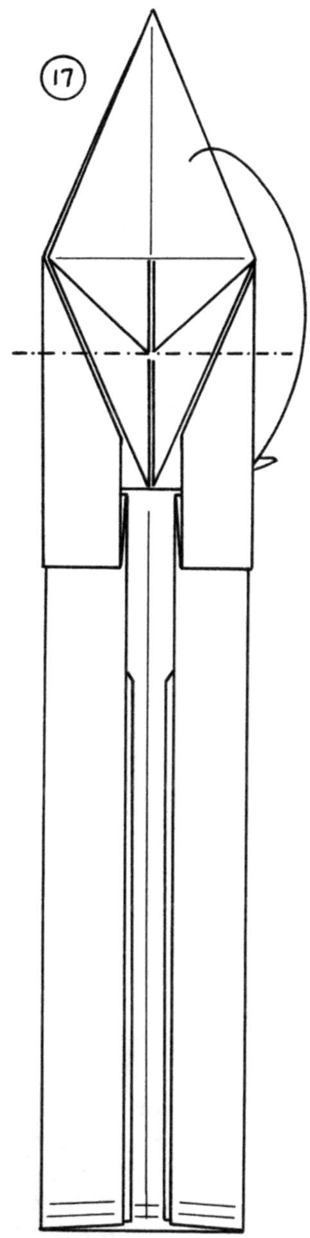

Mountain fold at tips of small triangular flaps, flipping entire hammer head section behind.
The hammer head section is now shown again in next picture.

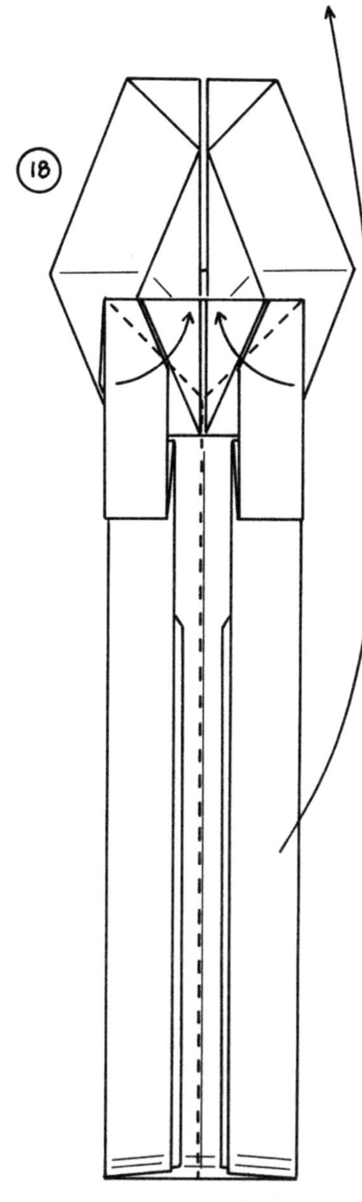

Rabbit ear end of handle flap. When finished, handle will be standing up perpendicularly to the surface.

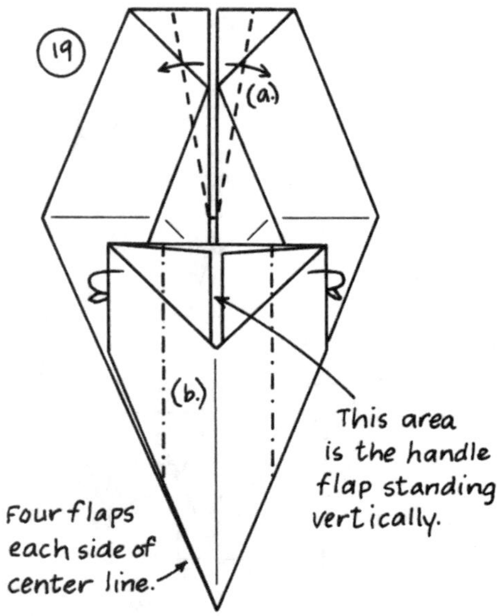

(a.) Valley fold to shape claw.
(b.) Mountain fold two (2) flaps inside to center line.

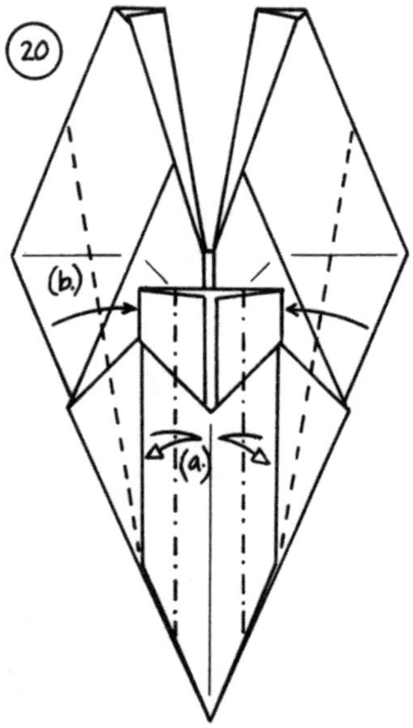

(a.) Mountain folds behind and unfold. Very thick.
(b.) Valley folds.

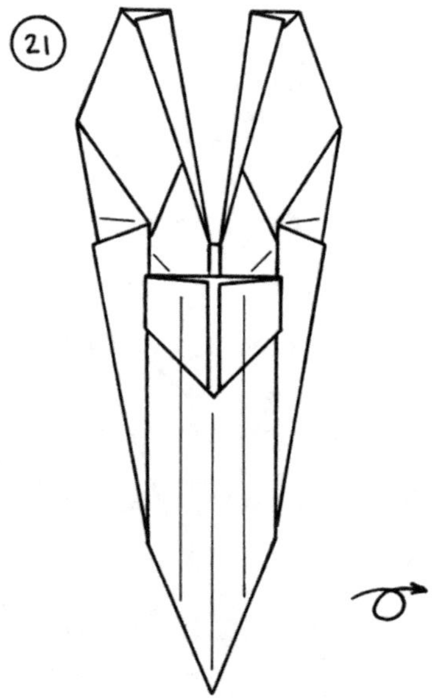

Step 20 finished. Turn model over.

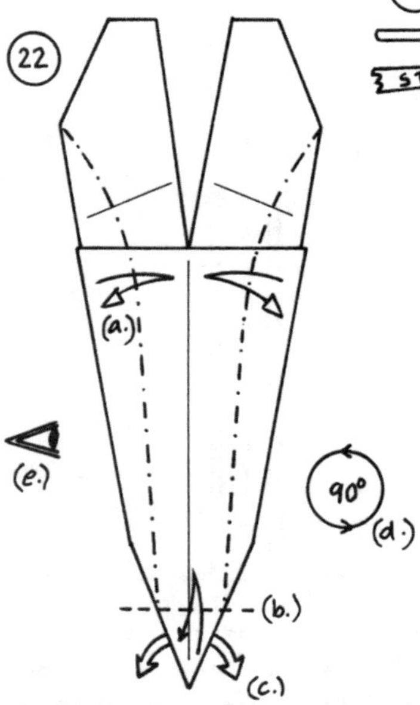

(a.) Mountain fold behind and unfold.
(b.) Valley fold and unfold.
(c.) Open out tip. There are eight flaps, but open out hexagonally, keeping bottom-most two pairs together. Crease "b" above is changed as needed to form a mountain fold perimeter around the hexagon-shaped hammer face.
(d. and e.) Rotate and look this way.

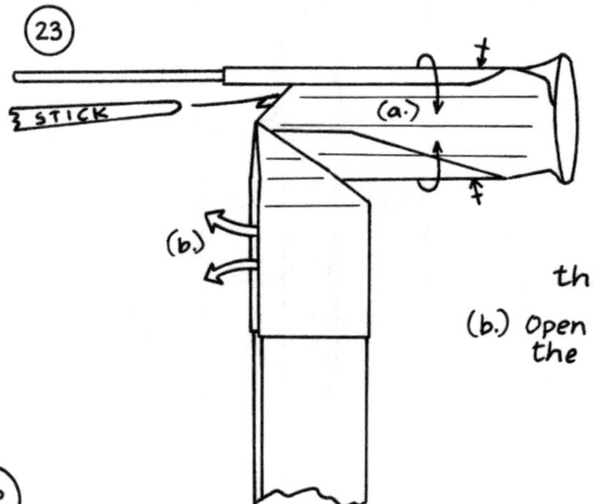

(a.) Refold the two pairs of mountain folds from steps 20"a" and 22"a" to shape the hammer head 3-D. Use a long thin stick to help. Fold at 90° angle only.
(b.) Open out inner flaps of the handle.

View of hammer face.

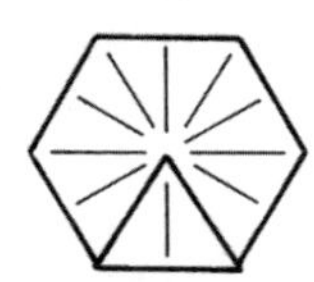

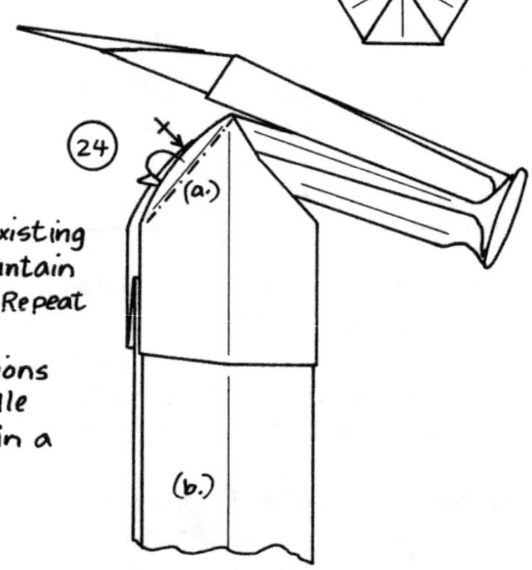

(a) Locate short existing crease and mountain fold it inside. Repeat behind.
(b.) Curl all sections of the handle lengthwise in a tube shape.

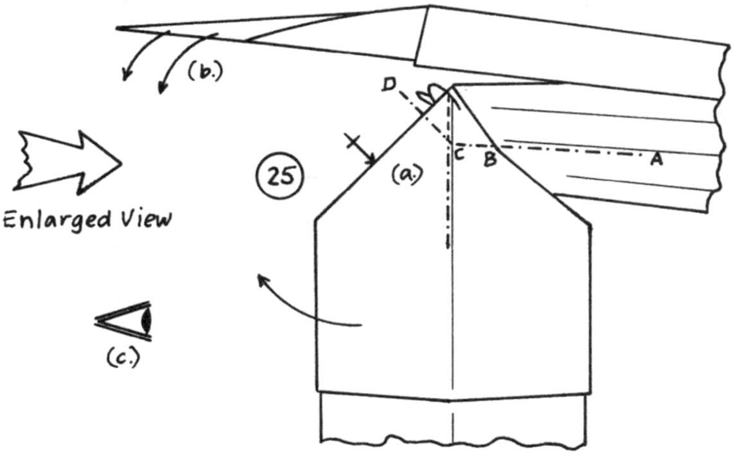

(a.) Crease AB is a mountain-folded edge. Mountain fold BC along same line as AB, then push left flap to the back as you pinch the small mountain fold CD. Repeat behind.
(b.) Curl the claw.
(c.) Rear View.

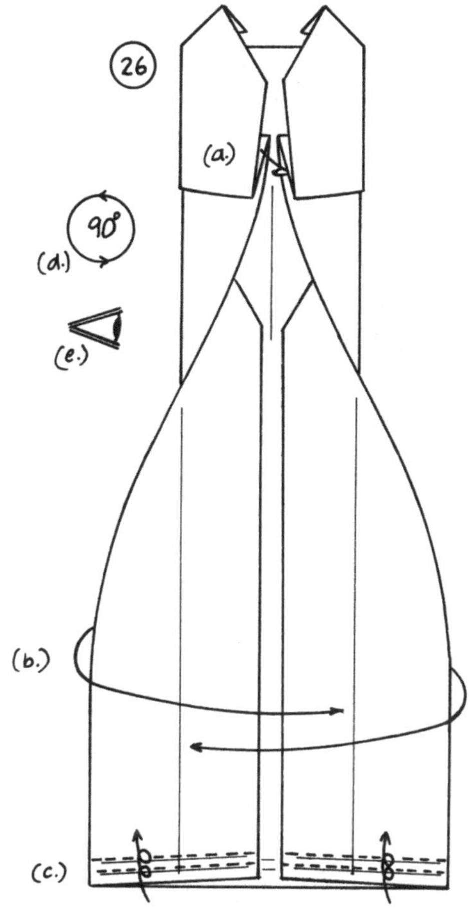

(a.) Insert one pleat into the other as far as possible.
(b.) Form handle into a tube shape, overlapping the left and right outer panels.
(c.) Fold thin hem fold inside to lock the end closed; then roll fold over once again.
(d.) Rotate, and look this way.

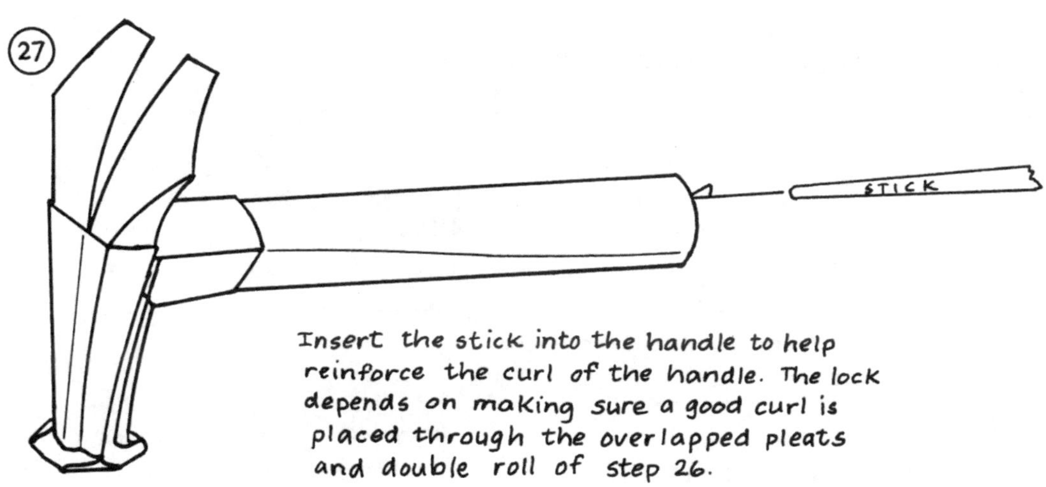

Insert the stick into the handle to help reinforce the curl of the handle. The lock depends on making sure a good curl is placed through the overlapped pleats and double roll of step 26.

DAFFODIL

This is a compound model, using a 6" square for the flower, a 13" square for the stem and leaves, and producing a finished model 6 1/4 " tall.

Thin, foil-backed paper is required to create and retain the shaping. Coloring can be done with liquid water color washes on the white surfaces, or by bonding colored tissue to the paper.

Make the flower first beginning yellow surface underneath. The square is first folded into a hexagonal shape, and it is not necessary to cut off any paper flaps created in steps 9 and 10.

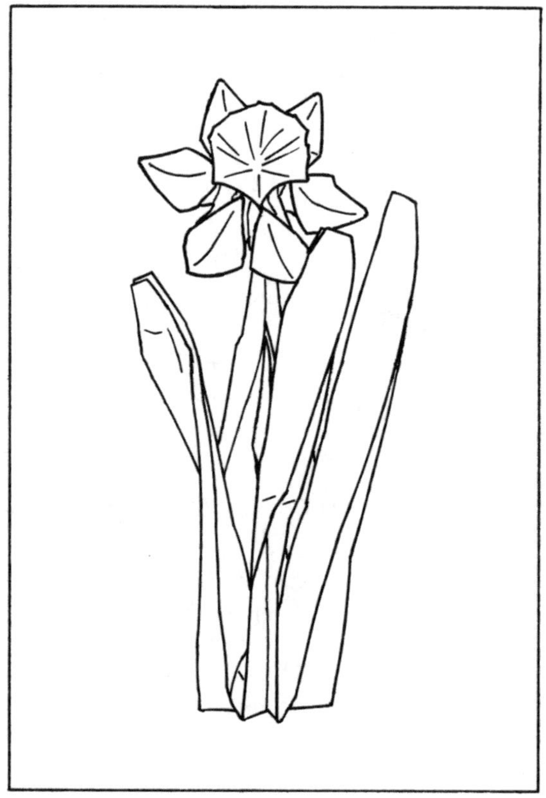

1

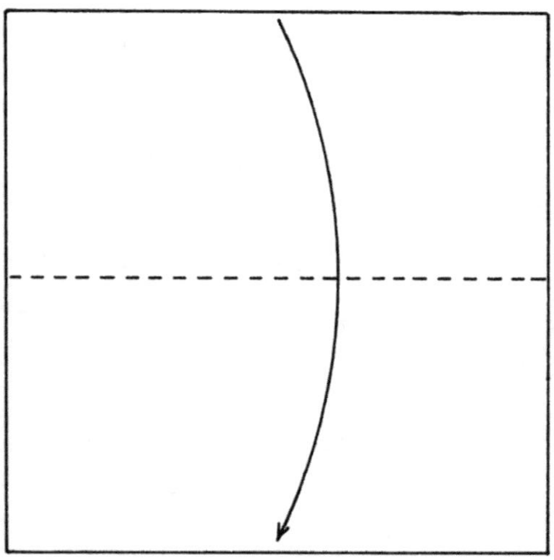

Fold in half, top-to-bottom.

2

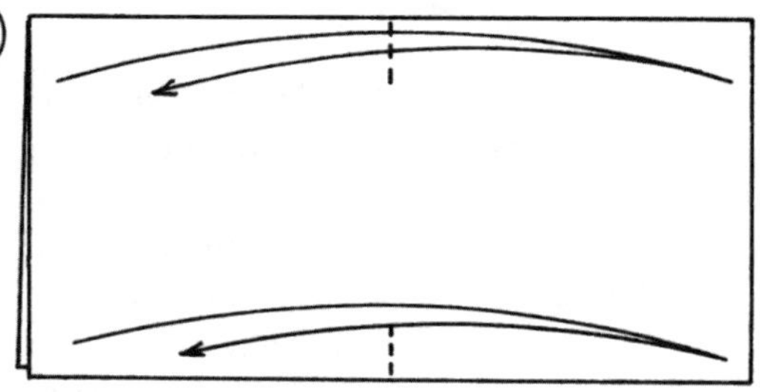

Crease landmarks at mid-points of the top and bottom edges.

3

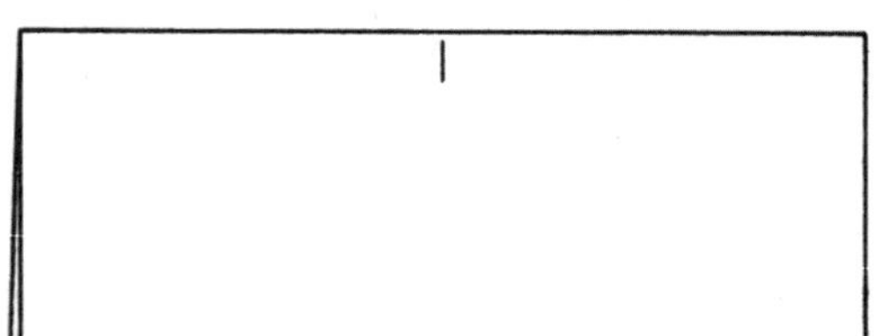

Crease landmark at mid-point between corner and center mark.

4

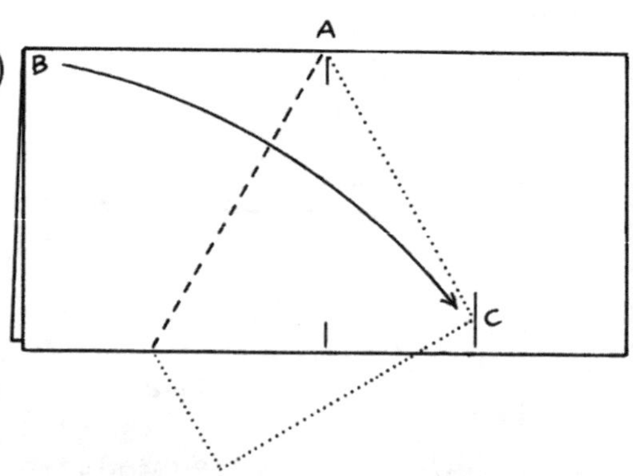

Begin valley fold landmark A, as corner B is placed at landmark C.

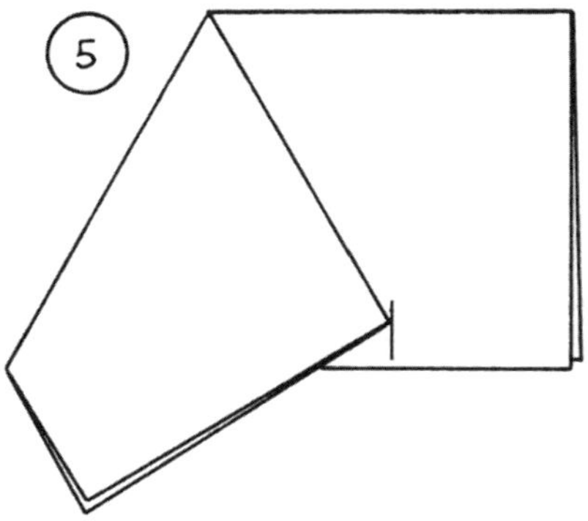

View of step 4 finished.
Turn model over side-to-side.

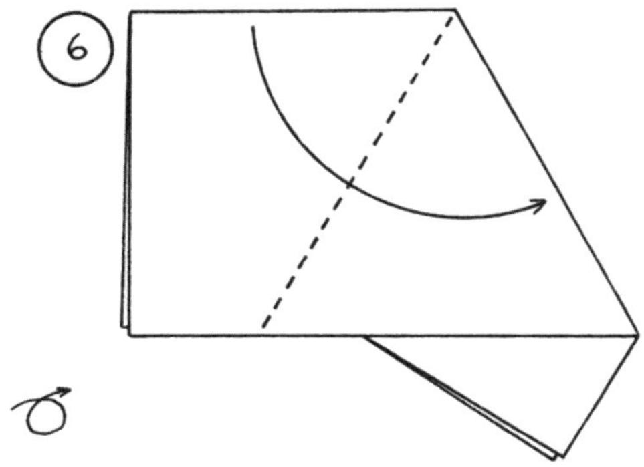

Valley fold the top edge over to the right edge.

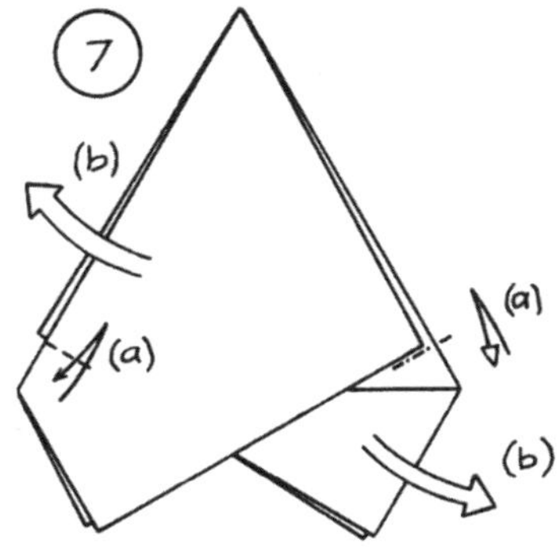

(a) Crease landmarks to match edges shown. (b) Unfold all and position color side down.

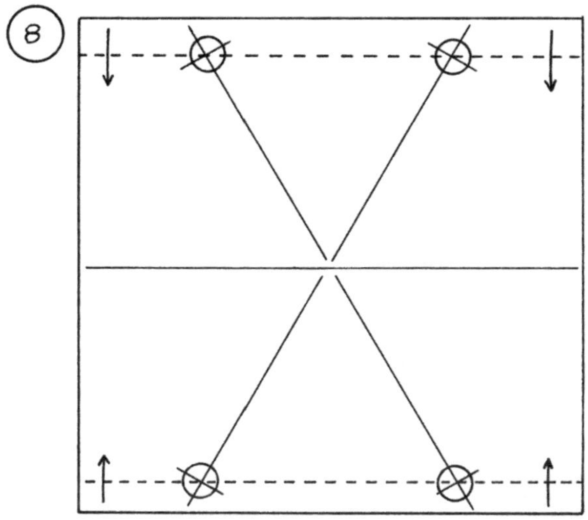

Valley fold through the intersections of the radii and landmarks from step 7.

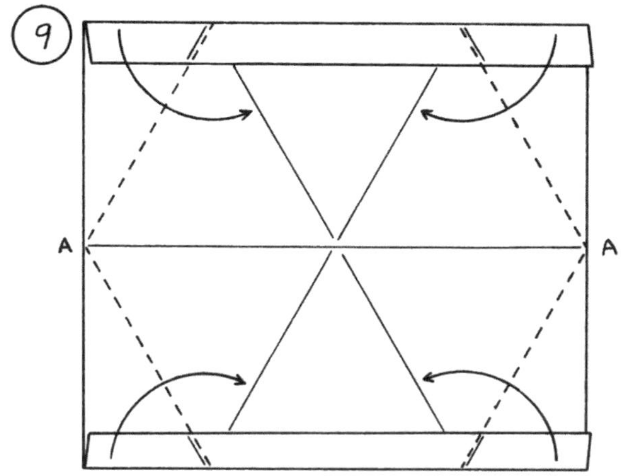

Form hexagon shape by valley folding each segment to crease. The folds might not intersect A, but this is OK.

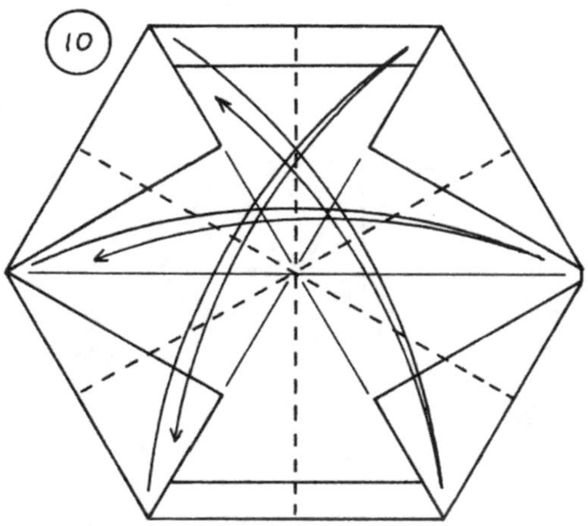

Make three valley folds by bringing opposite corners together. Fold and unfold in turn. Be sure creases intersect at center.

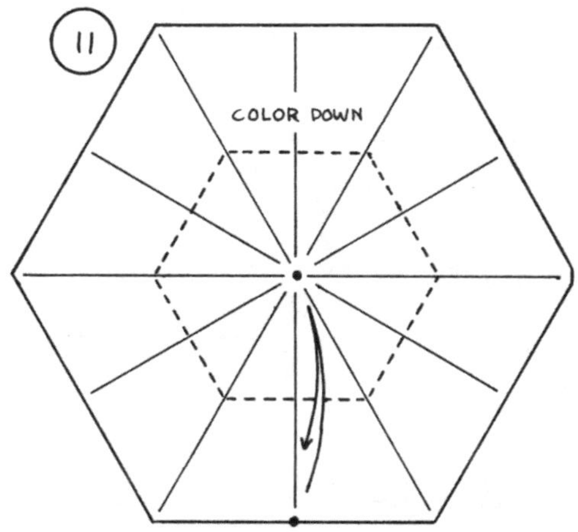

NOTE: Flaps not shown in remaining steps. Color side is down. Fold each edge to center and unfold, only creasing where shown.

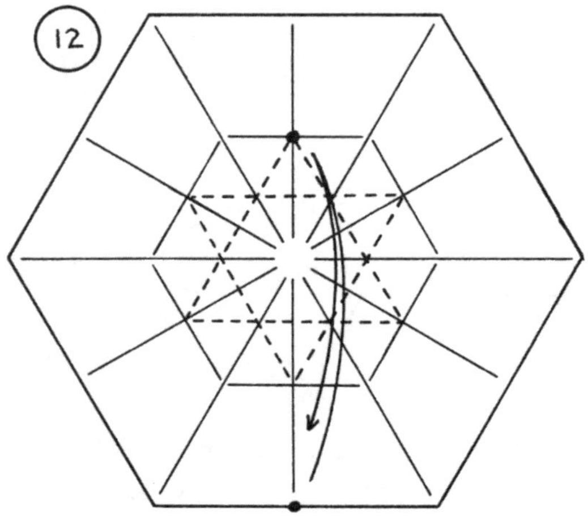

Valley fold each outside edge of hexagon to the most distant parallel crease. Crease only where shown. Turn over side-to-side.

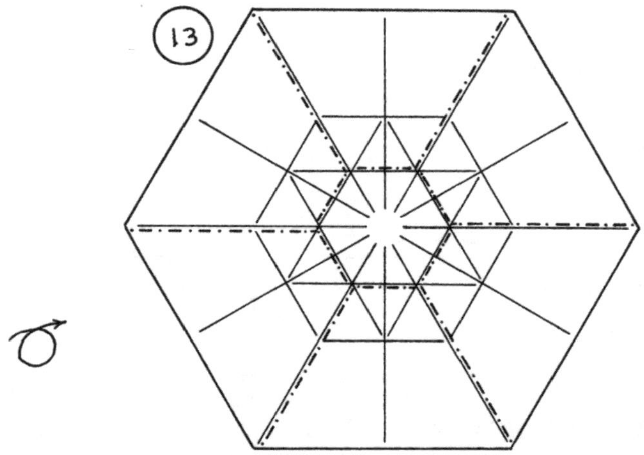

Mountain fold where shown, using existing creases - all around the smallest hexagon and the creases between its corners and outside corners. 3-D the model.

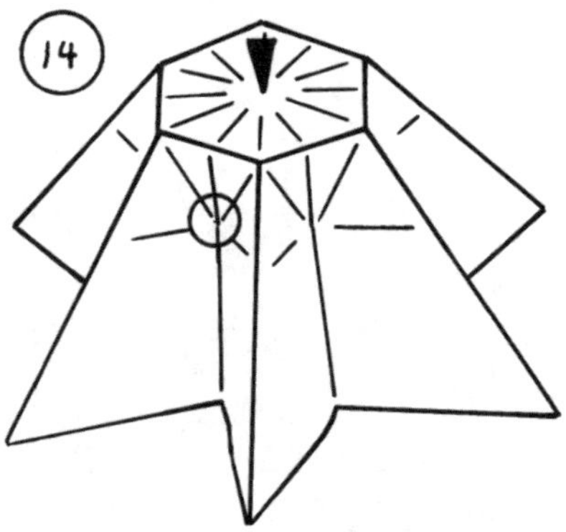

Patiently, make an open sink fold. The center point of the hexagon will meet, inside, the intersection circled above. Flatten model as in step 15. Picture gets larger.

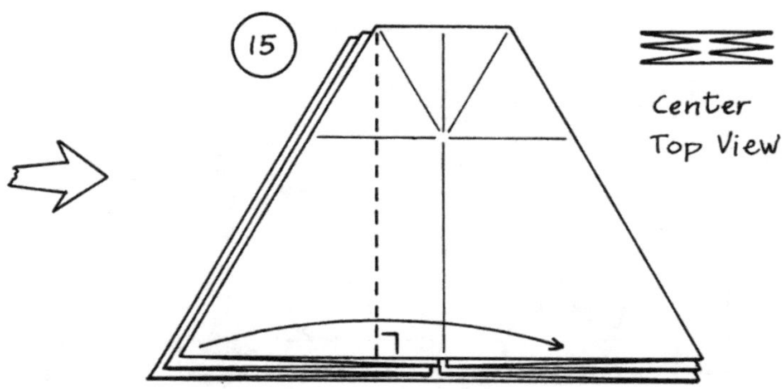

Valley fold top left flap only, at a right angle to bottom edge.

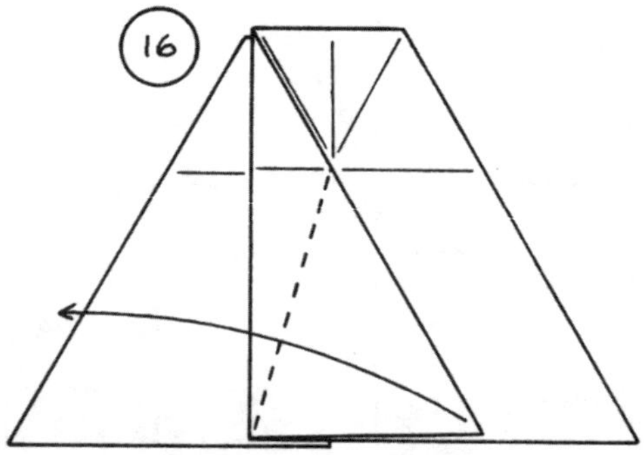

Some details omitted. Valley fold the flap between upper intersection and the lower left corner.

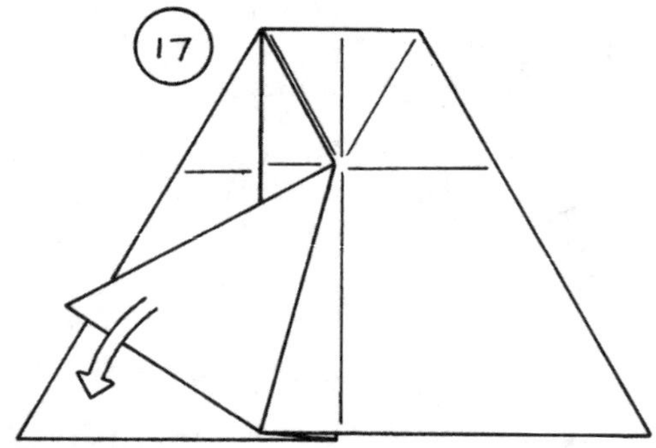

Unfold the two creases made in steps 15 and 16.

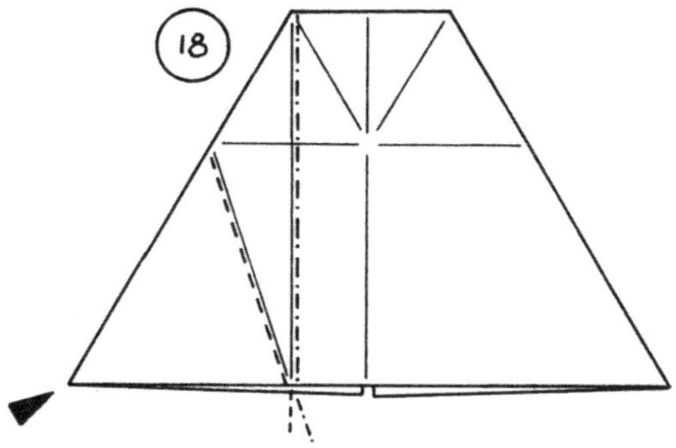

Form in order, (a), then (b), two inside reverse folds on the flap.

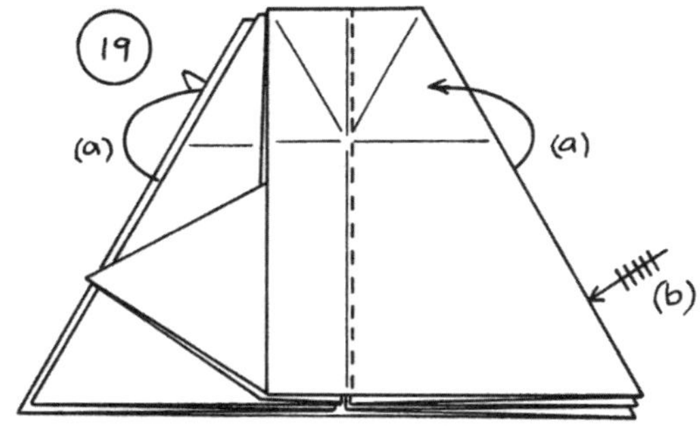

(a) Rearrange flaps: left-rear to the right and right-front to the left. (b) Repeat step 18. Continue rearranging flaps and repeating the step 18 folds until all 6 flaps are completed.

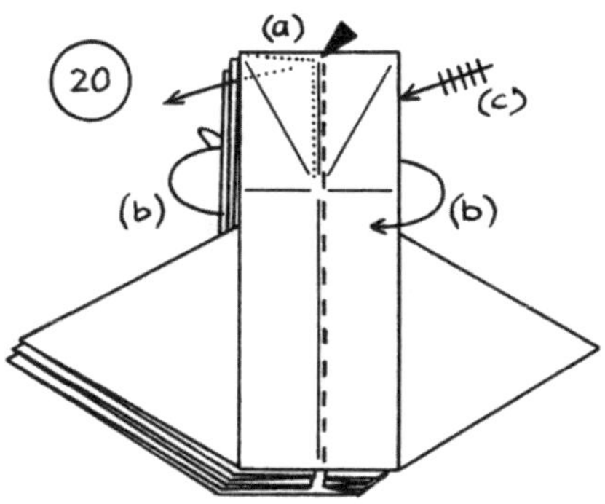

(a) In the upper left corner, reverse fold hidden inside flap outwards along existing creases. (b) Rearrange flaps as in step 19 and (c), repeat reverse fold (a) 5 more times. These folds unfold and refold as flaps are turned.

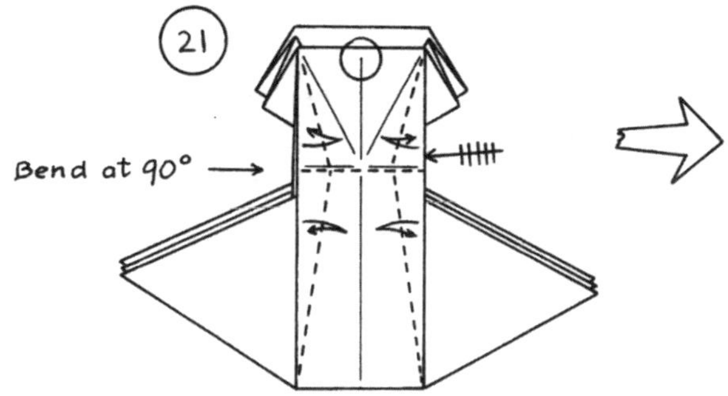

Grip top edge where circled, bending front surface at 90° angle along existing crease. Fold and unfold the slanted creases where shown. See step 20 for illustration of the folded position before unfolding. Rearrange flaps and repeat step 21 on 5 remaining surfaces. Picture gets larger.

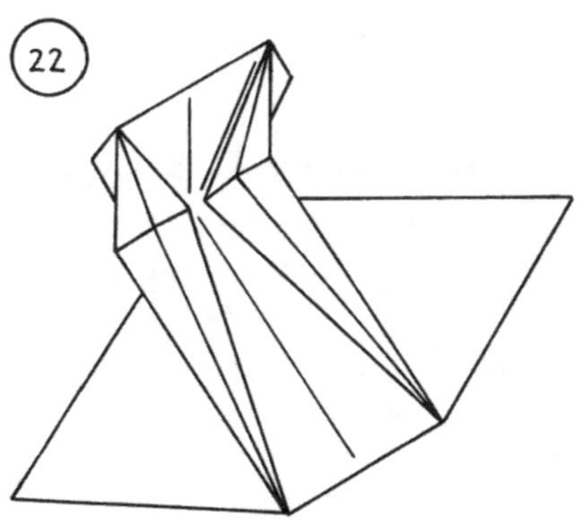

Illustration of front surface with step 21 folds, before unfolding them.

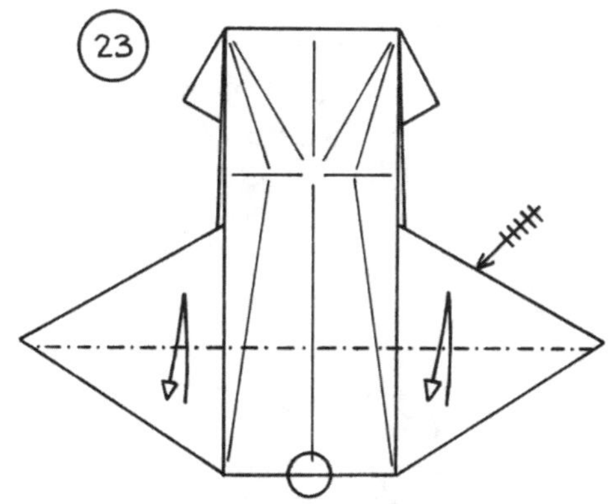

View of front surface only. Lift edge at circled spot. Note that mountain fold and unfold to be done is located slightly below tips. Rearrange flaps in turn, and repeat on other 5 surfaces.

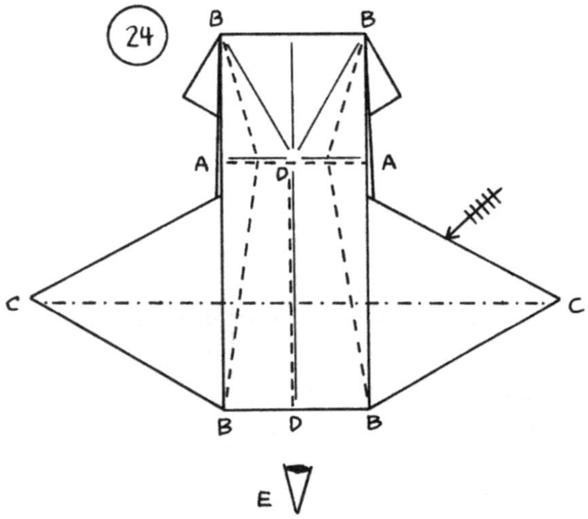

3-D the model as follows: Bend at AA and refold the pairs of creases BB, as in steps 21-22. Then, refold mountain CC, followed by valley folding DD. Rearrange flaps and repeat sequence on 5 other surfaces. Lastly, look this way (E) for underside view.

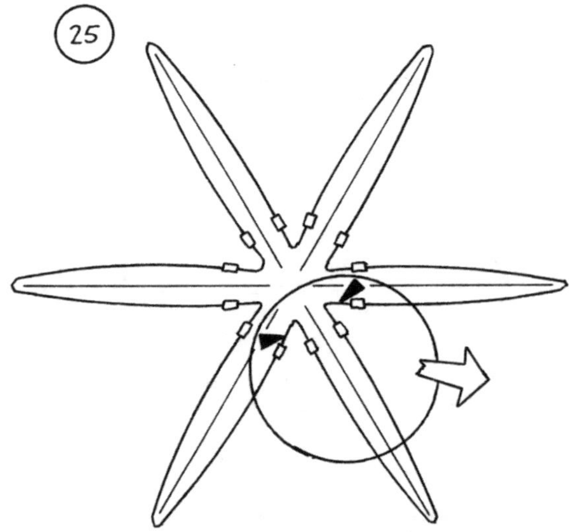

In this view the edges of the petals are the mountain folds CC, and the little "bumps" are a layer of paper formed by creases BB. With fingertips or tweezers, pinch two adjacent corners together. Next, see enlarged detail.

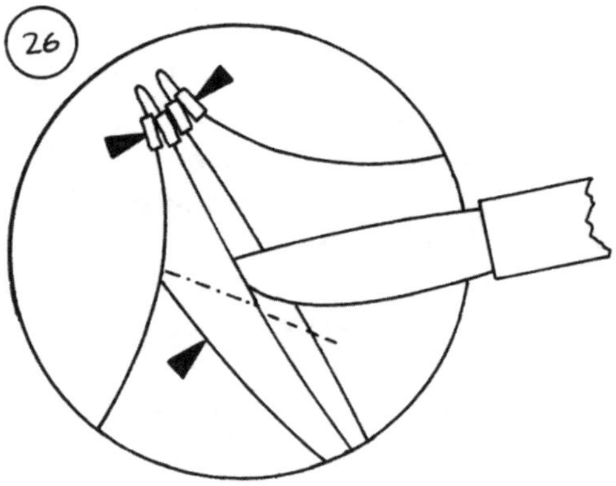

While pinching the inner ends of the petal, use a tool to spread it open, preliminary to making a squash fold. Turn model over and squash fold the petal.

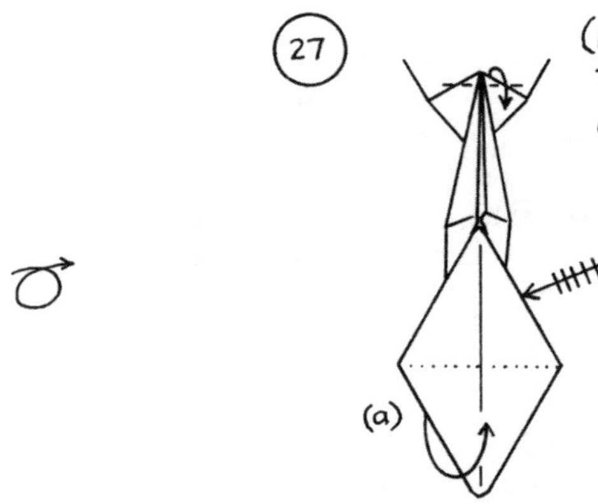

(b) View of lip of trumpet, above one petal.

(c) 25-27

(a) While continuing to pinch underneath, complete the squash fold as wide as possible, then curl tip upward along dotted line.
(b) Fold over the corner at top.
(c) Repeat steps 25-27 on 5 other petals.

Two Views
Finished Flower

DAFFODIL STEM AND LEAVES
color on the outside.

This piece is made from a standard bird base,

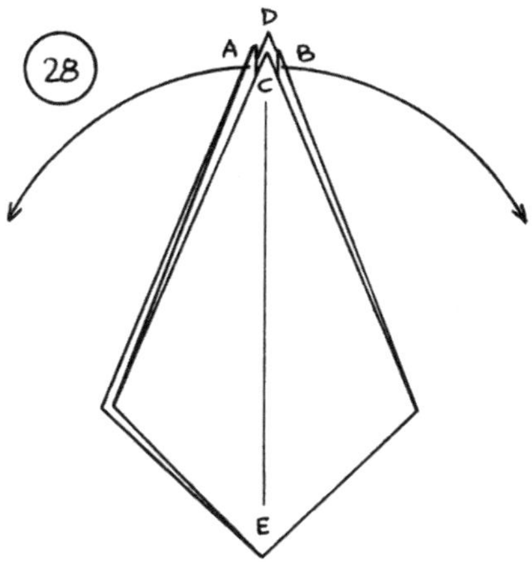

Notice that flaps A and B have grooves.
Grip A and B, pulling out and down.

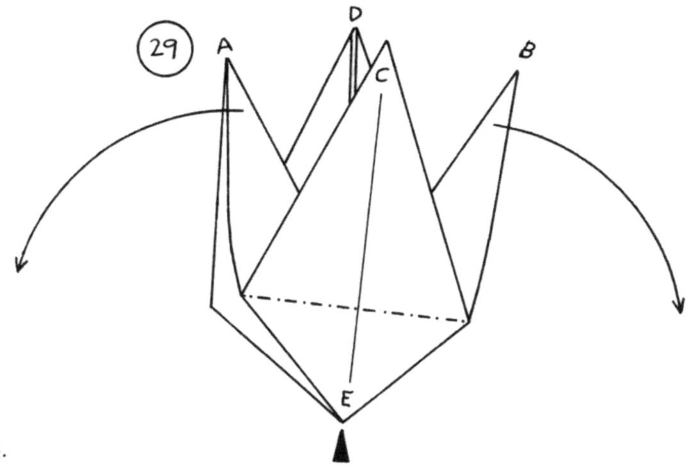

Continue pulling and stretching A and B. Grooves open wider and point E will snap inside. Form mountain fold front and back. Flatten model to shape in next step.

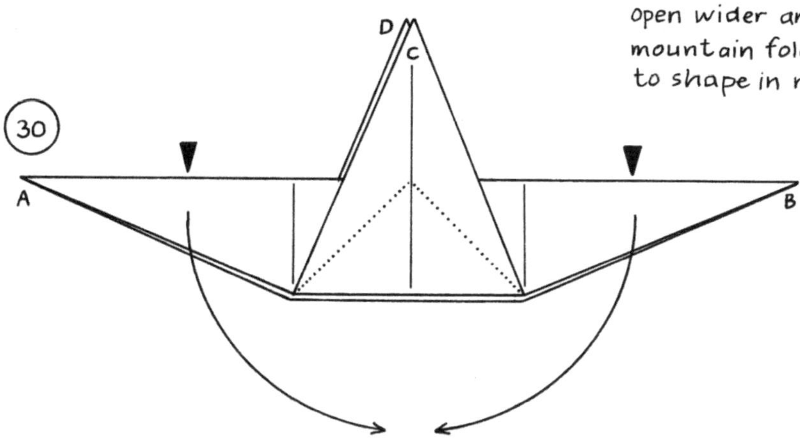

Dotted lines show locations of hidden creases. Reverse fold both long flaps down, using these creases.

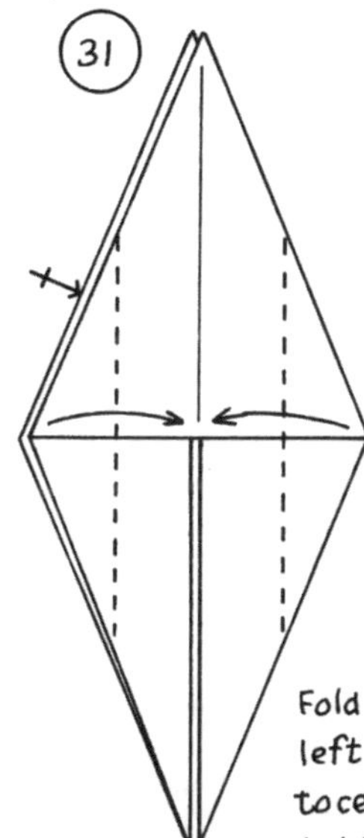

Fold the corners of left and right flaps to center. Repeat behind.

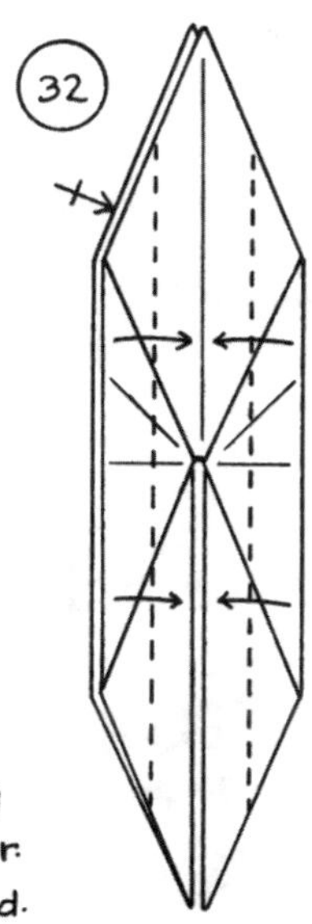

Valley fold long edges to center. Repeat behind.

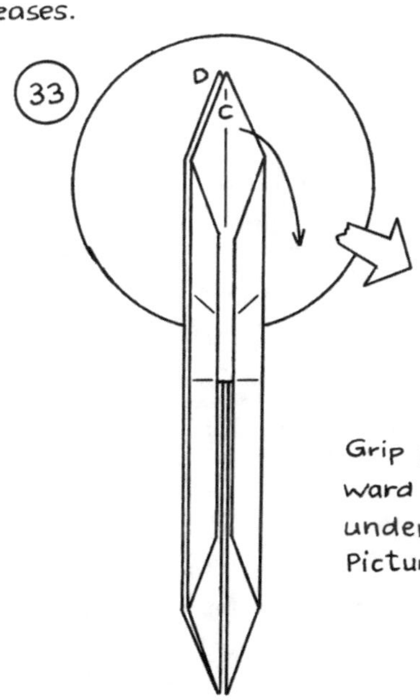

Grip point C, lift and curl it downward in order to see flap D underneath. Do not fold flap C. Picture gets larger.

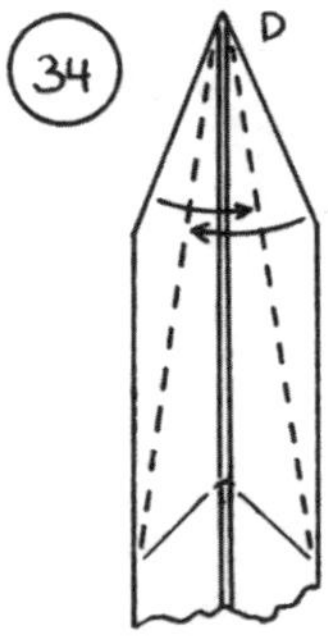

Flap C not shown. Make the two valley folds shown, extending from the tip to spot on edges met by existing creases.

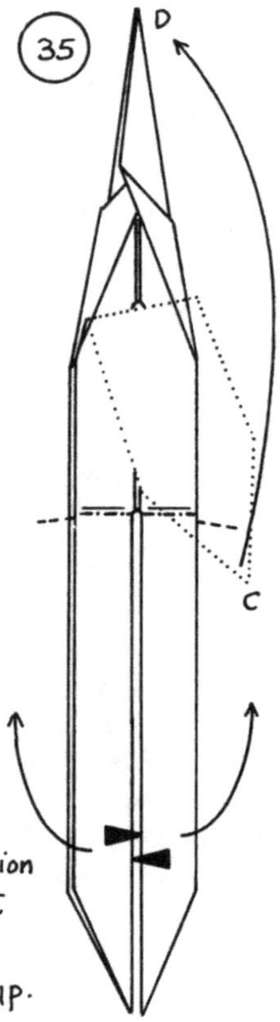

(a) Dotted lines show position of flap C. Now return it to lay flat. (b) Inside reverse fold long flaps up. Picture gets larger.

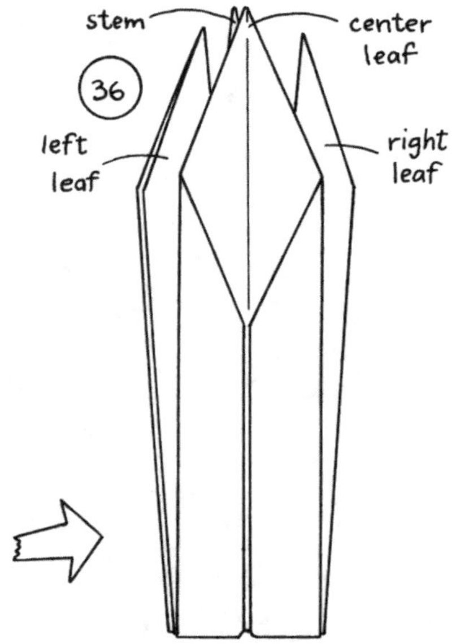

In next few steps the tips of the stem and leaves are first shaped, and lastly, the leaves are curled. Heights are also slightly varied, tallest first in this order: stem, right leaf, then center, then left.

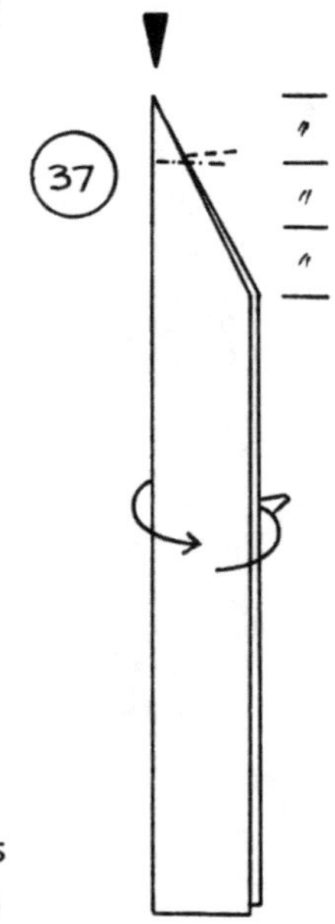

Right Leaf

Inside reverse fold about 1/3 the distance from tip to corner. Later, curl as shown.

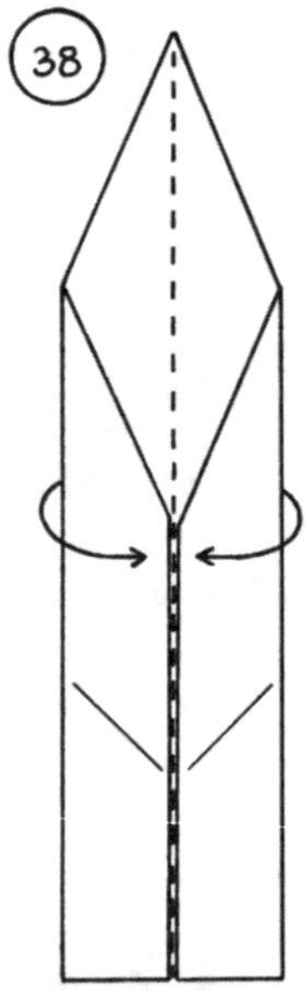

Center Leaf

Valley fold to bring side edges together. The lower section folds partly closed only.

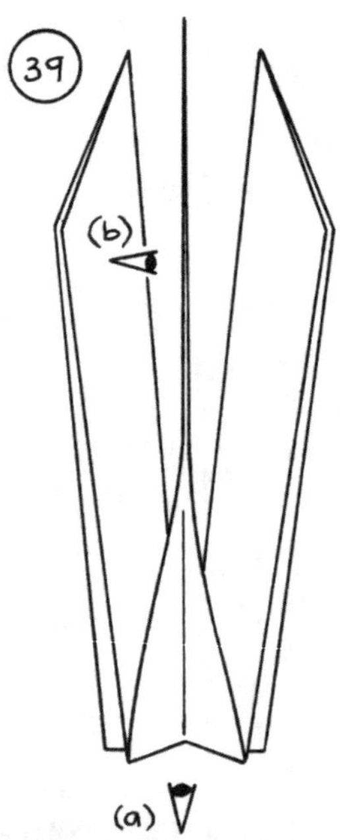

(a) Look to see how four thick edges spread so model may stand up. (b) Look this way for side view of center leaf.

Front surface center leaf.

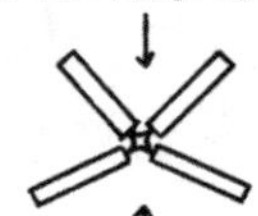

Rear surface of stem.

(a) Bottom view.

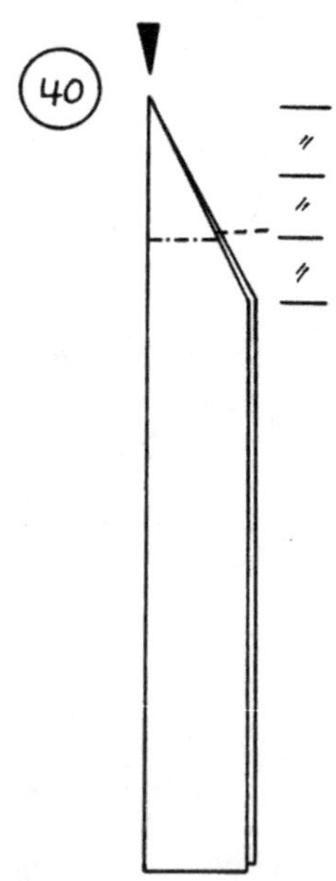

(b) Side view center leaf. Inside reverse fold about 2/3 the distance from the tip to corner.

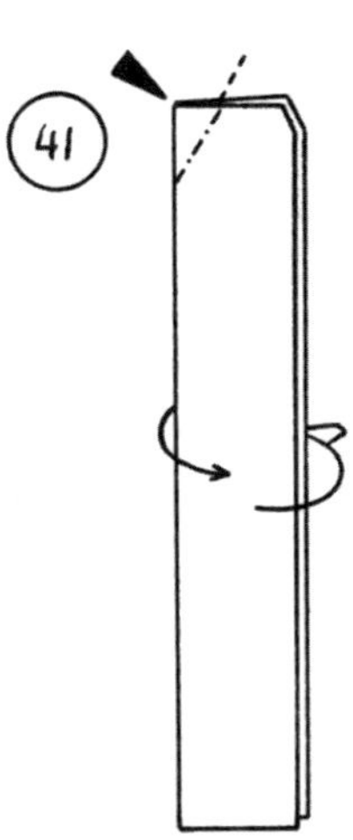

Inside reverse fold the corner. Later, curl as shown.

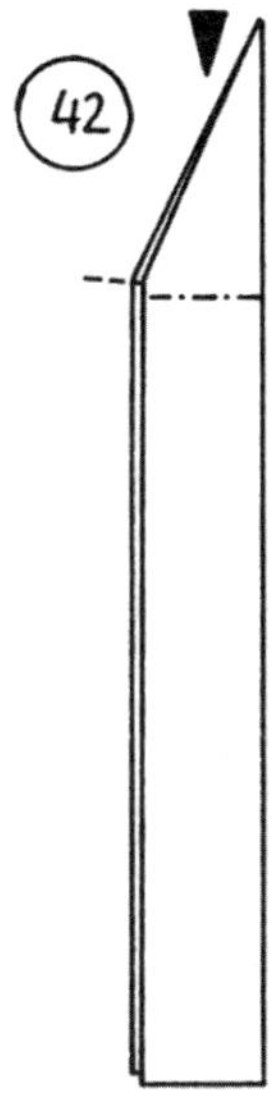

Inside reverse fold the tip, at or slightly below the corner.

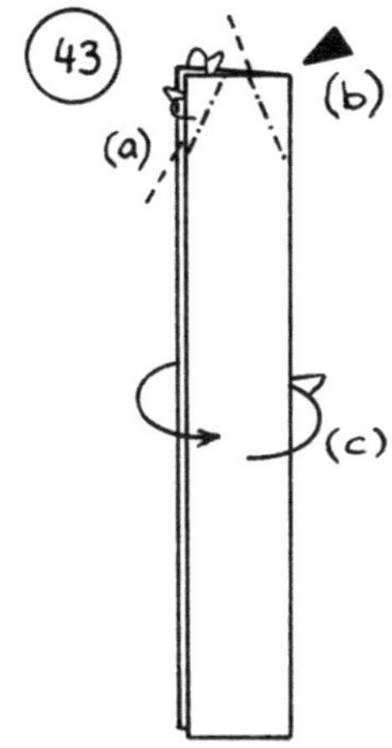

(a) Fold two left corners inside.
(b) Inside reverse fold right corner.
(c) Later, curl as shown.

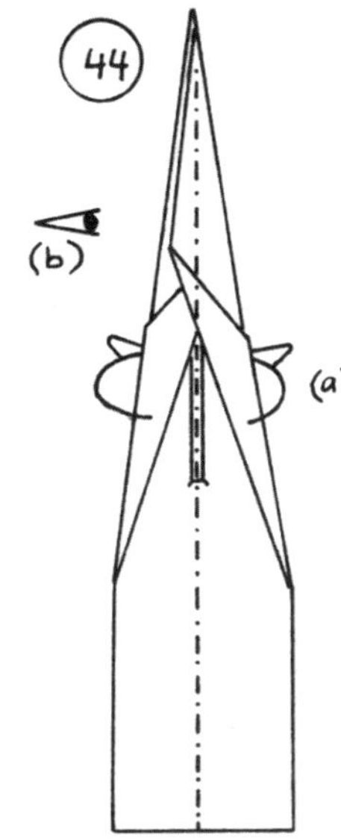

Front View of Stem
(a) Mountain fold the length. (b) Look this way for side view.

Some layers not shown. Outside reverse fold the tip.

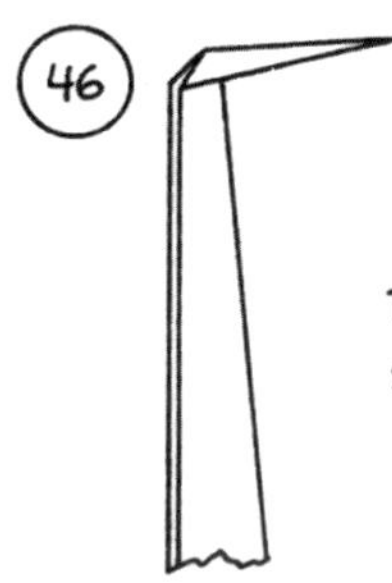

The angled end of the stem should face front.
GO BACK AND CURL THE LEAVES. See steps 37, 41, 43.

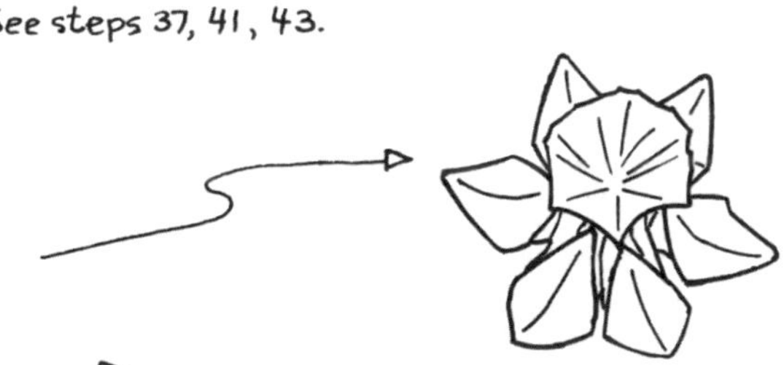

Find any convenient slot located near center of back of the flower, and insert stem.

Additional Model Information

The information presented here provides details about the models in this book that the diagrams do not include. Details vary by model, but include dates of original design and diagrams, approximate finished size of the model based on size of paper used, coloration technique, and prior publication of model. Some diagrams were previously published in the Friends of The Origami Center of America *Annual Collections*, abbreviated here as *FOCA*.

120° Module Series

Designed 1982 / Diagrammed 1982
Finished size from 2" X 3" pieces
(6 of these cut from a 6" square):
Soccer Ball = 3 ½" diameter
Dodecahedron = W 3 ¼", H 2 ¾"
Truncated Icosahedron = 7 ½" diameter

Prior Publication: *FOCA* 1982.

Canovi, Luisa, Giovanni Ravesi, and Dario Uri. *Il Libro dei Rompicapo: Topologia a Tre Dimensioni*. Firenze: G.C. Sansoni Editore, 1984.

Basket

Designed 1978 / Diagrammed 1984
Finished size from 5" x 15" rectangle:
Basket = base 2 ½" X 2 ½", height 2 5/8"

Prior Publication:
The Origamian, Vol. 16, #1 (1984?)

Candlestick

Designed 1979 / Diagrammed 1987
Finished size from 6" X 18" rectangle:
Candle = 4" tall

For a model with a colored candle, pre-color 1/3 end section of the paper prior to folding.

Claw Hammer

Designed 1979 / Diagrammed 1988
Finished size from: 5" X 15" rectangle
Hammer = 6" long, with head 3 ¼" long

Prior Publication: *FOCA* 1988

Crane Stickpin

Designed 1989 / Diagrammed 1989
Finished size from 6" square:
Crane Stickpin = 3 ½" from wing tip to pin tip

Insert into hat band, button hole, etc.
Model can also be inflated for 3-D display.

Prior Publication:
FOCA Newsletter, No. 33, 1989

Cross-Shaped Dish

Designed 1980 / Diagrammed 2005

Daffodil

Designed 1981 / Diagrammed 2005

Expanding Ball

Designed 1979 / Diagrammed 1984
Finished size from 3" squares:
Expanding Ball = 2 ¼" tall

Prior Publication: *FOCA* 1986

A very similar-looking model, Bauble, folded from a single rectangle, appears in Paul Jackson's 1991 book *Festive Folding*. In the book Jackson acknowledges that the model was by "an unknown author, possibly in the USA."

I was unaware of this book until seeing it in my public library in 2006. In an email exchange, Jackson could not recall with certainty from whom he obtained it, but believes he learned it about 1982-83, and most likely as a single-sheet model, rather than as a modular. We were unable to conclude whether Bauble somehow evolved from Expanding Ball, or whether the two models represent a type of simultaneous invention.

Flying Crane on a Stand

Designed 1989 / Diagrammed 2006

When folded with duo paper the crane will be the color of one side of the sheet, and the stand will be the opposite side color.

Friends' Logo

Designed 1985 / Diagrammed 1986
Finished size from 18" X 4 ½" rectangle:
Friends' Logo with 2 ½" diameter

The model is a representation of the logo of The Friends of the Origami Center of America, precursor to OrigamiUSA.

Letterfold

Designed 1984 / Diagrammed 1984
Finished size from 8 ½" X 11":
Letterfold = 6 ¼" X 3 ¼"

Prior Publication:
British Origami, No. 85

Cunliffe, John, ed. *Envelope and Letter Folding: American Emphasis.* London: British Origami Society, 2001.

Lily

Designed 1989 / Diagrammed 2002
Finished size from 10" square:
Lily = 4 ½" wide with 2" stem

Michael Shall's Coin Purse

Designed 1996 / Diagrammed 2000

Mouse

Designed 1980 / Diagrammed 1987
Finished size from 6" square:
Mouse = 5 ¼" long

Paper Chain

Designed 1978 / Diagrammed 1980
Finished size from 1 ½" x 6" strips
(4 of these cut from a 6" square):
Paper Chain Links = 1 ½" diameter

Prior Publication: *FOCA* 1983.

First Steps in Origami, 4th Collection, published by Origami Center of America for Japan Air Lines' "Exhibition in the Window."

Variation: "How Strong Is Your Currency" in Jackson, Paul. *Folding Money*. London: Argus and Robertson Publishers, 1986.

Variation reprinted in: Leo, May, ed. *Making More with Money*. New York: Origami USA, 1995.

Hall, Judy. *Christmas Origami: Favorite Holiday Projects*. Westport: Hugh Lauter Levin Associates, Inc., 2001.

Puzzle Cube

Designed 1961 / Diagrammed 2006

Rabbit

Designed 1991 / Diagrammed 1991
Finished size from 10" square:
Rabbit = 4 ¾" tall

Rowboat

Designed 1981 / Diagrammed 1981
Finished size from 6" square:
Rowboat = Length 4 ½" length,
Width 1 ½"

Prior Publication: *FOCA* 1981

Seamless Box and Lid

Designed 1979 / Diagrammed 1987
Finished size from 10" X 6 ½" rectangle:
Box = Length 3 1/8" and Width 1 ¾"

Prior Publication: *FOCA* 1987

Triangular Solid

Designed 1978 / Diagrammed 2004

Wristwatch

Designed 1980 / Diagrammed 1980

Prior Publication: *FOCA* 1981

Resources and Contacts

The popularity of origami has virtually exploded internationally over the past 10-15 years. Consequently there has been a huge increase in resources available for learning and teaching origami, participating in communities of fellow folders, or obtaining origami books, papers, and related materials. Within the scope of this book it is impossible to describe them all. Typing "origami" into an Internet search engine (such as Google or Yahoo) will return more information than you will *ever* be able to read.

Here I share a number of my personal favorites, selected for their usefulness in providing information directly, for their links to organizations and other information sources, for their sales of origami books and materials, or as a result of my involvement as a member.

Organizations & E-Mail Discussion Lists

OrigamiUSA — www.origami-usa.org

OrigamiUSA is a non-profit, educational organization dedicated to the sharing of paperfolding in America and around the world. The organization conducts conventions of paper folders, sells origami books and papers, provides contacts for international and local origami groups, provides an e-mail discussion list and Lending Library for members, and publishes an *Annual Collection* of new diagrams and the magazine *The Paper.*

British Origami Society — www.britishorigami.info

The British Origami Society is a worldwide group devoted to the art of paperfolding. The society publishes origami books and the bi-monthly magazine *British Origami,* conducts conventions for folders, and sponsors a members' e-mail discussion group. The BOS website also hosts David Lister's detailed writings on the history of origami *The Lister List,* and archives the Thoki Yenn website.

Origami Mailing List — lists.digitalorigami.com

An international e-mail forum of more than 800 members, for discussion of all things relating to the art of paperfolding - models, books, styles, paper, techniques, tools, etc.

Websites

Origami Database — **www.origamidatabase.com**

The world's largest index to published origami diagrams. Maintained by Dennis Walker, the index's contents, including images of book covers and folded models, were built and continue to grow through user contributions.

Joseph Wu's Origami Page — **www.origami.as**

This site provides a comprehensive list of links to origami websites around the world and in many languages, and includes photo galleries, articles, and diagrams.

Encyclopedia Origamica — **www.geocities.com/foldingca/origamica.html**

Dorothy Engleman's site is an immense compendium of everything origami providing detailed links to articles on origami history, diagrams, galleries, and folding groups.

Origami — **www.origami.com**

Alex Barber's extensive website provides gallery images, downloadable model diagrams, an index to diagrams, links to other origami folders, and other external links.

Dave's Origami Emporium — **members.aol.com/ukpetd**

David Petty's website offers a large collection of diagrams, including many traditional models, book recommendations, links to other sites, and articles on origami diagramming, copyright, and creativity.

Gilad's Origami Page — **www.giladorigami.com**

Gilad Aharoni's website provides a large collection of origami book reviews, diagrams, galleries of origami models, articles, and annotated links to other origami websites.

Flickr — **www.flickr.com**

Flickr, an online photo management and sharing website, is one of the best Internet sources for viewing images of origami models. Search the term "origami," then try sub-searches for groups, people and discussions.

For the production of this book
copies of the original hand-drawn and lettered diagrams
were scanned at 1200 dpi and saved as TIFF images.
In a few instances the layout was modified slightly,
and all diagram titles were replaced in a consistent style.
Otherwise the diagrams appear as originally produced.

Front cover and color pages:
Photos by David Shall

Back cover:
Family Tree - Celebration and Memorium (detail)
Quilt and Photo by Maxine Burkholder

Fonts used:
Covers and Pagination: Papyrus
Text: MC Wright

TIFF images and color photos manipulated in Photoshop Elements 4.0
All pages generated in Microsoft Word v.11.2
and converted to PDF on a MacBook Pro

Printed by:
Biltmore ProPrint, Phoenix, Arizona

Smyth-sewn Binding
Bound by:
Roswell Bookbinding, Phoenix, Arizona